THE COMPLETE HOME DECORATOR

Over 200 practical projects to transform your home, with more than 1000 color photographs

THE COMPLETE HOME DECORATOR

Over 200 practical projects to transform your home, with more than 1000 color photographs

STEWART AND SALLY WALTON

This edition is published by Hermes House

Hermes House is an imprint of Anness Publishing Ltd
Hermes House, 88–89 Blackfriars Road, London SE1 8HA
tel. 020 7401 2077; fax 020 7633 9499; info@anness.com

© Anness Publishing Ltd 2003

All rights reserved. No part of this publication may be reproduced, stored in a retrieval system, or transmitted in any way or by any means, electronic, mechanical, photocopying, recording or otherwise, without the prior written permission of the copyright holder.

Publisher: Joanna Lorenz
Senior Editor: Clare Nicholson
Photographer: Graham Rae
Stylist: Catherine Tully
Designer: Caroline Reeves

Printed and bound in Spain

1 3 5 7 9 10 8 6 4 2

CONTENTS

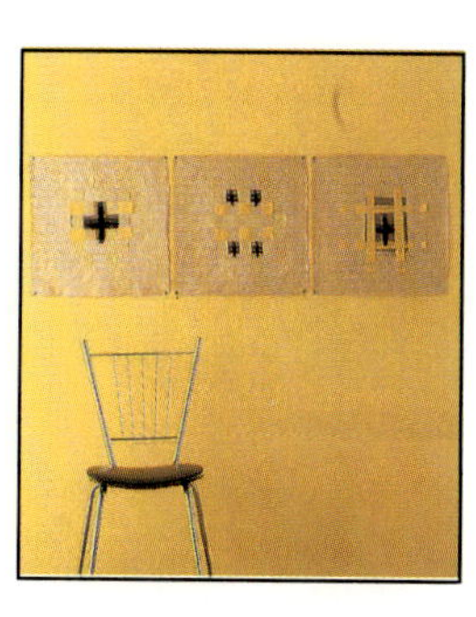

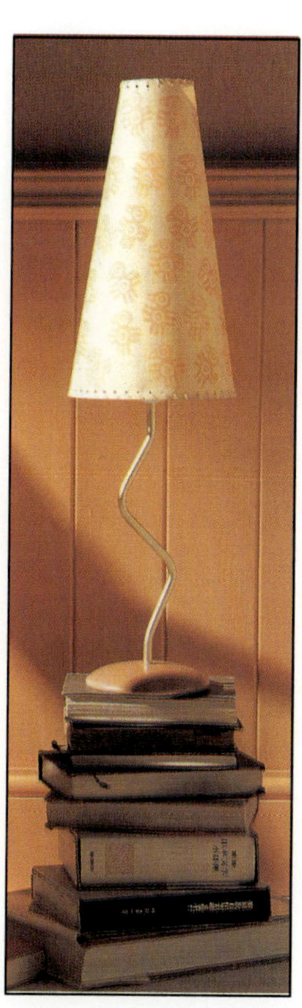

INTRODUCTION

INTRODUCTION

It is very easy to brighten dull shelves in the house by dressing them with different edgings made from string, paper, fabric or ribbons. Experiment to discover what you like, and if you fix your edgings with double-sided tape they can be removed and changed in an instant.

DECORATION, COLOR AND DESIGN—never have they been as important than in the modern home as the twenty-first century approaches. Yet, while everyone wants a beautiful home, our lives are busier, and fewer and fewer people have the time or money to devote to intricate, expensive decorative schemes.

This book is the ideal starting point for anyone who is looking for innovative new ideas to brighten the home and add those individual touches that distinguish the exceptional from the ordinary. In it you will find decorative projects for every room in the house, from bedrooms to kitchens, and there are separate chapters on lamps, lighting, and containers, essentials for every room.

The first thing you notice in a room is the windows. Whether you live in a basement, studio, apartment, house or mansion, you will find ideas in this book to revolutionize your windows at minimum cost. Armed with a staple gun and some inexpensive materials, you can make your windows the focal point of each room. With these inspirational ideas you will never have to visit a curtain department again. Many of the projects featured are inspired by examining familiar materials in a new light. This in itself carries you away from traditional methods and old-fashioned styles toward the freshness of experimental window dressing.

It is very important to emphasize the windows in a room—here, buttoned blankets have been used to make unusual curtains. Another simple touch is to decorate bags and aprons with colored felt shapes.

There are window projects to suit every taste and every budget, including quick stylish ideas for tie-backs, hanging treatments and color schemes and the simple effects that can be created by draping, tying, stapling, buttoning, hanging, clipping and gluing all kinds of fabrics.

After windows the most important elements in any room are the walls and floors. Our wall and floor projects, which can be used throughout the house, are all original and innovative. Our terrific treatments go far beyond simple paint effects and concentrate on new and creative approaches. These range from using photocopies for graphic black-and-white effects, draping fabric to disguise an irregular surface, creating mosiacs from broken china, applying solid panels of color to liven up a neutral space or attaching colored strips of wood to the wall to add interest and texture. Applying simple paper cut-outs, designing your own stencils, hanging fabric—all these projects will provide a rich source of ideas to help you make the most of colors and textures, and they are all illustrated with the help of simple step-by-step photographs.

Floors are expensive to re-cover. New carpets are expensive, and it is essential to make the right choice, so all floor treatments must be carefully considered. Having said that, there are many ideas here that

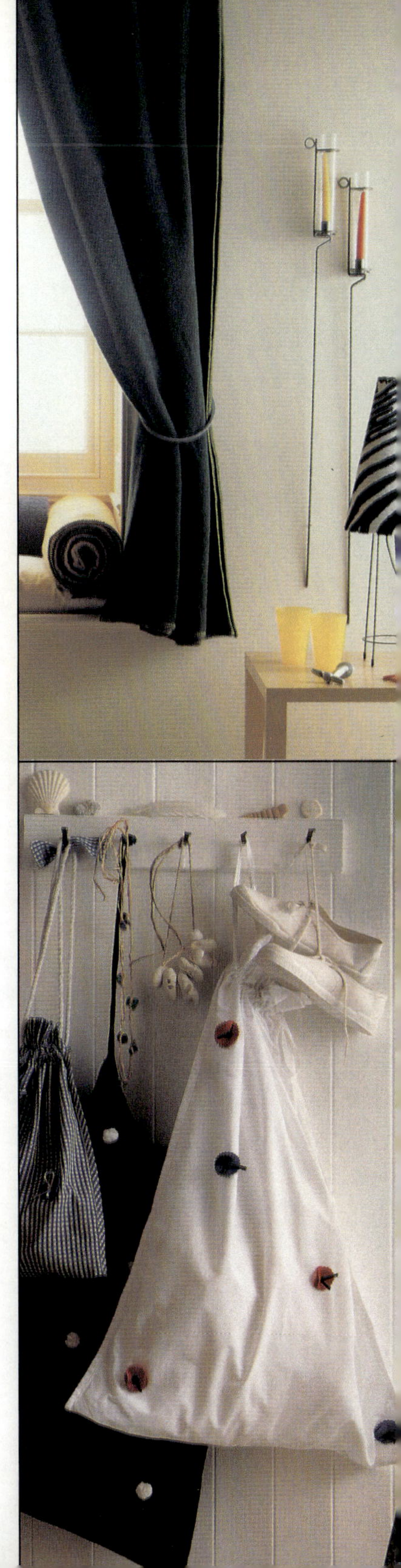

are relatively inexpensive and will change the look of the whole room—all you need is a clean, level floor. If you are working on bare boards check that they are securely fastened to their joists and sand them down thoroughly—it is probably best to rent a sanding machine—before you start work. If you do this carefully you can create marble-effect floors or scintillating three-dimensional linoleum patterns. In one room we even suggest a giant backgammon board made from carpet squares.

Here, a simple wooden chair has been painted and decorated with script lettering, transforming an everyday object into something quite outstanding.

Two of the most important elements in any home are the chairs and tables. There are tables and chairs in nearly every room, from the elegant, luxurious sofas in the living room to the spaces used by everyone every single day—the kitchen and the family room. These are the places where tables and chairs get a lot of wear and tear. They are expensive to replace but very often they can be refurbished at little cost with just a little bit of effort and ingenuity. Sometimes furniture needs no more than a new cover to give it a new lease on life, so you certainly won't have to sacrifice every weekend for months to take on a project. Another excellent way to replace old furniture is to haunt flea markets and antique stores. If you make a point of

Blinds made from grass beach mats are both cheap and elegant. Another idea for an unusual wall treatment is to make a large, color photocopy of a map and antique and varnish it. This makes a stylish wall covering for a study or den.

seeking out yard sales you will discover that old furniture can be bought extremely cheaply, and if you revamp it carefully, you can create an individual masterpiece of your own and give your home a sense of personal style that you cannot get in any other way.

All these projects and ideas are collected and listed under the various rooms in the house, from living rooms and kitchens, to studies, hallways, novelty and children's rooms, but particular attention is paid to bedrooms and bathrooms. In these rooms you can let your imagination run riot. These projects are for people who want the opportunity to try out something unusual and original, from making a canopy bed to surrounding the bed in beach matting. There are countless ideas for transforming bedheads and making unusual cushions to give your bedroom the individual touch that you desire. The two indispensable tools are the glue gun and the stapler, which together provide freedom from the conventional methods of construction, attaching and draping, and let you both achieve the impossible and keep it in place.

All the techniques used here are clearly photographed for each project and are designed to be easy to follow. Throw inhibition to the wind and enjoy creating stylish effects that will change the look of your home at next to no cost.

Moses Basket

THESE GENEROUS-SIZED WOVEN BASKETS were originally designed as easy, convenient and comfortable transport for young babies. Sadly, these old-fashioned cradles do not conform to stringent modern safety regulations, so present-day newborns have safer, but rather less charming, plastic and metal contraptions instead. Moses baskets are not completely obsolete, however. They are used here as fresh and airy hanging containers for clothes and also provide an attractive decorative feature for a bathroom or bedroom. Alternatively, you could use them for easy toy storage in a child's nursery.

YOU WILL NEED

plank of wood
tape measure
saw
sandpaper
drill, with wood and masonry bits
1 long or 2 short branches (or poles)
penknife (or wood carving knife)
dowels (optional)
2 Moses baskets
wood glue
hammer
plastic anchors and screws
screwdriver

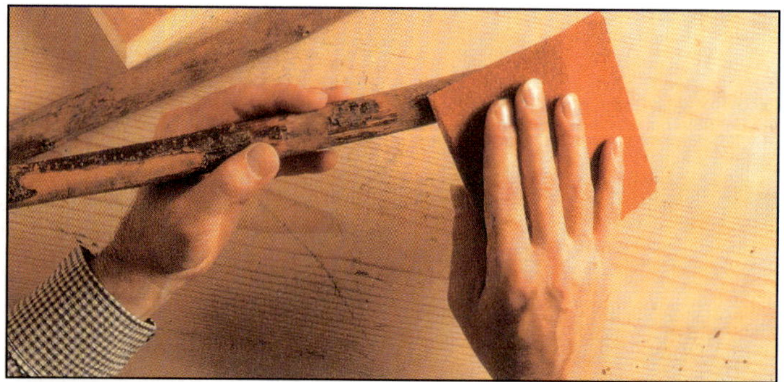

one *Cut two squares of wood at least 4¾ x 4¾ inches and 2 inches deep. Sandpaper the edges and drill a hole through the middle of each square, slightly smaller than the diameter of the branches. Carve away the branch ends so that they fit tightly into the holes. Sandpaper them slightly.*

two *Use dowels or scraps from the branches for the pegs. Taper the ends.*

three *Measure the distance across the basket between the basket handles and drill two holes the same distance apart on top of each branch. Apply wood glue to each branch and tap them into each square.*

four *Apply wood glue to the peg ends and fit them into each branch. To attach the top branch to the wall, drill holes in the four corners of the square of wood, and four corresponding holes in the wall. Using the plastic anchors and screws, screw the branch to the wall. Attach the lower branch to the wall allowing about 4 inches of clearance between the two baskets.*

PRETTY POTS

MINIATURE TOPIARY WILL LOOK both eye-catching and charming on a windowsill or collected on a table, but don't forget to make the most of their containers. Terra-cotta pots have their own special appeal, but can also be treated to a variety of embellishments, from tassels to tape. Subtle, natural colors are best as they look best with the pots themselves and with the small pebbles used to conceal the florist's foam.

YOU WILL NEED

florist's dry foam block
sharp knife
3 old terra-cotta pots
2 straight twigs
glue gun and glue sticks
2 florist's dry foam balls
fresh foliage, such as box
selection of pebbles
curtain weight
fine string
string tassels
masking tape
craft knife
self-healing cutting mat
matte varnish
paintbrush

one *Cut the florist's foam block in half and cut each block to fit into two of the pots. Position the foam in the pots. Insert the twigs and then glue them in place, to act as the stems of the trees. Glue the foam balls on top.*

two *Cut small pieces of foliage to the required size and insert them at random in the foam balls, to create a casual, carefree effect.*

three *Cover the foam in the pots with a layer of small pebbles so that it is completely concealed.*

four *Thread the curtain weight onto string and tie it around one of the pots. Decorate the other pots with tassels or designs cut from masking tape with a craft knife. Varnish to make the masking tape secure.*

ALL BOXED UP

THERE IS A HUGE VARIETY of boxes available, ranging from plain and simple white wooden boxes to shoe boxes to oval trinket boxes. Make a set of three using easily available natural materials. Boxes can be trimmed with almost anything you want: bottle caps, paper clips, string, rope or a collage of stamps. Linen tape (used in upholstery) is available at notions departments.

YOU WILL NEED

plain wooden box
tape measure
scissors
linen tape
needle
matching sewing thread
2 wooden beads
glue gun and glue sticks
twig
small slatted wooden box
small package of potpourri
small Shaker-style box
dried leaves and fir cones

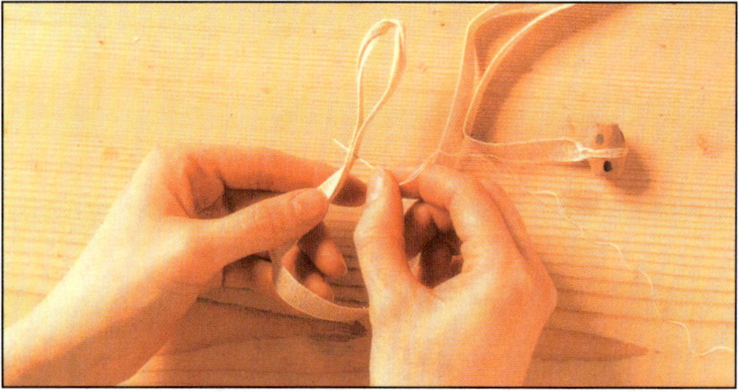

one *Measure the plain wooden box. Allow an extra ¾ inch at one end for the bead and about 3 inches for the loop. Cut two lengths of linen tape to this length. Sew a loop in the end of each tape and attach the wooden beads to be used as toggles.*

two *Secure the tape to one end of the box with glue, leaving the toggle and loop free so the lid can be opened. Repeat on the other side. Glue a twig to the top of the lid, as a decorative "handle."*

three *For the slatted wooden box, sort through the potpourri and choose the items you would like to use. Glue them to the lid. Glue the dried leaves and cones to the Shaker box, and glue linen tape around the sides.*

Maths montage, pp. 106-7

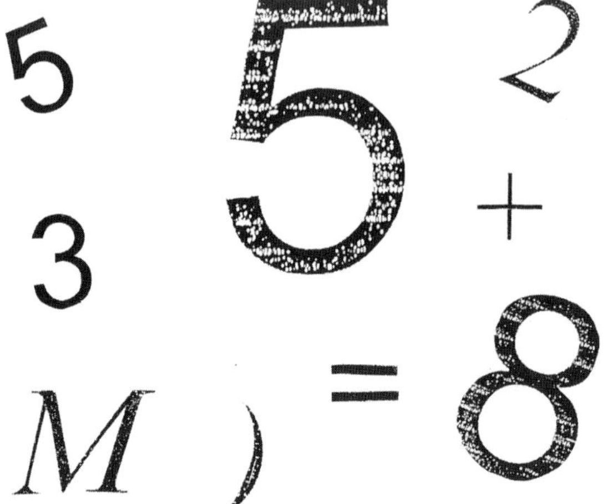

Country-style shelf, pp. 130-31

Fish footstool, pp. 386-7

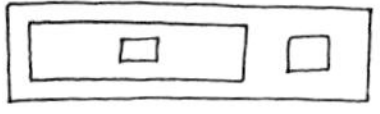

Escher-style wall, pp. 110-11

Sprigged curtains, pp. 78-9

Flag stencils, pp. 298-9

Escher deckchair, pp. 112-13

Trompe l'oeil linoleum, pp. 162-3

Vermeer-style marble, pp. 166-7

INDEX

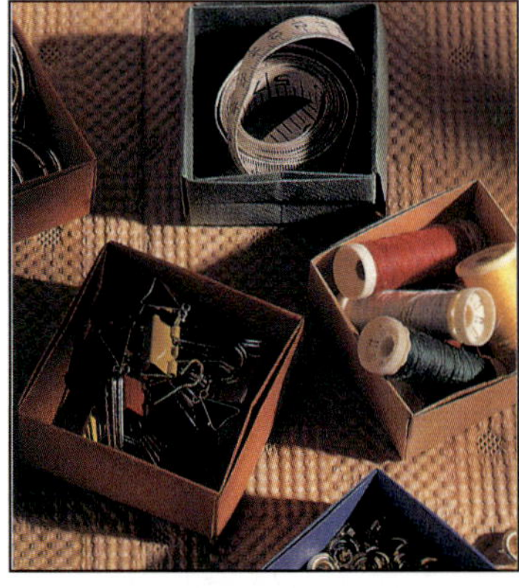

LIVING AND DINING ROOMS

LIVING AND DINING ROOMS

IMAGINE A ROOM FULL of light with cool, bleached tones and welcoming textures. Imagine it with bold strokes of color, imaginative details and a hint of elegant understatement. Think beach house, vacation, friends: relaxed, informal, calming. Now imagine this vision of cool as your own living or dining room.

An impossible, or impossibly expensive, dream? Not so. Transforming your living or dining room doesn't mean committing yourself to sweeping changes, or paying a bevy of professionals to take care of everything from the light bulbs down. It doesn't mean discarding all your favorite things. It does mean using what you already have and concentrating on the details.

A modern laced chair provides a stylish touch that will brighten any room in the house. Covers such as this can be changed to suit the room.

Details are important, and in this chapter we look at ways in which an imaginative approach and quality execution can have an effect nothing short of miraculous. We have lots of ideas for both small and larger scale projects to point you in the right direction and loads of tips and shortcuts that can bring even the most professional-looking living/dining room decorating solutions well within anyone's reach.

Disguising an old lampbase or adding your own unique touches to unadorned cushions sound like minor changes, but when done imaginatively as part of a grand plan the results can be stunning.

Also, tackling bigger jobs is easier than ever these days. You can turn uninspiring or even damaged walls or floor surfaces into works of art. Narrow strips of wood, painted and then attached at regular intervals to a wall, add interest out of all proportion to the materials used and the skill needed.

Fledgling decorators can even make grand statements with upholstery and curtains—usually mentioned in the same breath as being both expensive and difficult—thanks to the staple gun and iron-on hemming. These days you don't even have to sew.

That totally uplifting new living or dining room is just around the corner.

SUPER SOFA

TRIM A PERFECTLY PLAIN sofa using only a strand of rope that curves gently down the edge of the arm and across the base. This type of decoration works extremely well in a white-on-white color scheme because the eye is aware of the shape, but the embellishment doesn't jump out at you. Other types of trimming that could be used to add a stylish personal touch to your sofa are raffia edging, linen tassels and fringing.

YOU WILL NEED

graph or plain paper
pencil
rope, the length of the area to be trimmed
clear tape
scissors
dressmaker's pins
needle
strong sewing thread

one *Try different designs for the rope on paper, to see what works best; this style seemed to go well with the shape of the arm of the sofa and the lines of the seat.*

two *Bind clear tape around the ends of the rope so that the ends do not fray once the rope is in position.*

three *Cut as close to the end of the tape as you can so that as little is left as possible, but it still holds the rope firmly. Pin the rope onto the sofa and hand-stitch in place.*

CREAM TOPPING

MAKE A GRAND STATEMENT at the window by creating a valance with a curved edge trimmed with rope. The gentle wave of the valance gives a very gracious, elegant appearance to the treatment, which could, if desired, be echoed in the edging of a loose cover on a chair or sofa. Another wonderful idea is to continue the valance right around the top of the room, so it acts as a wavy trim to the whole area. In this case make sure the valance is the same color as the ceiling so the contrast doesn't jar the eye. Valances can be any shape or size; experiment with pointed V's with bells on, castellations and other variations. Cut the shape out of paper first, and pin it above the curtains to see what effect it will have upon the window and the room as a whole.

YOU WILL NEED

tape measure
2 plates
paper, for template
pencil
valance fabric
dressmaker's scissors
interfacing
dressmaker's pins
needle and basting thread
sewing machine
matching sewing thread
iron
rope
thin strip of wood
hammer and nails or Velcro

one *Measure the window and decide on the dimensions of the valance. Allow an extra 2 inches to attach to the strip of wood. Use plates to make a template.*

two *Cut two pieces of fabric for the back and the front of the valance. Cut out interfacing to stiffen the valance, and pin the three layers together with right sides facing.*

three *Draw around the template onto the valance piece with a pencil. Pin the fabric just inside the outline.*

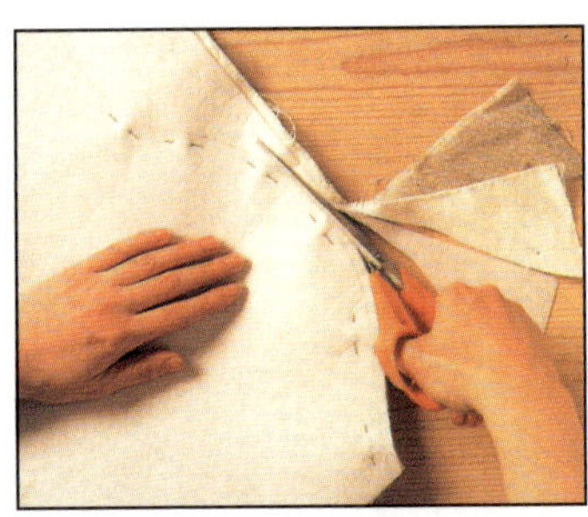

four *Cut out the scallops about ½ inch from the outline. Baste along the edge, then machine-stitch.*

five *Trim the interfacing and clip the seam allowance so that the curves will lie flat when turned right side out.*

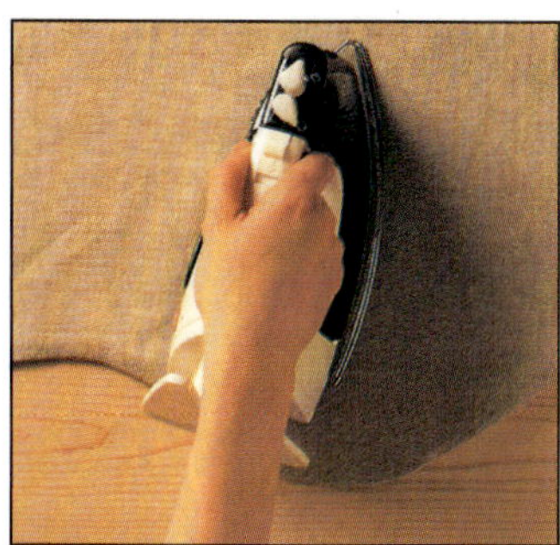

six *Turn the valance right side out and press the scalloped edge. Turn under the straight edge of the valance, then pin and machine-stitch.*

seven *Measure the scalloped edge, and cut a length of rope to fit. Experiment with design options for the rope; for example, you could use two different colors and weights of rope.*

eight *Pin the rope to the valance and hand-sew it in place. To attach the valance to the wall, use a thin strip of wood and nail the valance to it; alternatively, use Velcro to make the valance easy to remove.*

No-PROBLEM LINKS

WHAT LENGTHS WILL YOU GO TO for a bargain? If you find the fabric of your dreams in the remnant bin, but it's just a bit too short for your window, it's no longer a problem. Use curtain rings to connect the different lengths of fabric you have found—you can use as many as you need for the drop. Nobody will ever suspect that the linked effect was anything other than a deliberate design decision.

YOU WILL NEED

drill

metal curtain rod and attachment hardware

level

plastic anchors and screws

screwdriver

assorted lengths of fabric remnants

iron-on hem tape

iron

needle and matching sewing thread

split curtain rings

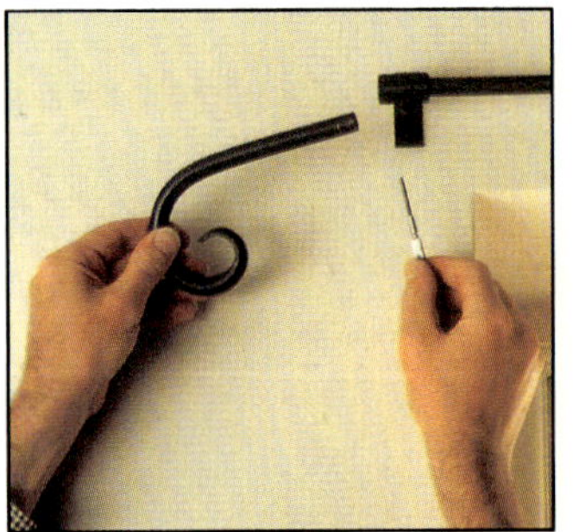

one *Attach the rod hardware above the window. Check with a level before you screw it to the wall. Assemble the curtain rod and hardware.*

‹ two *Hem all the rough edges of the fabric, either with hem tape or by hand. Sew small split rings along the top edge of the curtain to link into the rod rings. Sew rings in the same positions along the bottom of the first piece of fabric.*

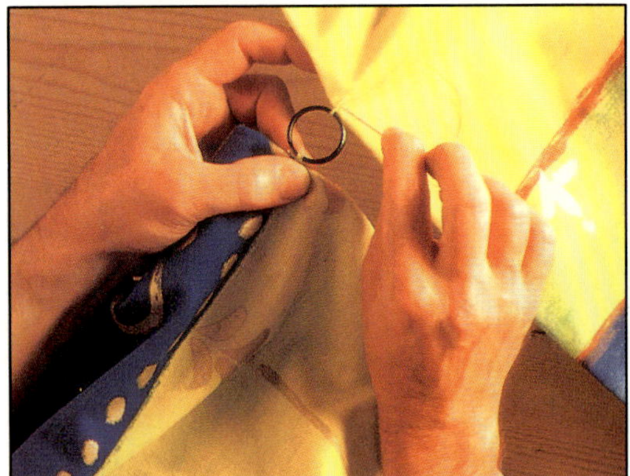

three *Line the curtain up with the next piece of fabric and mark the positions for attaching the rings. Make sure they line up exactly with the first curtain if you have a geometric or striped pattern. Sew the rings to the second piece of fabric along the whole width, then hang in place.*

Above: The curtains can be linked with split rings, single rings or interconnecting rings, like these.

CURVING ROPE DESIGN

A PATTERN IN ROPE makes a simple, textured wall finish, perfectly in keeping with today's trend for natural materials in interiors. Rope makes good curves, so the design can be as twisting as you like. For a small area or to make a focal point in a room, mark out squares and put a different, simple design in each square. You could also use the rope to create borders or frames within a room at chair-rail and picture-rail height for posters or paintings.

YOU WILL NEED

scrap paper
pencil
level
straightedge
rope
glue gun and glue sticks or strong adhesive
masking tape
craft knife
white latex paint
paintbrush

one *Plan and draw your design to scale on paper.*

two *Transfer your design to the wall using a level and a straightedge.*

three *Use a glue gun or other suitable adhesive to attach the rope to the wall. Use paint cans or other round objects to help you to make smooth curves. It is easier to cut through the tape if you wrap masking tape around it.*

four *Paint over the wall and rope with white latex paint; you may need a few coats to get an even finish.*

FABRIC WALL

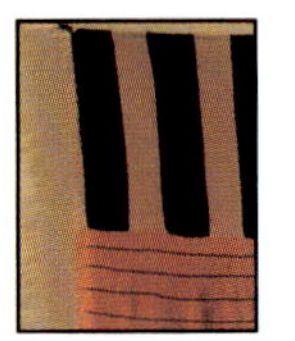

NO SPECIAL SEWING SKILLS are needed to achieve this dramatic wall treatment. Draping fabric on a wall is a good way to disguise lumps and bumps and add a lot of interest for little effort. When you have a modern fabric design, however, such as this eye-catching blanket, it may not seem appropriate to drape it on the wall in baroque folds. Instead, create a contemporary look by pulling it as taut as possible with colored string at the corners and middle of the fabric.

YOU WILL NEED

tape measure
fabric or blanket
pencil
drill, with masonry bit
plastic anchors
screw eyelets
colored string
matching strong cotton thread

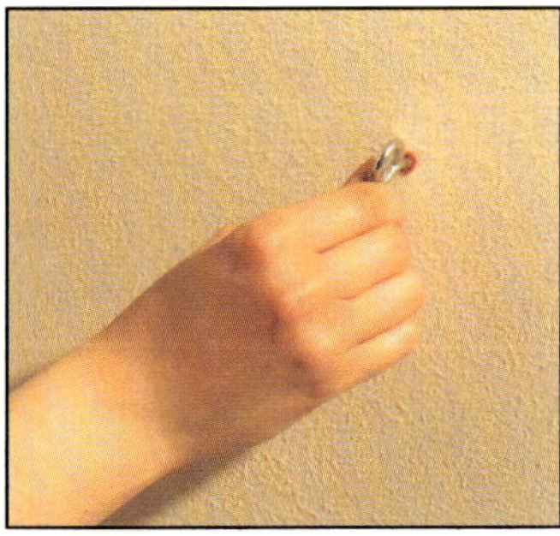

one *Measure the fabric or blanket and mark on the wall the positions for the screw eyelets, bearing in mind that you want the fabric to be pulled very taut. Drill and insert plastic anchors at the pencil marks. Screw the eyelets securely into the wall.*

two *Wrap lengths of string tightly around the corners of the fabric and around a small pinch of fabric in the middle of the two long edges.*

three *Feed the strings through the eyelets, pull them tight and secure them by looping the string back on itself. Bind the string with cotton, for a neat finish.*

LIFE'S LITTLE LUXURIES

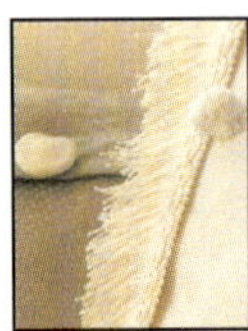

CUSHIONS ARE THE PERFECT way to add a certain style, as well as an element of comfort, to any room. Here, the choice of natural tones and fabrics perfectly complements the simplicity of the sofa. Interest was added to the restrained look with decorative ties, looped buttons and a simple rope trim. If you want a change from the neutral color scheme shown here, add splashes of vibrant color with blues, reds, oranges and purples. Alternatively, blue and white always look fresh and pretty.

one *For the rope-trimmed cushion cover, use a fine-gauge rope to experiment with different designs. When you are happy with the result, pin the rope onto the cover. Hand-stitch the rope to the cover, neatly finishing off the ends. Insert the cushion pad.*

two *For the cushion with ties, measure the cushion pad and cut one piece of cotton canvas the depth of the cushion plus ⅝ inch all around for seams, and a second piece twice the length plus 6½ inches for turning. Pin, baste, press and sew the seams on the wrong side. Turn it right side out.*

three *For the ties, cut six pieces of cotton canvas 2¼ x 11 inches. Fold each in half lengthwise with wrong sides together and pin, baste, press and machine-stitch a ½-inch seam around two sides. Clip the seams and corners. Turn the ties right side out and slip-stitch the ends closed. Position the ties in pairs and topstitch securely.*

four *For the cushion with loops and buttons, measure the width and length of the cushion pad. Double the length and add 4 inches for the flap opening, plus 1¼ inches for seams all around. You will also need to cut a 3-inch wide strip, the depth of the cushion plus seams. Cut the linen to this size and fold it in half.*

YOU WILL NEED

ROPE-TRIMMED CUSHION

about 2 yards fine-gauge rope
dressmaker's pins
plain linen cushion cover
needle
matching sewing thread
cushion pad

CUSHION WITH TIES

cushion pad
tape measure
cotton canvas
dressmaker's scissors
dressmaker's pins
needle
basting thread
iron
sewing machine
matching sewing thread

LOOP AND BUTTON CUSHION

cushion pad
1 yard linen
dressmaker's scissors
dressmaker's pins
needle
basting thread
sewing machine
matching sewing thread
small safety pin
iron
8–10 small buttons

five *To make the piping for the button loops cut a length of linen about 1 inch wide, on the cross. With wrong sides together, pin, baste and machine-stitch the fabric. Trim close to the stitching and, using a small safety pin, turn through to the right side. Press flat.*

six *Measure the buttons and cut the loops to the correct size. Turn over the seam allowance on the cover, then pin and baste the loops in position. Pin, baste and sew the interfacing strip for the back opening on the edge of the cover with the loops.*

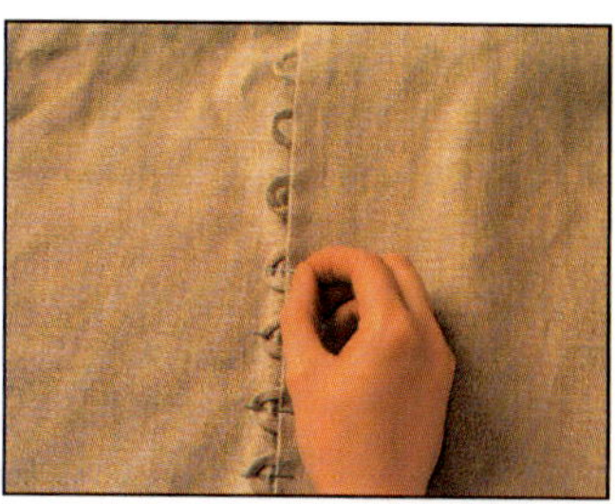

seven *With the right sides together, sew a seam all around the cushion cover. Turn it right side out and press. Mark the positions of the buttons with pins, and hand-sew them in place. Insert the cushion pad.*

CORK-STAMPED FLOOR

THIS PRETTY STAMP has been made from seven wine bottle corks. They have been taped together in a daisy shaped bundle and the pattern shapes are cut from the surface of the cork bundle with a scalpel. Dense cork like this is a good material to carve into, as it is both soft and very smooth. With a dark woodstain, use the stamp on dust-free sanded wood or on cork tiles. Let the stamp stand and soak up the stain for ten minutes, then blot it on paper towels before you begin printing. Use the paper strips to ensure that the pattern is an even distance from the wall.

YOU WILL NEED

7 wine bottle corks
wood glue or white glue
masking tape
felt-tipped pen
scalpel
2 paper strips of equal width
dark woodstain
bowl
paper towels

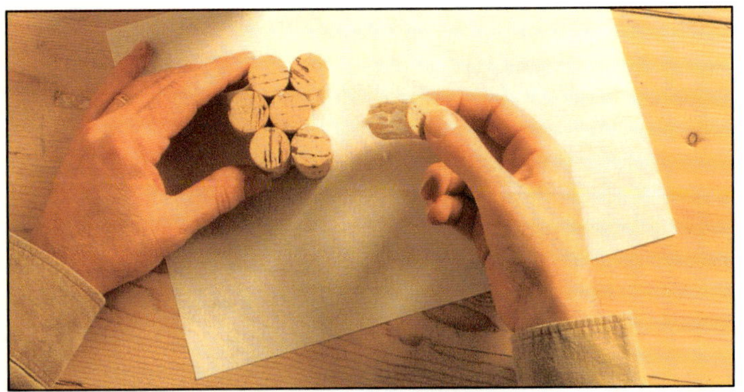

one *Glue the corks in a daisy formation, standing the ends flat on a piece of paper. This will provide a level printing surface. Bind the corks together with masking tape once the glue has become tacky.*

two *Draw the pattern onto the cork surface with a felt-tipped pen. Cut out the background pieces with a scalpel.*

three *Start by stamping the design at each corner of the floor, placing the paper against the baseboard, as guide.*

four *Move the strips along the straight baseboard and stamp a motif about halfway between the first two. Stamp a row of evenly spaced motifs between the existing prints. Continue to stamp a border all around the room.*

FAUX-SOAPSTONE FLOOR

BLACK CORK TILES covering the whole floor in this room were too severe, but when the middle section of the room was treated to this wonderful soapstone effect, they became an important part of the overall grand gesture. The cork tiles in the center were replaced with a large piece of fiberboard, to which a maze pattern was applied. This could simply have been painted on plywood or fiberboard as a two-dimensional effect, but here the surface has been enhanced by routing the maze pattern (take it to a local carpenter; routing really isn't for the inexperienced) and then painted to create a soapstone effect. You could also imitate slate, by using a wave design and the black leading that was used in the nineteenth century for cleaning cast-iron fireplaces and grates (available at specialty stores). Sand or prepare your floor before beginning.

YOU WILL NEED

paper
pencil
sheet of medium density fiberboard
plastic wood or wood filler, if necessary
fine-grade sandpaper
matte latex paint: white, dark gray and medium gray
paintbrushes
wax candle
scraper
soft brush
matte varnish

one *For a new floor, plan your design on paper, using this picture as a guide. Draw it onto the sheet of fiberboard. Take it to a carpenter to be routed and ask him or her to attach it in place on your floor. For an existing floor, draw the maze on the floor directly and ask a carpenter to do the routing in situ.*

two *Fill in any mistakes or flaws with plastic wood or wood filler, following the manufacturer's instructions. Don't try to achieve a perfectly flush surface at this stage. Let dry.*

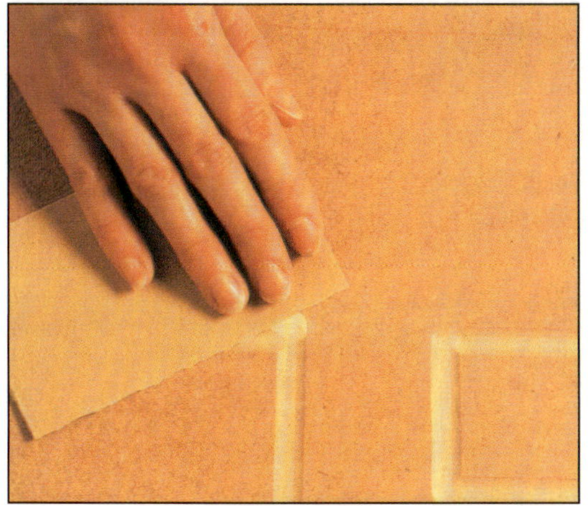

three *When dry, gently sand until you have a level surface.*

four *Paint the whole surface white and let it dry.*

five *Paint over the whole surface of the floor in dark gray.*

six *Using a candle, apply a generous coating of wax with circular movements to the surface of the floor.*

seven *Take off most of the candle wax, using a scraper.*

eight *Follow this with a coat of medium gray latex paint.*

CONTINUED OVER ➤

nine *Apply another coat of wax. Take off the wax with the scraper.*

ten *Apply white paint with a dry soft brush, to soften the whole effect. Seal with matte varnish. If you are surrounding the fiberboard with cork tiles, lay them at the end and make sure they meet neatly at the edges.*

Hanging Around

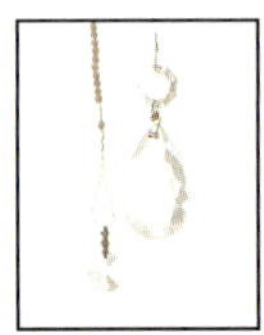

Make the prettiest of chandelier-hangings with simple deciduous twigs such as apple or pear branches. Select a few branches with gnarled, interesting shapes and bind them together to make an eye-catching structure, then hang the finished chandelier in the center of a window, suspended from a length of gold twine. Trim the branches with sparkling trinkets such as crystal droplets and tiny pearls, all attached with the finest of gold cord. This project would also look stunning hanging from a ceiling rose or as a wall decoration.

YOU WILL NEED

- 2–3 apple or pear tree branches
- fine gold wire
- scissors
- gold cord
- crystal droplets
- gold beading wire
- small pearls
- gilded decorations

one *Take the branches and move them around until they form a pretty shape. Bind the branches together at the top with fine gold wire.*

two *Attach a length of gold cord to hang the branches.*

three *Thread crystal droplets onto gold wire. Make short strings of pearls.*

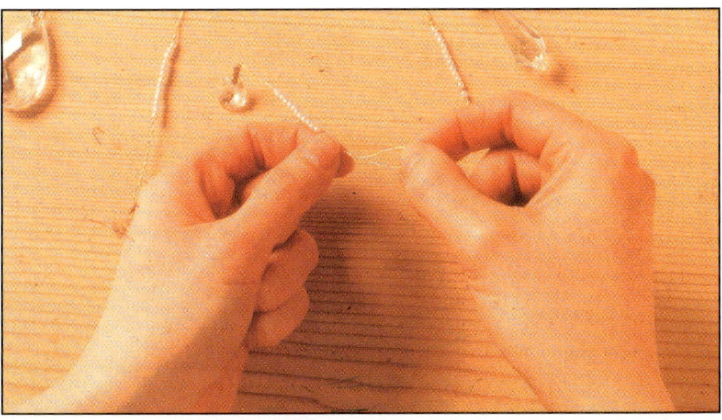

four *Wire the remaining decorations, then twist the wires to make hanging loops. Position the twig chandelier and hang on the jewels.*

COLORED STRIPS OF WOOD

SOMETIMES THE SIMPLEST IDEAS are the most effective. Strips of wood spaced on the wall at regular intervals can create an unusual and very dramatic look. Use them on a single wall or in smaller areas, such as the back of an alcove. The key is to keep the colors either tones of the same shade or very contrasting and bold. If time permits, paint the top and bottom of the wood in slightly different shades of the same color to add extra interest. The strips of wood used here are 2 x 1 inch.

YOU WILL NEED

- tape measure
- wood strips
- pencil
- saw
- matte latex paint: blue and white
- paintbrush
- level
- drill, with masonry and wood bits
- wall plugs
- wood screws
- ruler

one *Measure the height and width of the wall to make sure you will have equal spacing all the way up the wall. Cut the wood strips to the required length. Paint the wood strips; you could paint all three sides that will show in different colors, for a more interesting look, or in tones of the same shade, for subtlety.*

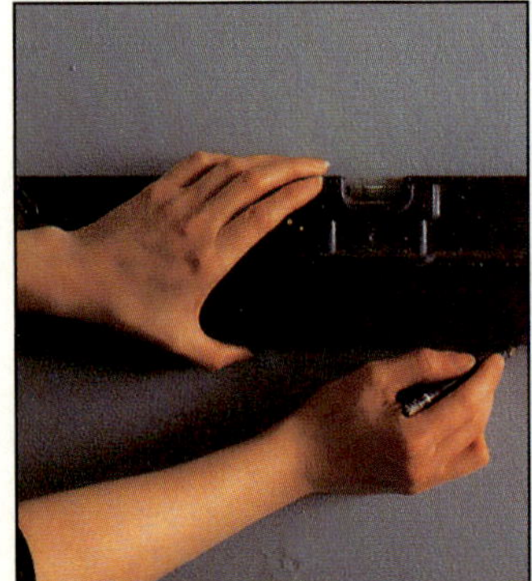

two *Use a level to mark a guideline for the first strip, to make sure the wood is absolutely level.*

three *Drill holes in the wall and insert wall plugs. Drill holes in the wood and then screw the strip in place. Mark out the position for the next wood strip; the space between strips must be absolutely even to create the right effect.*

PHOTOCOPY MONTAGE

THIS EFFECT IS REMINISCENT of the wonderful painted floors of the great European palaces. Few of us can afford to commission frescoes and floor painting, but we might still aspire to a home decorated in a style fit for Marie Antoinette. Using photocopied images on a freshly prepared floor can turn these dreams into reality. Choose any theme: Our photograph shows a composition of landscapes, but architectural drawings, classical motifs such as columns, garden urns and statues, or even still lifes of fruit or vegetables could be made into successful montages. Using the same techniques, you could create a totally modern feeling using color photocopies of, say, flowers; instead of stenciling the borders, add freehand leaves and scrolls.

YOU WILL NEED

- cream and green eggshell latex paint
- paintbrushes
- photocopied images
- long metal ruler
- craft knife
- self-healing cutting mat
- artist's watercolor or acrylic paints
- gum arabic tape (optional)
- pencil
- masking tape
- acetate sheet
- bleed-proof paper (such as tracing paper)
- green stencil paint
- stencil brush
- wallpaper paste
- matte varnish

one *Starting with a well-prepared hardboard or marine-plywood floor, paint on an undercoat of cream eggshell paint, followed by a top coat. Let dry completely.*

‹ two *Experiment with images in different sizes and settle on an arrangement that looks good on your floor. Trim the images so that you are left with just the pictures.*

three *If your images are black-and-white, use watercolor or acrylic paints to put soft washes of color over the prints. You may need to stretch the paper, using gum arabic tape, depending on the quality of the paper—test a small area first.*

four *Arrange the images on the floor and draw the borders you want. Mask off the boxes for the images with masking tape. Paint between the lines of masking tape with green eggshell paint. When the paint is almost dry, gently peel off the masking tape.*

five *Make the stencil from the acetate sheet. Apply the stencil to the floor with masking tape and stipple with green paint. Glue the photocopies to the floor with wallpaper paste. Varnish the floor several times.*

COLOR-WASHED PARQUET

HERRINGBONE PATTERNS ON FLOORS give instant classical elegance, suggestive of the wonderful dark oak parquet floors found in large old houses. However, a fresher look is often wanted, yet with all the interest of the old floors; the introduction of a pale, soft color lifts gloomy dark wood into the realms of light Atlantic beach houses or modern Swedish homes. To keep the interest of the grain of the wood running in different directions, paint each individual piece separately.

YOU WILL NEED

- marine-plywood, cut into manageable lengths
- miter saw
- tape measure
- sandpaper
- matte latex paint: cream, blue and white
- paintbrushes
- matte water-based glaze
- lint-free cloth
- floor adhesive
- matte varnish

one *Make sure the floor is clean, dry and level. Miter the edges of the marine-plywood strips, using a miter saw. Remember that you must have left- and right-hand miters in equal numbers. Measure your required length for the herringbone pattern and cut as many as you need for the floor.*

two *Smooth any rough edges with sandpaper. Undercoat all the boards with cream matte latex and let them dry completely.*

three *Mix up at least four variations of blue with a very slight tonal difference between them. Add a little matte water-based glaze to each, to delay the drying time. Thin one of the colors with water to make it even more translucent. Paint equal numbers of the boards in each color.*

four *With the lint-free cloth, wipe off most of the paint randomly while it is still wet, so that the undercoat shows through. Wipe in the direction of the grain of the wood.*

five *For an even more weathered look, sand some areas of some boards when the paint is dry; this will give contrast when the floor is down. Lay the floor following the instructions for the Parquet project. Finally, ensure that the floor is dry and dust-free, then seal the whole floor with at least two coats of matte varnish.*

SHELL TIE-BACKS

CURTAIN TIE-BACKS can be made in a tremendously wide range of styles so you can use them to create whatever decorative effect you like. Though we normally think of a simple braid or tassel, tie-backs can be decorated to make them a focal point in any room. Here, a fishing net was festooned with different types and sizes of shells. You could wire a mass of very small shells onto the net or even edge the curtain with a widely spaced line of matching shells.

YOU WILL NEED

fishing net
shells
fine wire
wire cutters
glue gun and glue sticks or electric drill, with very fine drill bit
string (optional)

one *Take the fishing net and arrange it in graceful folds. Gather a mass of shells and see how they look best when arranged on the net. Cut lengths of fine wire. These can then be glued to the back of the shells so that they can be wired onto the net.*

two *Alternatively, drill holes in the shells. Thread string through the holes for attaching to the net.*

three *Attach the shells to the fishing net. Make another tie-back in the same way. Loop the tie-backs around the curtains and onto the wall.*

GEOMETRIC WALL-BOARD

YOU DO NOT NEED to be an artist to make a work of art for your wall and even make sure it's the right size and in complementary colors for the room. With a piece of fiberboard, a simple, repetitive design and a little time and patience, you can create a wall decoration at very little cost. A stencil is all that's needed and, if you stick to a design made of simple squares and circles, it is no problem to create your own stencil. Alternatively, it is worth looking at the commercial stencils available. There are so many designs to choose from, you are certain to find one you like.

one *Choose your colors. You may consider complementing your existing furnishings. Plan out the whole design to scale on paper. Here, a wrapping paper design was used for inspiration.*

two *Cut the fiberboard to size, apply the blue base coat and let dry. Draw a grid of squares on the painted fiberboard. Use a ruler and compass to draw the stencil on the sheet of acetate. Cut out the stencil carefully using the craft knife on a cutting mat.*

three *Tape the stencil over one of the squares on the grid. Stencil all the yellow circles and surrounds, then stencil the red circles and surrounds.*

four *Touch up any smudges with the artist's brush. When the paint is completely dry, rub out any visible pencil lines.*

YOU WILL NEED

- scrap paper
- pencil
- ruler
- medium-density fiberboard
- tape measure
- saw
- latex paint: blue, yellow and red
- paintbrushes
- compass
- sheet of acetate
- craft knife
- self-healing cutting mat
- masking tape
- stencil brush
- small artist's brush
- rubber
- clear varnish
- varnish brush
- screw eyelets
- picture-hanging wire
- picture hook
- hammer
- drill, with masonry and wood bits (optional)
- plastic anchors (optional)
- wood screws (optional)

five *Apply a coat of varnish. Attach the wall-board to the wall by inserting screw eyelets and stringing picture-hanging wire between them. Hammer in a strong picture hook and hang the board as you would a painting. Alternatively, drill holes in the wall and insert plastic anchors, screw the board to the wall and fill and make good the screw holes.*

WOOD-GRAIN FLOORING

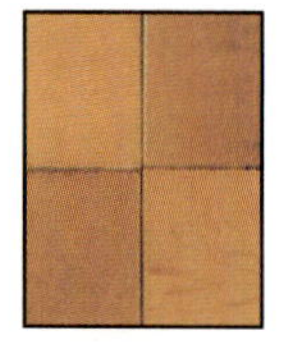

CHECKERBOARD FLOORS ARE a popular theme for flooring but are rarely seen in natural wood. If you are starting from a concrete or wooden floor, have the new floor covering cut into squares the size you want. If your floor is already covered in sheets of plywood, fiberboard or hardboard, mark a checkerboard pattern, ignoring the natural seams. Woodgraining does not have to be done painstakingly carefully. Obtain a sample of the wood effect you want; we used oak, grained to resemble wood treated in different ways, half "polished" and half "rough-sawn and sandblasted." You can use two different wood effects if desired.

YOU WILL NEED

pencil
tape measure
long ruler or straight edge
masking tape
2 cream oil-based eggshell paints
paintbrushes
wood sample
artist's oil paint to match wood sample
oil-based or glaze
paint thinner
dry-graining brush
graining comb
satin varnish
soft cloth
non-slip polish

one *Make sure the surface is smooth and mark into checkerboard squares. Edge alternate squares with strips of masking tape and paint them, using two different cream eggshell paints.*

two *Mix the oil colors into the glaze, to match the wood sample. Thin if necessary. For the "lighter" squares, brush on the glaze in the direction you want the grain to run.*

three *Add random strokes, let dry for a few minutes and then drag a dry-graining brush over the glaze to give the graining effect.*

four *To introduce the chevrons of the wood grain, use a darker oil paint and draw them in with a fine artist's brush. Soften with a broad brush, adding thinner if the paint has dried.*

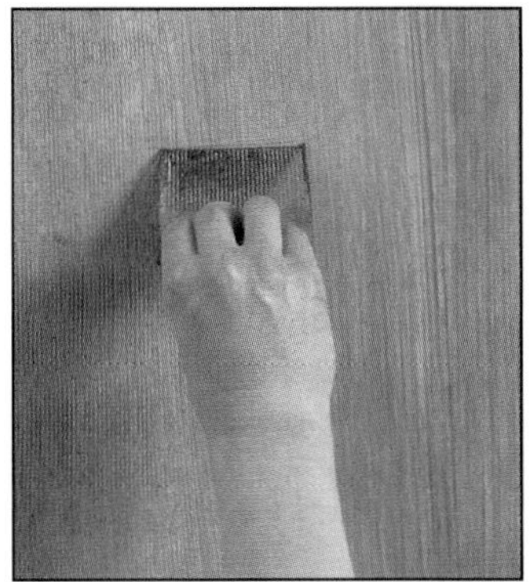

five *For the "darker" squares, repeat step 2 and then step 3, using a graining comb rather than a dry-graining brush so the grain looks wider.*

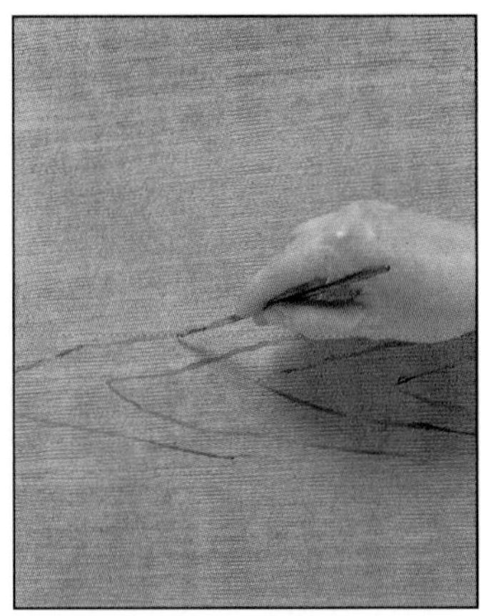

six *Paint on darker chevrons as before, following the grain of the glaze.*

seven *Soften the effect, using the graining comb, then the brush. Apply two coats of satin varnish and let dry. Burnish with non-slip polish.*

LIVING ROOM SECRETS

JUST BECAUSE YOU INVEST heavily in some great curtain fabric, you should not feel committed to spending at least as much again on having it made up. This is a totally no-sew curtain and valance idea that could easily pass for the work of a professional. To figure out how much material you need, just measure the drop and allow three times that length. The seams are all iron-on and the rest is done with a staple gun and string. It's hard to imagine that such an elegant draped valance could be put together without sewing a stitch. Follow the steps to discover the hidden secrets that lie behind this living room window.

YOU WILL NEED

striped fabric
tape measure
scissors
iron-on hem tape or double-sided carpet tape (optional)
iron
2 narrow strips wood, window width, plus 12 inches each side
level
drill
plastic anchors and screws
screwdriver
staple gun
string

one *Divide the fabric into three equal lengths, two for the curtains and one for the valance. Turn over the hems on both ends of the valance and one end of each of the curtains. Attach the hems with iron-on hem tape, or carpet tape if the fabric is very heavy. Attach the thin side of one of the strips of wood to the wall so that the ends overlap the window equally—use a level to check the position. Screw the other strip of wood onto it at a right angle.* ➤

two *Starting at one end, staple the edge of one curtain to the front of the strip of wood. Staple the other corner of the curtain to the middle of the wood. Most of the curtain will now hang loose in the middle.*

three *For the pleats, hold the curtain away from the window and find the middle. Staple this to the middle of the wood. Find the middle of the two loose sections and staple them to the middle of the strip of wood. Keep subdividing the strip of wood and the fabric until you have reached the pleat width you want. Repeat for the other curtain.*

four *Fold the valance fabric in half lengthwise and line up with the center of the window. Starting at the center, staple along one edge to the top of the strip of wood, close to the wall. Lift the side drops and gather up the fabric at the corners. Put a row of staples under the gather so that the stripes line up with the curtain stripes below.*

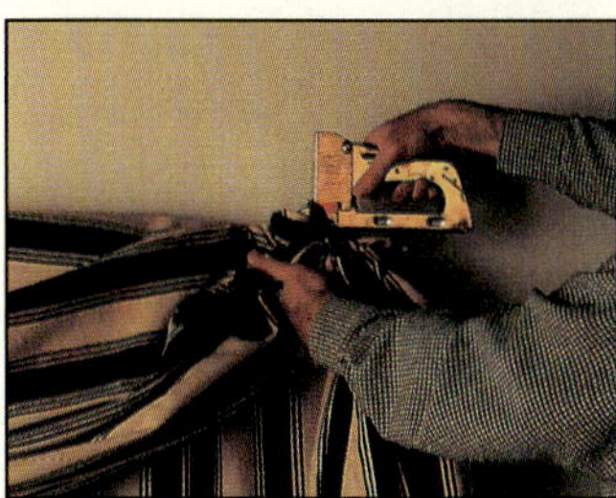

five *Bunch up the fabric at each corner and tie it with string. Be aware of the way the fabric folds at this stage —you may need to practice folding and tying a few times until you achieve the desired effect. Staple the string to the strip of wood. It won't show, so use as many staples as you need to make it secure.*

six *Tie another piece of string around the drop of the valance, about 12 inches down. Tie it tightly, leaving enough string to let you tie another knot to raise this section to the top corner.*

seven *Pull the fabric up to the corner and tie the string ends tightly around the first knot. Push the knots inside the remaining fabric to puff the front out. If necessary, add staples to hold this in place along the top of the strip of wood. Finally, arrange the pleats and folds.*

No-FRILLS NAVY

BLOCK OUT THE LIGHT with these crisp, stylish navy blue curtains. Cotton canvas is as heavy as denim, but to add firmness and thickness to the tops, you can use double-sided carpet tape to bond them together. This also means that you get a good fit with the large brass eyelets that are made for tent canvas and sails. You will need to buy fabric about one-and-a-half times the width of your window plus an allowance of 2 inches at the top and bottom to get perfect pleats. It is always a good idea to err on the generous side with curtains, so stretch the budget rather than the fabric on this project.

YOU WILL NEED

double-sided carpet tape
craft knife
navy cotton canvas
backing cardboard
ruler
pencil
hole punch
hammer
brass eyelets
rigging wire, window width
2 wire rope grips
2 thimbles
pliers
drill
2 plastic anchors and large hooks

one *Stick a length of double-sided carpet tape along the top of the fabric, just in from the edge. Peel off the top paper. Fold the top hem over the tape, smoothing as you go to ensure a crisp, wrinkle-free finish.*

two *Place the curtain on a sheet of backing cardboard. Using a ruler and a pencil, mark the positions for the holes at 8-inch intervals. Put the back part of the hole punch in position behind the fabric to make the first hole.*

three *Position the top part of the hole punch and bang it firmly with a hammer. Place the back part of the eyelet in the back part of the hole punch. Place the middle of the eyelet through the punched hole.*

four *Place the top half of the eyelet on top of the bottom half. Position the tool provided with the eyelets and bang it firmly with a hammer. Continue positioning the eyelets at the marked intervals along the top of the curtains.*

five *Thread the rigging wire through the wire grip to form a loop. Place the thimble inside the loop and pull the wire taut. Using a hammer on a hard surface, bang the wire grip closed. You may also need to squeeze it with pliers.*

six *Drill holes and attach one of the hooks in the window recess. Loop the rigging wire over it. Thread the curtains onto the rigging wire through the eyelets.*

seven *Thread the other end through the wire grip as before, then attach to a hook. Screw the hook into a pre-drilled and plugged hole. This will ensure even pleats.*

SCOTLAND THE BRAVE

HERE IS THE PERFECT WAY to show off bright tartan wool rugs. Draped and pinned over a wooden rod, they will add a baronial touch to the plainest of windows.

Tartan has quite a masculine feel and looks good alongside old leather cases and other "practical" accessories. This window would suit a study or hallway with plain walls that would contrast with the richness and pattern of the tartan. Attach the curtain rod above the window, extending it about 12 inches on each side.

YOU WILL NEED

wooden curtain rod
level
drill
plastic anchors and screws
screwdriver
3 different colored tartan rugs
6 kilt pins

one *Attach the curtain rod according to the package instructions. Begin on the left with one corner of a rug. Take the corner over from the back and pin it about 12 inches down the rug.*

two *Drape the second rug over the rail, also on the left, but arrange it so that the drape is more or less equal at the front and back. Lift it in places and pin it onto the first rug using kilt pins.*

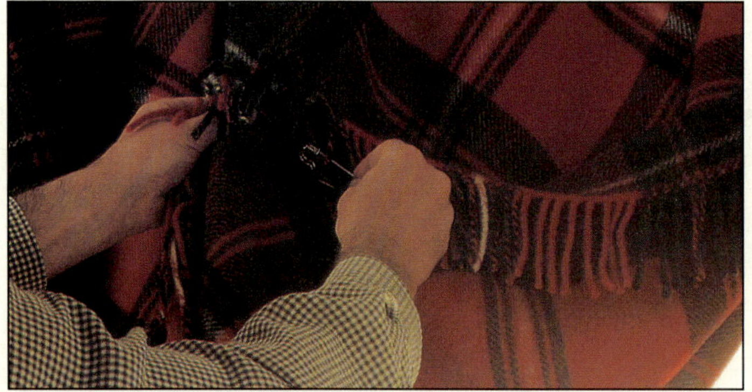

three *Drape the third tartan rug along the rest of the pole diagonally so that the fringed edge can be seen hanging down from the right corner. Lift sections of this rug and pin it so that it drapes by attaching it with kilt pins to the second rug.*

four *Stand back and check the effect, then use any remaining pins to hold the rugs in place, making a feature of the fringing and the pins.*

DRAPED DIRECTOR'S CHAIR

COMPLETELY DRAPED IN A slip cover, a folding director's chair loses its functional character and takes on the role of an armchair. Avoid complicated fitting by cutting a simple tunic-style slip cover, based on squares and rectangles that are just tied together. You can then put the cover straight onto the chair without ironing, since it can be removed and stored flat when the chair is folded away.

YOU WILL NEED

director's chair
measuring tape
2½ yards of 54-inch fabric
fabric marker
triangle and ruler
scissors
dressmaker's pins
matching thread
sewing machine

one *Measure: (a) from floor to top edge of back; (b) from top edge of back to back of seat; (c) length of seat; (d) width of seat; (e) from center of wooden armrest to inside base of seat; (f) from center of armrest to floor; (g) from front edge of seat to floor.*

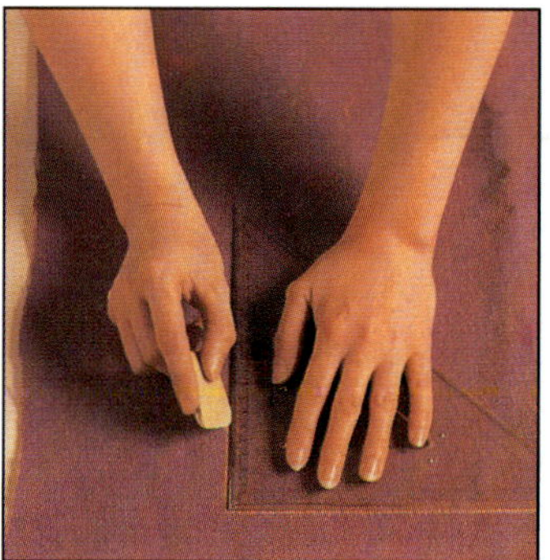

two *Measure and draw the pattern pieces directly onto the fabric, with a seam allowance all around each piece. Cut out, then pin, baste and sew the pieces together following the diagram at the back of the book.*

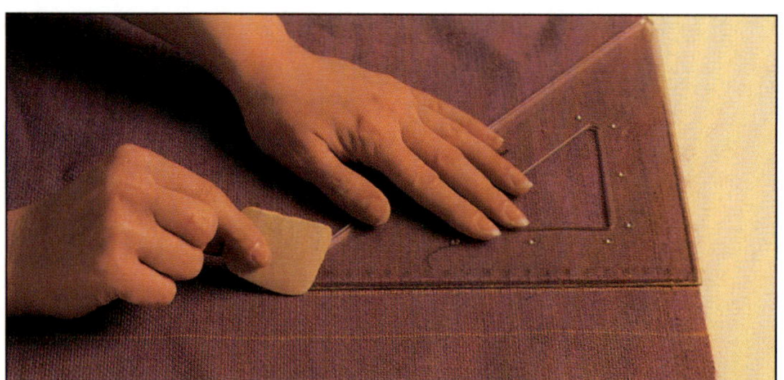

three *Mark and cut strips of fabric to make ties of a finished size of about 1 inch wide and 16 inches long. Put right sides together and sew the long edges together. Then turn them out and slip-stitch the ends.*

four *Assemble the tunic as a cross (see diagram). Slip the finished cover over the chair and knot the ties firmly.*

DRESSING FOR DINNER

FOR VERY SPECIAL OCCASIONS, why not dress up your table and chairs? Choose a style of corsage suited to the style of your chairs. A simple unvarnished country chair, for instance, calls for understated trimmings, whereas a fancy French one requires something much more elaborate. Trim the table to match. The individual flower arrangements can be given to your guests to take home. These ideas could not be simpler, but will add to the festivities.

YOU WILL NEED

florist's wire
silk or fresh flowers
fresh greenery
scissors
2½ yards organza ribbon and piece of organza
potpourri and star anises
fine string
glue gun and glue sticks
beads

A CHAIR WITH STYLE

one *Use florist's wire to join the flowers together at the stems. Silk flowers are best because they are bendable.*

two *Continue binding in flowers and greenery to make an attractive corsage. Trim the stems and tuck in any ends.*

three *Finish with a ribbon bow. Make a wire hook to attach the corsage to the chair.*

LIVENING UP THE TABLE

one *Fill a teapot with potpourri. Then cut a circle from organza, fill it with potpourri and tie the top with string. Twist a cinnamon stick into the tie and tie the bag to the lid.*

two *Make a bottle a necklace by pulling apart a piece of fine string into separate strands and gluing star anises to one strand.*

three *Decorate a decanter or jar with a piece of organza ribbon tied into bows, or threaded with beads.*

LACED DINING CHAIR

TRANSFORM A DULL CHAIR into a modern piece with added comfort and dramatic color. These covers can be permanent or changed at whim. Any bright canvas fabric is suitable; economic cotton canvas has been used here. The fabric must have a little body or you will need to add a backing fabric. Ticking, canvas or linen are all suitable.

Self-covering buttons with cord loops or, for the more skilled, buttonholes are good alternatives to lacing eyelets. Loops and toggles or frogging give a military look, especially with a bright scarlet fabric.

YOU WILL NEED

- dining chair
- measuring tape
- foam or rubberized horse hair (to fit the back of the chair)
- scissors
- tape for ties
- thin batting (to fit the back of the chair)
- upholstery tacks
- tissue or pattern-cutting paper
- felt-tipped pen
- 3 yards of 50-inch-wide cotton canvas
- dressmaker's pins
- sewing machine
- matching thread
- iron
- safety pins
- fabric marker
- hole-punching tool
- hammer
- 8 eyelets
- eyelet pliers
- 3 yards cotton tape

one *Measure the chair back for the size of the foam backing or rubberized horse hair. Cut the backing to size and attach it to the chair back with ties at the top and bottom.*

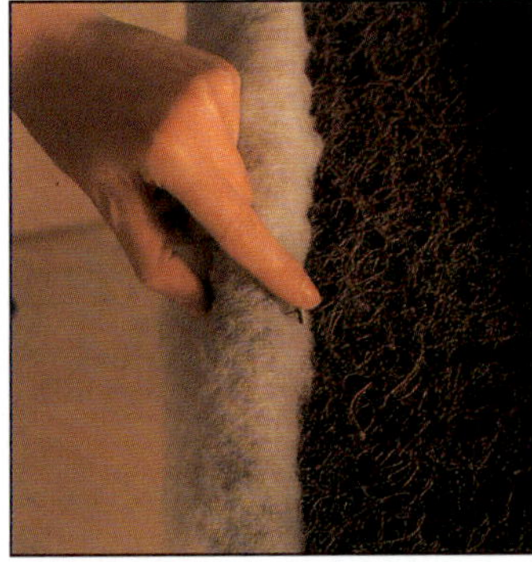

two *Cover the foam or horse hair loosely with thin batting and secure the batting with tacks.*

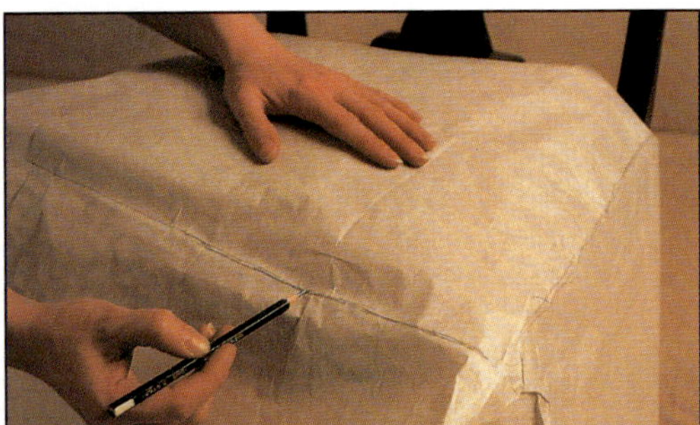

three *Lay the pattern-cutting paper on the seat and draw around it, adding a 1½-inch seam allowance. Make a pattern for the front of the seat back.*

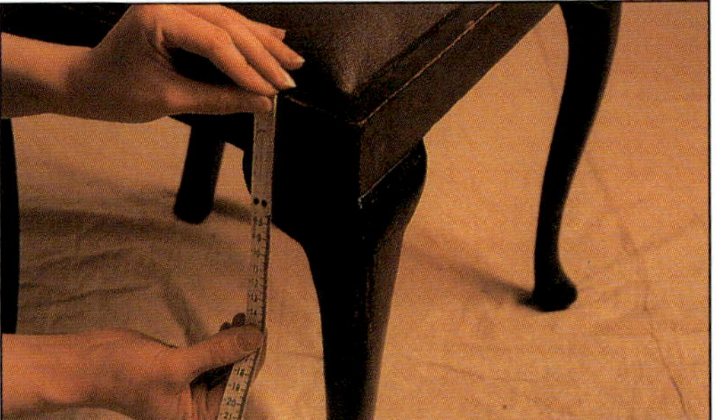

four *Decide how deep the skirt will be, then figure out the dimensions for the back. The back panel incorporates a box pleat to allow easy removal (see diagram). Draw a pattern.*

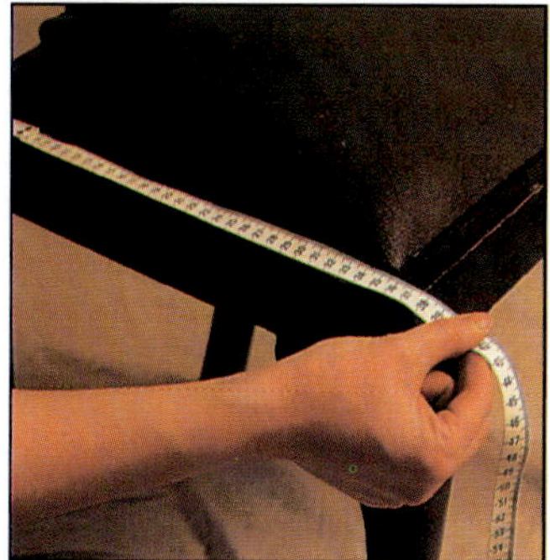

five *For the skirt, measure the two sides and front of the seat, then add 12 inches for each of the four box pleats. Add 1½ inches to the depth as a seam allowance. Make a pattern.*

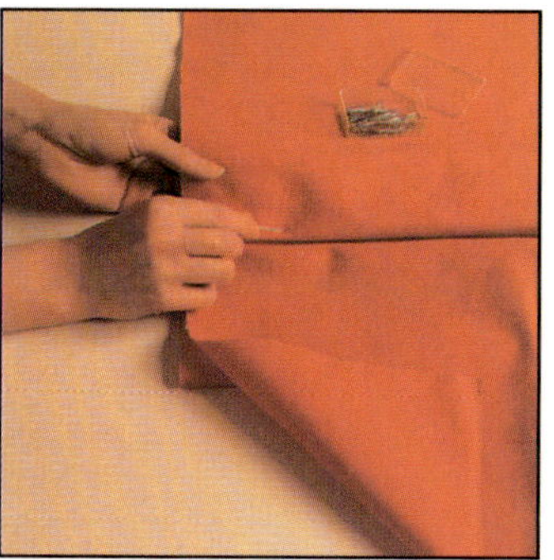

six *Lay the patterns on your material and cut out each piece. Take the back panel and pin, then stitch the central box pleat down to 1½ inches from the top of the seat and press it.*

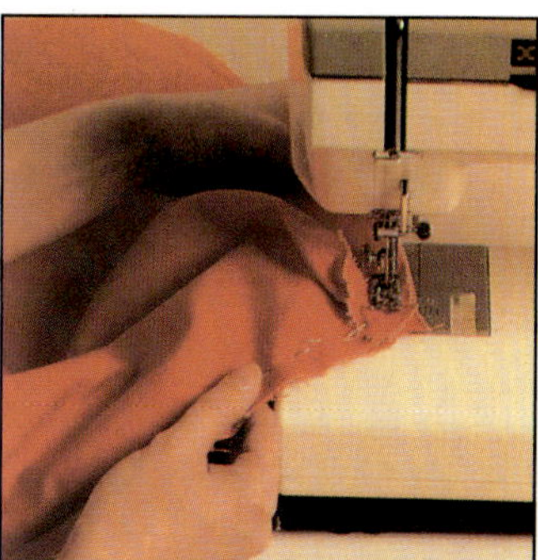

seven *Stitch the front panel to the top of the seat panel with the right sides together. Trim and press open all the seams as you go.*

eight *Stitch the front panel to the back at the top and sides. Hem the bottom edge of the skirt. Fold and pin the box pleats so they fall in the corners of the seat. Machine-stitch the seat and skirt in place along the top edges.*

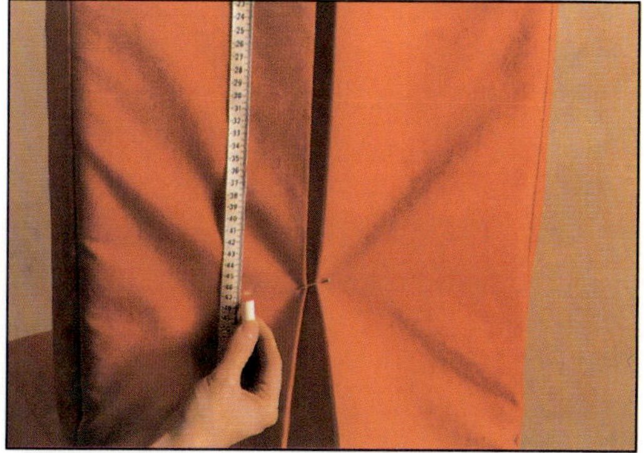

nine *Put the cover on the seat, close the back pleat with safety pins and mark where the eyelets are to be with a fabric marker.*

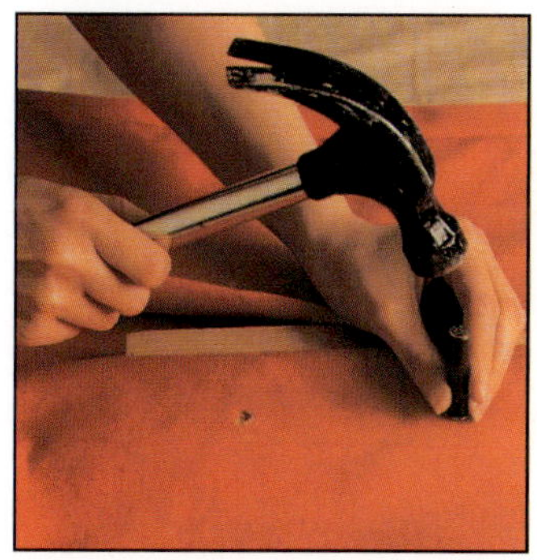

ten *Remove the cover. Using a hole-punching tool, make holes for the eyelets.*

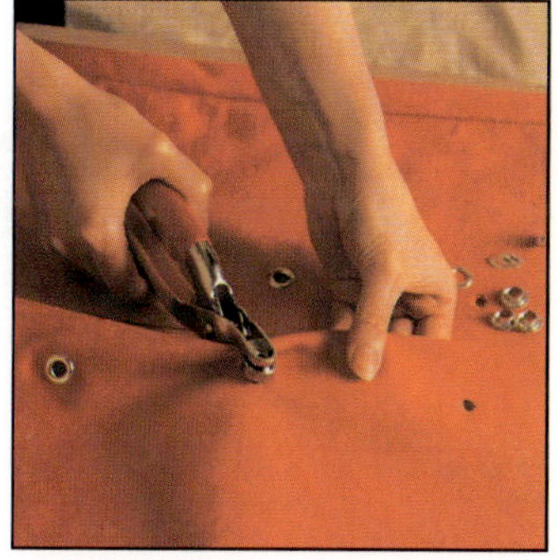

eleven *Following the manufacturer's instructions, attach the eyelets.*

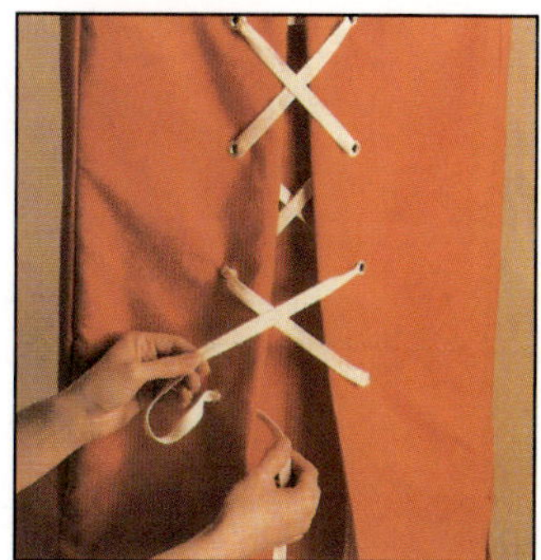

twelve *Put the cover on the chair and lace up the back with cotton tape.*

CONTINUED OVER ➤

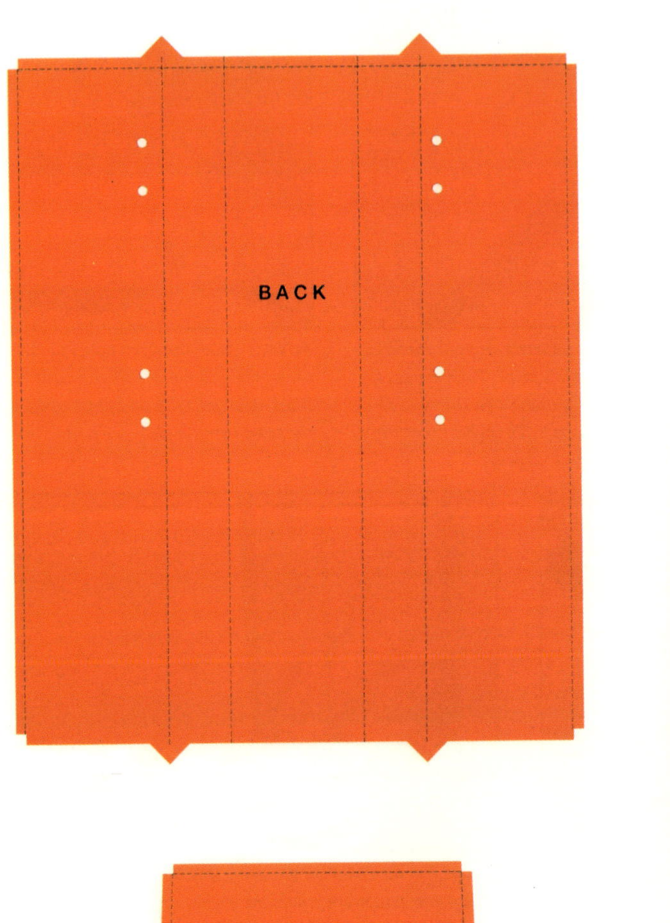

SEAT

EDGING

AFRICAN CUSHIONS

NEW CUSHIONS ARE ONE of the best and easiest ways to brighten up a room, and this glorious pile of striking orange-brown cushions decorated with stamps based on traditional animal motifs from Africa creates a distinctive look. Stamps of this type are perfect for making a themed, but not identical, set of cushions to display together. The covers are made from rough homespun fabric that has been vegetable-dyed in rich spicy shades. The combination of primitive stamped shapes and textured fabric is doubly effective.

YOU WILL NEED

fabric-stamping ink in black

3 African-style rubber stamps

loose-weave cushion covers

sheet of cardboard

one *Apply the fabric ink directly to the stamp and make a test print on a scrap of the fabric to ensure that the stamp is not overloaded.*

two *Place a sheet of cardboard inside the cover to protect the other side.*

three *Re-ink the stamp and print a row of small motifs around the edges to create a border.*

four *Stamp a row of the larger motif at even intervals above the border. Use a combination of all three stamps to complete the cushion design. Arrange the stamps differently on the other covers, either radiating from the center or in circles.*

EGYPTIAN TABLE-TOP

THE BEAUTY OF THIS TABLE-TOP design lies in its simplicity. Just one color was used on a bold blue background, with three similar images stamped in regimented rows. The table used here has a lower shelf, but the design would work equally well on most tables. The salmon pink prints show up well on the rich background, making it look even bluer. The stamps are pre-cut and are taken from Egyptian hieroglyphs. The finished table could be the surprising and eye-catching centerpiece of a room decorated in subdued colors.

YOU WILL NEED

3 hieroglyph rubber stamps
ruler and triangle
2 cardboard strips, one the length and one the width of the table, for position guides
felt-tipped pen
small paint roller
salmon pink latex or acrylic paint
piece of cardboard or plastic

one *Use the stamps and ruler to measure out the stamp positions. Place a cardboard strip along the edge of the table and mark as many stamp lengths as will fit along, leaving spaces between them. Mark stamp widths along the second cardboard strip.*

two *Place the cardboard strips at 90-degree angles to each other to mark the position of the first row. Coat the roller with paint on a piece of cardboard.*

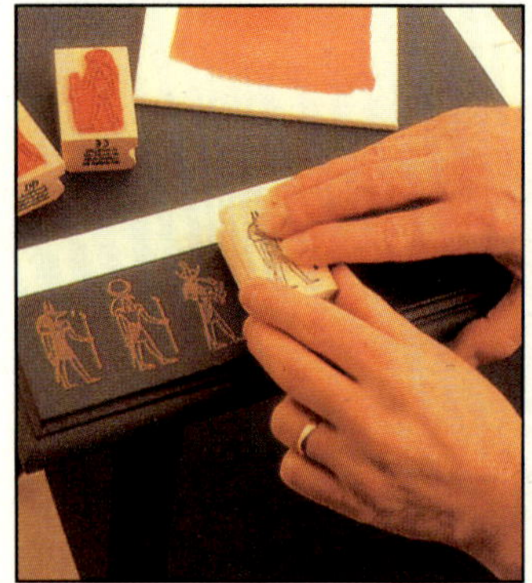

three *Coat the hieroglyphs and stamp in sequence along the first row.*

four *Move the long strip up one stamp-space on the short strip, check that it is at 90 degrees and stamp a second row. Continue until the table is covered.*

ROPE-BOUND CHAIR

COLONIAL-STYLE AND VERANDA CHAIRS have gained considerable popularity recently but, sadly, originals are extremely difficult to find. This is a good technique for a chair whose character would be lost if it were painted or stripped and yet which needs some form of embellishment. Natural trimmings, such as twine or burlap tape, can be expensive, as you will need about 90 yards. Look for less expensive forms of the same product, such as the thick rope used here. You could also use garden twine, clothesline or builder's scrim.

YOU WILL NEED

old chair

6 to 8 12-yard bales of thick rope

glue gun

one *Starting at the back of the chair, secure the end of the rope with a small amount of glue from the gun.*

two *Begin wrapping the chair with rope, according to your chosen design.*

three *You can use two lengths at a time for the arms, starting with a slip knot.*

four *When you reach the end of the length, secure it by tucking it in at the back of the chair and then glue.*

Parquet

GOOD PARQUET IS A very manageable kind of flooring. There are numerous patterns to be made from combining these wooden blocks. One good technique is to figure out the pattern starting from the center and make it as big a perfect square as you can, then lay a simple border to accommodate all the tricky outside edges. Parquet is often in oak but you could dye it with stain or varnish for a richer effect.

YOU WILL NEED

string
pencil
ridged adhesive spreader
floor adhesive
parquet blocks
strip of wood
matte varnish
paintbrush
fine-grade sandpaper

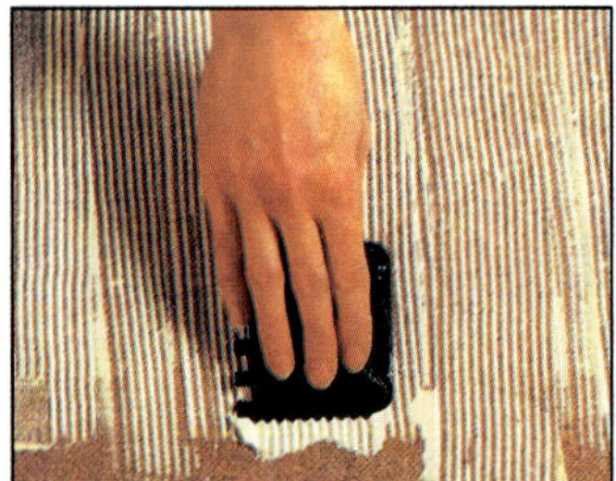

one *Make sure your floor surface is clean, dry and level. Find your starting point by stretching string from corner to corner as for tiles and draw guidelines on the floor. Using a ridged spreader, coat a small area of floor with adhesive.*

two *Apply parquet blocks to the adhesive. Use a strip of wood laid across the blocks to check that they all lie flush. Repeat until the floor is covered. Seal the floor with two or three coats of varnish, sanding between coats.*

GROOVY FLOOR

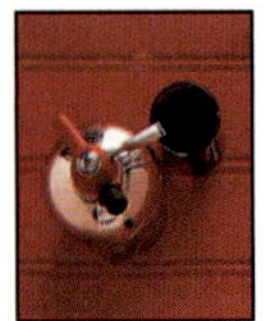

TONGUE-AND-GROOVE BOARDS look wonderful with a gleaming shine. Gloss paint or floor paint is durable and easily renewed if it's ever damaged. Use this floor in a room with a large window and enjoy the dramatic effect of the sun streaming across it. Gloss paint shows up detail, so it was a natural choice for these brand new tongue-and-groove boards but, if you like the effect of the dramatic color but have an old floor, a matte finish would be more forgiving. To lay a new floor of this type, a perfectly smooth and level subfloor is vital.

YOU WILL NEED

tongue-and-groove boards
hammer
drill, with pilot drill bit
flooring pins
pin hammer
nail punch
power sander and sandpaper
undercoat and paintbrushes
high-gloss floor paint

one *Slot the tongue-and-groove boards together and, using a scrap of wood to protect the exposed tongue, tap the next board into place until it fits tightly. If the boards are warped, pin one end first and work along the board; in this way you will be able to straighten out the warp.*

two *To prevent the tongues from splitting, pre-drill pilot holes. Tap pins in gently, using a pin hammer, at a slight angle back toward the boards.*

three *Punch the pins in with a nail punch so the next board can butt up.*

four *When the floor is laid, and before finishing it, sand it, first with a coarse-grade sandpaper and then with medium-grade and finally with fine-grade. Always sand in line with the wood grain. With long, even strokes, in line with the boards, undercoat the floor. Let dry. Lightly sand again and paint with gloss paint.*

JEWEL-BRIGHT ARMCHAIR

MANY ELEGANTLY SHAPED armchairs are disguised beneath several layers of ugly orange or dark brown varnish and dowdy upholstery fabrics. Once the covers have been removed and the old varnish has been sanded away, however, these chairs can be transformed instantly into desirable objects. Stretchy fabrics make it easier to achieve a neat, professional finish, but any upholstery fabric is suitable.

YOU WILL NEED

armchair
medium-grade sandpaper
clear wax or silicone polish
rubber fabric
scissors
staple gun
rubber adhesive
paintbrush
hammer
upholstery tacks
thick artist's cardboard

one *Remove all the old covers. Sand the varnish from the frame. Seal with clear wax or silicone polish. Using the existing cover pieces as patterns, cut the fabric to the size of the back rest, with a generous allowance to turn to the back surface. Stretch it over the back rest until it is hand-tight and staple it in place. Secure, in order, the top, bottom and sides, with one or two staples in the center, before applying lines of staples to keep the fabric taut.*

two *Cut a piece of fabric to fit the back surface of the backrest and use rubber adhesive to stick the fabric to the chair so that it covers the staples and the turned-over edges of the first layer. Hammer a tack into each corner.*

three *For the cushion, trace its shape onto the cardboard. Cut out and staple to the cushion. Wrap the fabric around the cushion, tucking in the corners neatly, and staple to the cardboard. Attach a layer of fabric to the underside of the cushion (following step 2), using rubber adhesive.*

BOLD BLOCKS OF COLOR

FOR THE BOLDEST LOOK of all, paint vibrant blocks of color all over the walls to create an effect like a painting by the Dutch Cubist Piet Mondrian. Using a basic square grid, work across and up and down to create strong patterns and changes of color. Although this example has been created in very brightly colored paints, you could choose a more subdued or even subtle look, using complementary tones or much paler colors. Use this effect on all the walls in a room, if you're feeling brave, or confine it to one area, such as above a chair-rail in a hall, for a less intense effect.

YOU WILL NEED

level
straightedge
pencil
scrap paper
latex paint in several colors
small and medium paintbrushes
masking tape

one *Draw a basic grid of squares directly onto the wall, using the level, straightedge and pencil.*

two *Decide on your colors. Putting small samples together on a sheet of paper may help you to decide which ones work together best.*

three *Mask off the areas for the first color. The blocks can be squares or oblongs, and they can turn corners. Use as many or as few squares of the grid as you like.*

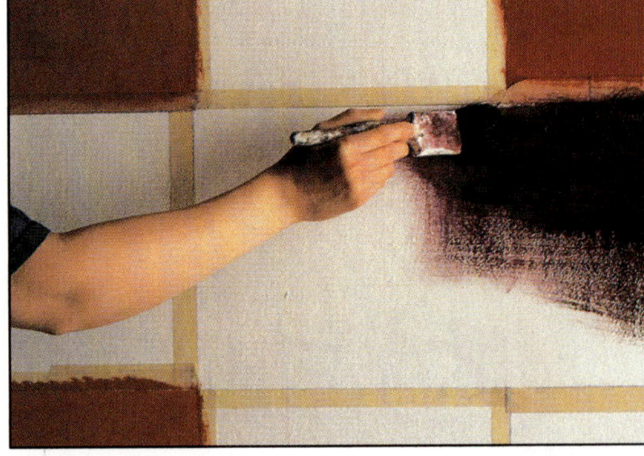

four *Paint the blocks. Remove the tape immediately and let dry. Repeat the process for each of the subsequent colors in your scheme.*

FLOATING FLOOR

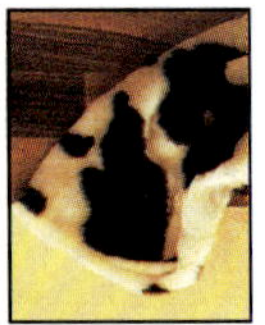

WOOD-STRIP FLOORING IS a good way of creating instant elegance. It comes in a huge variety of finishes and lengths, so you can combine different woods without difficulty. Once you have mastered the principles of how to lay it, you can work out many different combinations and patterns. The main photograph shows walnut interspersed with wide, light-colored maple boards. Alternatively, choose just one wood and lay it in different patterns. Laminated types of wood strip are generally pre-finished but others need to be sealed once they have been laid.

YOU WILL NEED

cushioned underlay (if necessary)
tape
metal joint clips
hammer
wood-strip flooring
spacers
wood glue
saw
tacks and quadrant beading (optional)
pencil
drill, with wood bit

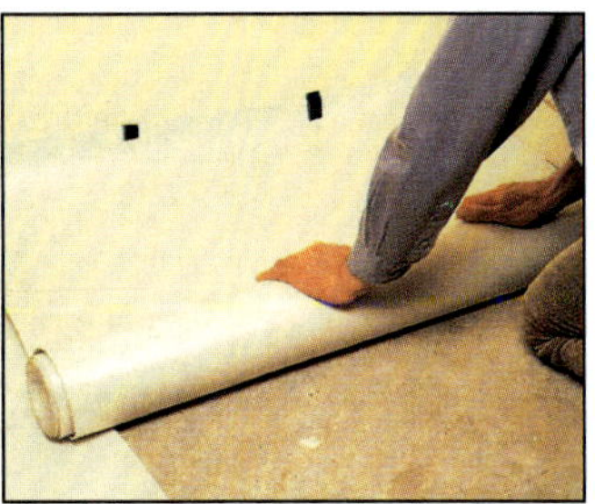

one *If you are using underlay, unroll it and tape one end to keep it in place. Prepare all the boards of wood-strip by hammering the special metal joint clips into the groove on the underside of the board, along the tongued edge.*

two *Lay the first length, clips toward you, against the walls, using spacers. Glue the ends of butt-jointed lengths. Position the second row of boards, tapping them together with a hammer and a scrap of wood, so that the clips engage in the groove of the second row.*

three *Cut the last board to width, allowing for spacers, and apply glue along its grooved edge. Insert, packing against the wall before levering the strip into place. Hammer it down level, using a scrap of wood for protection.*

four *Replace the skirtings or tack lengths of quadrant beading to hide the expansion gap; make sure the skirting fits tightly against the floor.*

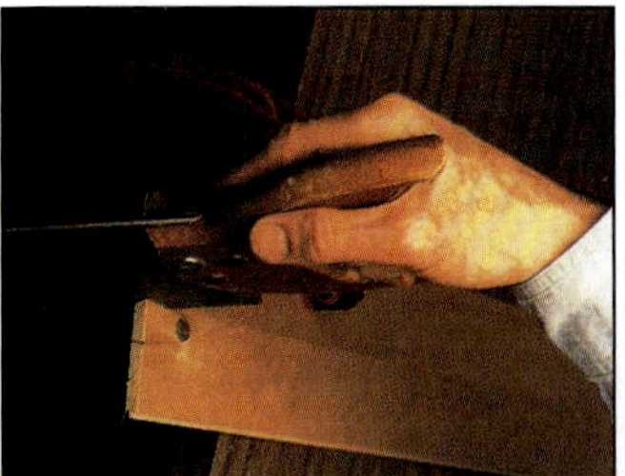

five *To fit a board around a pipe, mark its position and drill a suitably sized hole. Then cut out a tapered wedge, which can be glued back after placing the board.*

SPRIGGED CURTAINS

NATURAL CALICO HAS A lovely creamy color, especially when the sun shines through it. However, it is usually used as a lining fabric, and this association can make it look unfinished. This stamped floral sprig lifts the humble calico into another dimension, giving it a sophisticated finish. Calico is prone to shrinkage, so wash the fabric before you stamp it and make the curtains. The design for the calico stamp is in the template section at the back of the book.

YOU WILL NEED

calico fabric
linoleum block stamp
scrap paper
fabric ink: green and dark blue
scalpel
ruler
cardboard
pencil

one *Lay the fabric out on a flat surface, such as a wallpaper-pasting table. Make several prints of the linoleum block stamp on scrap paper, cut them out with a scalpel and use them to plan the position of the motifs on the fabric.*

two *Decide on the distance between the sprigs, and cut out a square of cardboard with the same dimensions to act as a measuring guide. Use it diagonally, making a pencil mark at each corner over the surface of the fabric.*

three *Apply green ink directly to the edges of the linoleum block stamp. Fill in the middle of the stamp with dark blue ink. Make an initial print on a scrap of fabric to determine the density of the stamped image.*

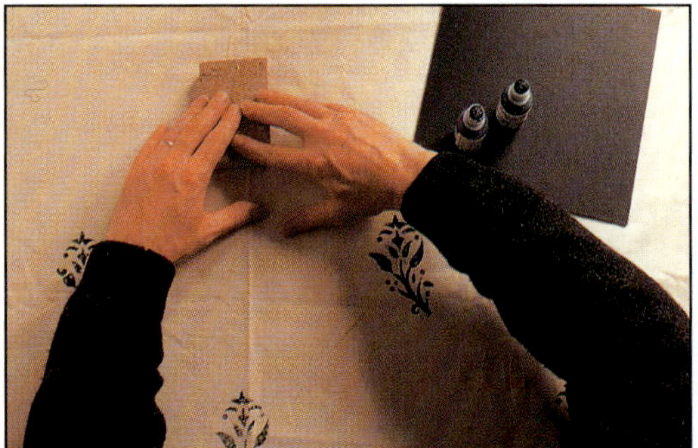

four *Stamp the floral sprig onto the calico, using the pencil marks to position the base of the stamp. You need to apply gentle pressure to the back of the stamp and allow a couple of seconds for the ink to transfer. Don't rush; the result will be all the better for the extra time taken.*

DISTRESSED FLOORBOARDS

OLD WOODEN FLOORS ARE often appealing because of their subtle variations of color. Wood stains can help to imitate that look in only a few hours. The look of driftwood or weathered teak or other hardwood decking, like that of beach houses, is the aim. Achieve the outdoor look using three different wood stains and a wash of white latex, diluted almost to water. This technique would give a bleached effect to any wood stain.

YOU WILL NEED

nail punch
hammer
power sander and fine-grade sandpaper
wire brush
3 different wood stains of the same make
lint-free cloth or paintbrushes
rubber gloves
latex paint: white or cream
dry cloth
matte polyurethane floor varnish

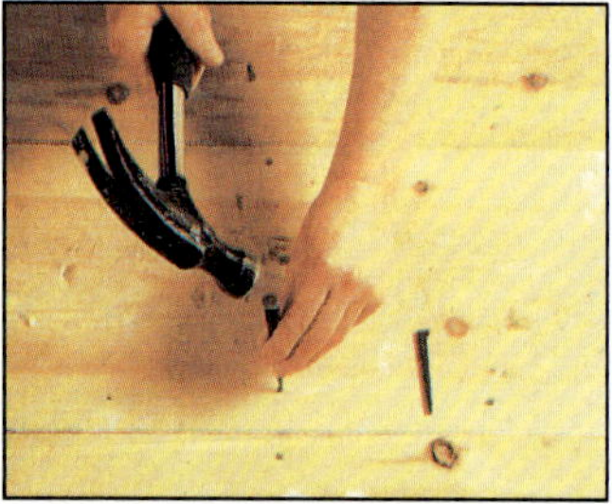

one *It is important that floors have no sharp or protruding nails, so knock in any you find with a nail punch before you begin. Remove old paint spills using a sander. Remember to change the sandpaper frequently, or you will damage the rubber seal of the sander.*

two *Brush the boards with a wire brush, along the direction of the grain, with the occasional contrasting stroke to give a distressed effect. Experiment with the stains, combining colors—a little should go a long way. Use scrap wood to test the effect before you commit yourself by staining the floor.*

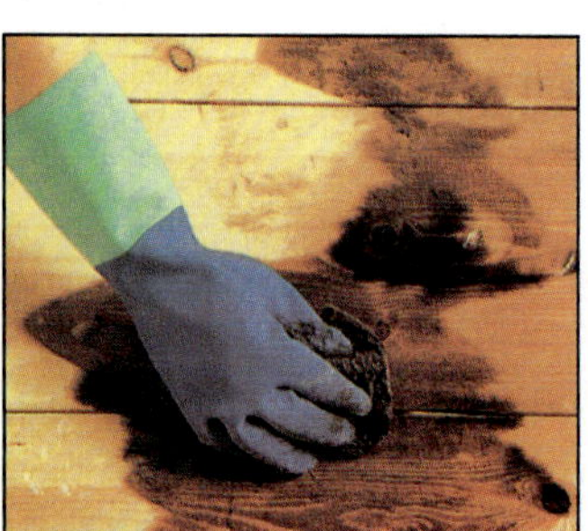

three *With either a lint-free cloth or a paintbrush, apply the stain. This will stain anything porous, so wear rubber gloves and old clothes.*

four *Start by applying quite a generous quantity of stain, but rub most of the surplus off. Don't stop until you've finished the floor or there will be a definite line; keep the seams between areas random and avoid overlapping parallel bands of stain.*

five *It is better to do one thin coat all over and then go back to apply additional coats. To give an uneven, weathered look you can work the stain into the knots or grooves with a brush.*

six *While the stain is still wet, brush on a wash of the diluted white or cream paint, about one part latex to four parts water.*

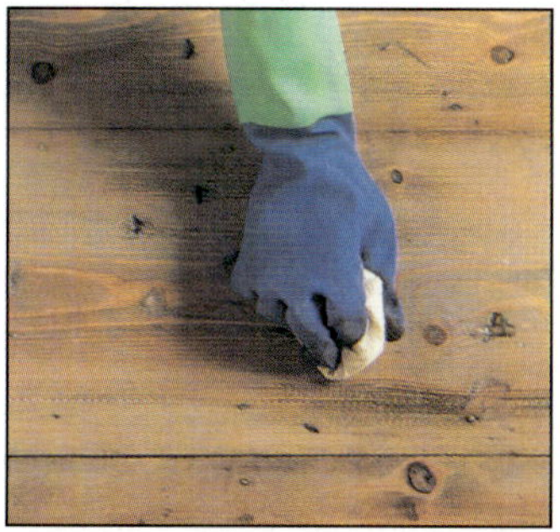

seven *Using a dry cloth, rub off the surplus or apply more until you have the effect you want.*

eight *Apply at least two coats of varnish, sanding very lightly between coats.*

CONTEMPORARY SHELF

ALTHOUGH A POPULAR CHILDISH METHOD has been used to decorate this shelf, the result is an incredibly sophisticated room feature. The shelf pattern has been cut into one half of a potato, with all the colors painted on at the same time, to allow one-step printing. A row of potato stamps like this has a three-dimensional quality, which is enhanced by the choice and positioning of the colors. This is an easy project to carry out, which has an effect far beyond its simple origins.

YOU WILL NEED

ruler

potato

felt-tipped pen

scalpel

knife

gouache, poster or acrylic paint: red, light blue, dark blue, green and yellow

paintbrush

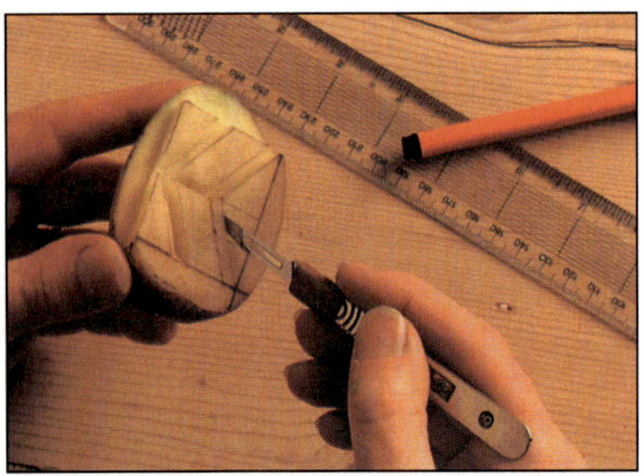

one *Measure the width of the shelf edge and cut the potato to fit. Copy the pattern shapes onto the potato. Cut down with a scalpel to outline the shape, then cut across with a knife to remove the background.*

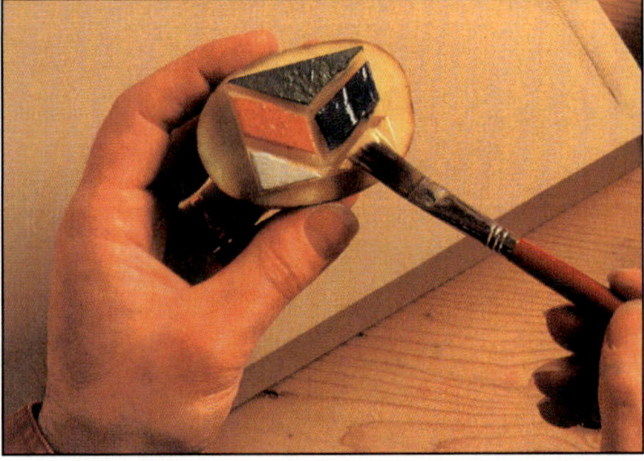

two *Mix the paint, then apply each color to a separate part of the design with a paintbrush.*

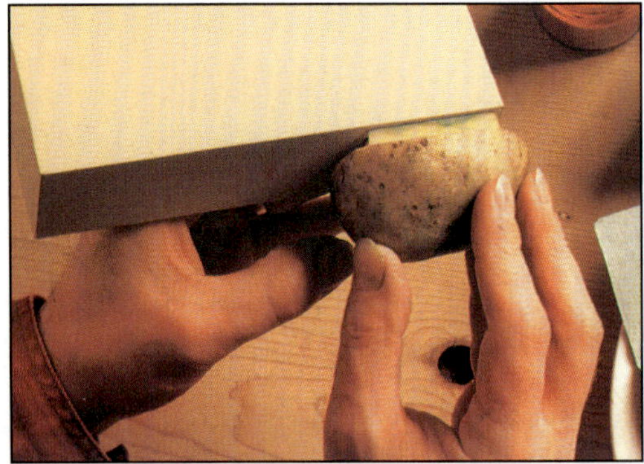

three *Begin printing the shelf edge, making the first print on the short side section that will be nearest the wall.*

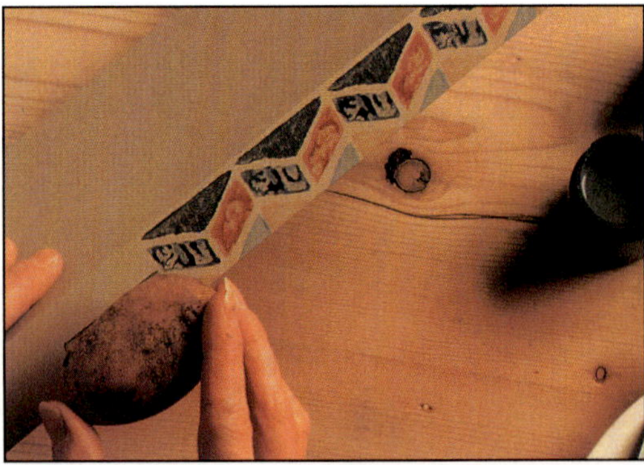

four *Continue to apply the paint as before and stamp the pattern to cover all the shelf edges.*

STUDIES AND HALLWAYS

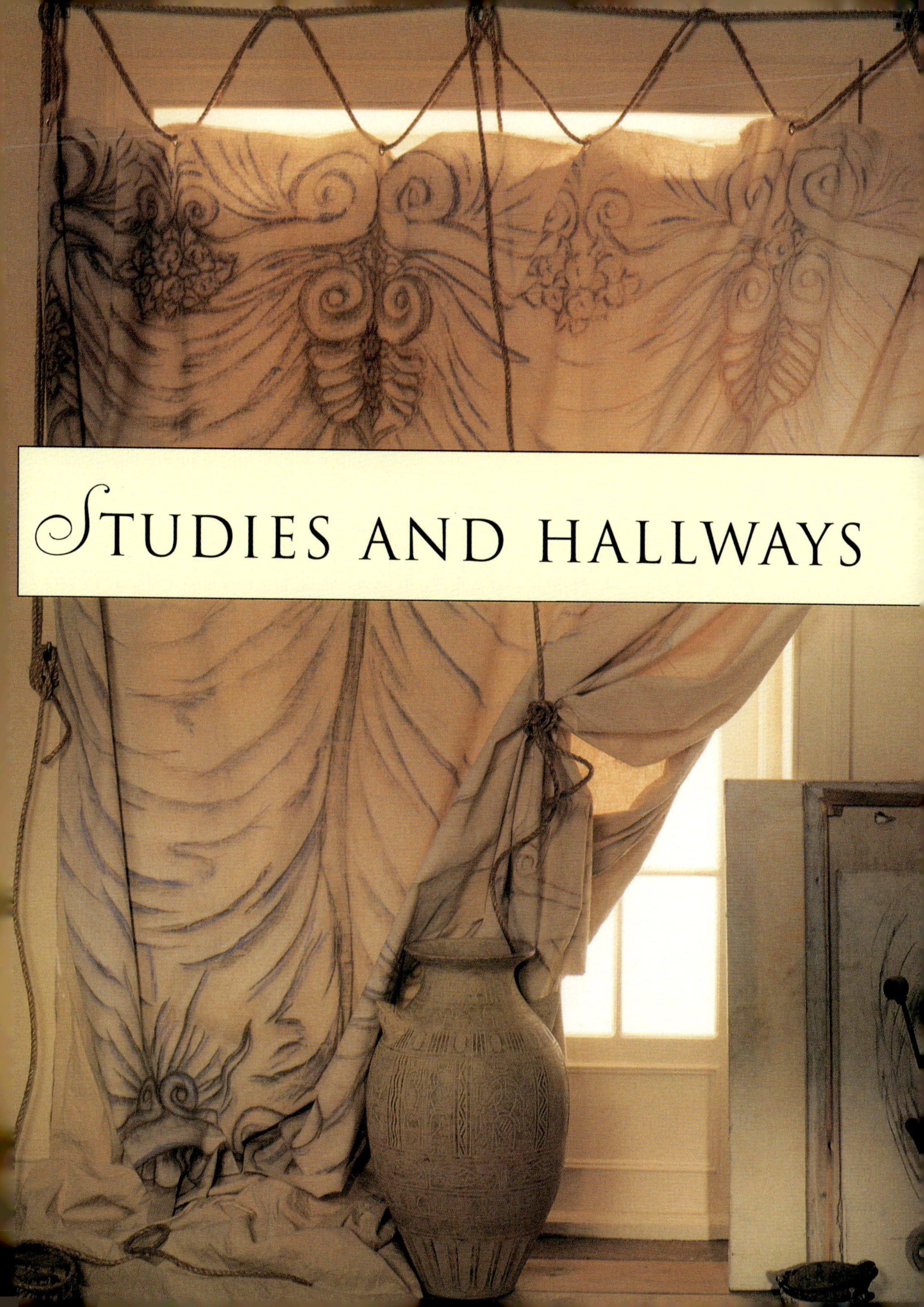

STUDIES AND HALLWAYS

STUDIES AND HALLWAYS ARE OFTEN the most neglected areas of the house, repositories for everything that cannot find a home elsewhere. No wonder that sometimes these spaces are a mess. They don't have to be so cluttered — and you don't have to throw everything out and start again. The clever way to transform these areas is to use what you already have.

The hall, in particular, is an important space. It provides that lasting first impression in any house and should give a hint of what lies beyond. There is little sense, after all, in having wonderfully light and bright rooms linked by a gloomy corridor crammed full of mismatched furniture.

Studies and dens can be hard to get right simply because they often need to double as TV rooms, spare bedrooms, storerooms or playrooms. Decorated to reflect your personality, they can be havens for work and creative passions, while still retaining their multiple functions.

Mismatched though everything may be, you can still make everything look coordinated. Light fittings and lampshades, even the lounge chair that has seen better days, all can be given a fresh new look that can revitalize your space.

Antique maps make wonderful wall coverings. They can be enlarged on color photocopying machines, varnished and then stuck onto the walls for maximum effect.

Imagine what you can put on the walls of these rooms! A big wall map given a coat of tinted varnish makes any study look like a million dollars. Wallpaper can be fun too, especially when you customize it or even make your own. The Escher-inspired wall covering of gray and black geometric patterns looks sensational and is really very easy to do.

You can even use a photocopier, creating striking wall treatments at the push of a button. Take a favorite subject, make lots of photocopies, cut them out and glue them onto the wall. It's hard to imagine that anything so simple could look so good and produce such successful decorative results.

WILD WEST CHAIR

IF YOU HAVE AN old armchair of these robust proportions, it will lend itself to this fun treatment reminiscent of the pioneer days of the Wild West. Update it with animal-skin prints and leather fringing for a new and imaginative look, as well as a cozy and comfortable feel. You could also use leatherette for the cushion covers or blankets, which would still be in keeping with this chunky, masculine look.

YOU WILL NEED

armchair
fake-fur or animal-skin fabric
upholstery needle
strong thread
tape measure
leather or suede
self-healing cutting mat
ruler
craft knife
leather glue
double-sided tape
pencil
softwood block
studs
hammer
rubber or softwood scrap

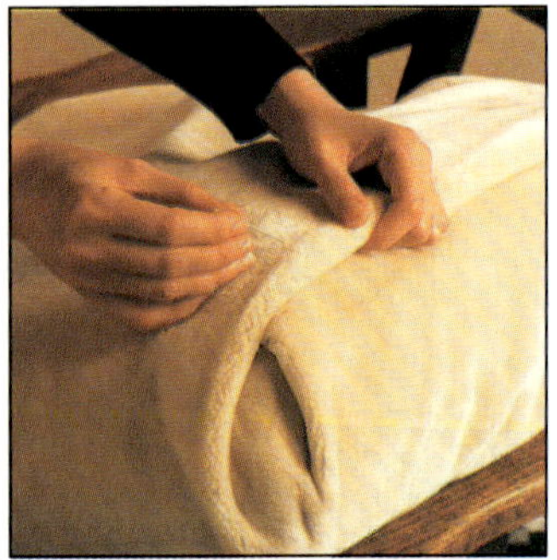

one *Remove the seat cushions of the armchair and wrap in fake-fur or animal-skin fabric, leaving sufficient fabric to make a continuous flap the length of the cushion. Stitch securely. Decide on the length of fringing needed to decorate the inside and outside edges of the arms of the chair.*

two *Decide how deep you want the fringe on the leather or suede to be. Measure and cut the fringe with a craft knife on a cutting mat, leaving sufficient uncut material to make a hem. Apply glue to the edge of the leather or suede and fold over the hem. Press it down firmly.*

three *Apply double-sided tape to the chair arms and stick on the fringing, matching it on both arms.*

four *Mark the positions of the studs with a pencil, using a block of wood to gauge the distance between each. Position the studs with your thumb, press and then tap with a hammer, protecting the stud with a scrap of rubber or a piece of softwood.*

PURE PLASTIC

A PLASTIC TABLECLOTH is invaluable on a table that gets a lot of use—in a family breakfast room, for example—as it can be wiped clean in seconds and doesn't stain. As a rule, however, ready-made plastic cloths tend to be very plain or extremely garish. To make an attractive as well as practical cloth, why not cut a shaped trim from plain white plastic and make a simple design along the edge using a hole punch? Inexpensive, quick and very easy to make—what could be better? You could also make a matching cloth for a sideboard or serving area.

YOU WILL NEED

tape measure
plastic fabric
dressmaker's scissors
pencil
cardboard
scissors
hole punch
ribbon, string or rope (optional)

one *Measure your table and cut the plastic fabric to the required size. Draw and cut out a cardboard template for the scalloped edge; choose a different shape if you prefer. Draw lightly around the template on the wrong side of the plastic fabric with a pencil.*

two *Cut the edging shape with sharp dressmaker's scissors, keeping the scallops rounded and even.*

three *Punch out a design with a hole punch. You could thread ribbon, string or rope through the holes to add even more interest and, perhaps, a splash of color.*

EASTERN PROMISE

DIRECTOR'S CHAIRS ARE INEXPENSIVE, but because the backrest and the seat are made of cloth they are very comfortable. Plain canvas seats are the standard form, but by customizing you can create a fun and rather chic effect. Kilim fabric is very long-lasting and has beautiful muted colors derived from traditional carpet designs, but any fabric that is strong and without too much "give" can be used; tapestry, burlap or carpet are all suitable. For even more character, stain the frame of the chair to match the muted tones of the kilim.

YOU WILL NEED

director's chair

wood stain and paintbrush (optional)

kilim carpet or fabric

dressmaker's pins

scissors

large darning or upholstery needle

strong darning yarn

package of chrome studs (at least 6)

hammer

one *Remove the old seat and back of the chair. Stain the wood of the chair, if desired. Choose the most decorative part of the kilim carpet or fabric and pin the old fabric to it as a pattern. Carefully cut out new seat and back pieces.*

two *Thread the needle with the yarn and neatly blanket-stitch the edges to bind them.*

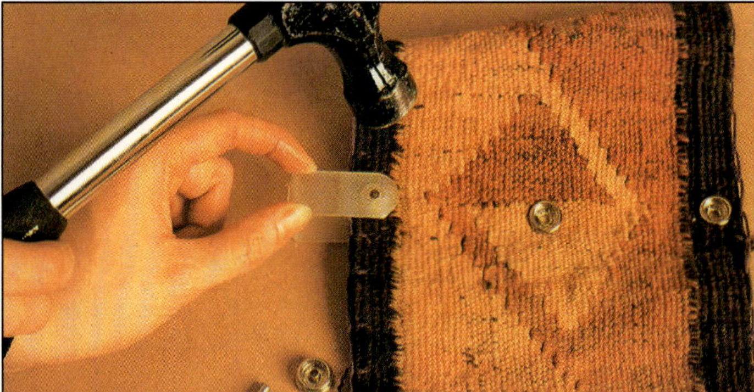

three *Fold over the edges of the back and fasten with chrome poppers, then slip over the uprights. Slot the seat back into position and secure firmly.*

ARTIST'S STUDIO

THIS IS THE IDEAL WAY to cover a large studio window, and as canvas comes in so many sizes, you're bound to find a piece to fit your own home's window. If you have never considered the possibility of becoming a painter, then this is a good way to start—curtains can also be art.

Here, chalks were used to draw on the canvas and change the flat panel into a boldly gathered backdrop. You could use this idea as your inspiration, or you could flick colors across the canvas in Jackson Pollock style, or simply add a few minimalist squiggles. If your window receives a lot of light, you may want to suspend a builder's dust-sheet in front of the window. This will provide a lining for the main curtain.

YOU WILL NEED

canvas, 1½ x window width
chalks or acrylic paints and paintbrush
drill
4 chunky garage hooks
screwdriver
metal cleat
rope
double-sided carpet tape
brass eyelets
hammer

one *Draw, paint or print onto the canvas using whatever style or design you have chosen—the bolder the better, as the canvas will cover a large area.*

two *Fix the garage hooks securely into the wall above the window, spaced at equal intervals.*

three *Screw the cleat to the wall, about halfway down the side of the window, then wind one end of the rope around it several times.*

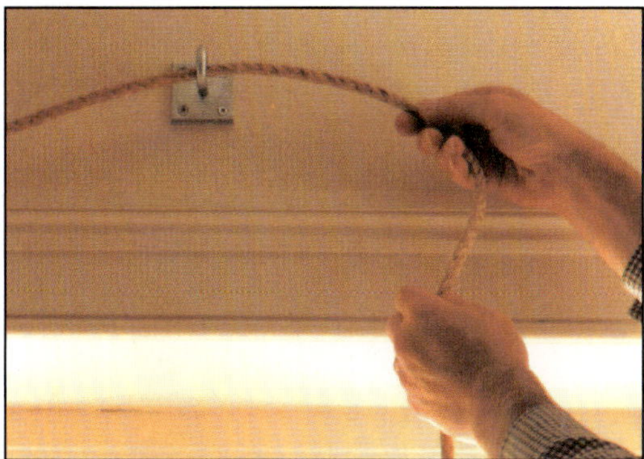

four *Take the long end of the rope up and through the hooks along the top.*

five *Pull the rope taut and tie it onto the end hook. Then attach the eyelets to the canvas following the manufacturer's instructions.*

six *Thread the rope through the first eyelet from behind, allowing about 6¼ inches between the hook and the eyelet. Then, leaving the same distance again, twist a loop in the rope and put it on the hook.*

seven *Take the rope down and through the back of the next eyelet, then up and over the back taut rope, which now forms a "rail" for the rope to rest on.*

nine *Take the rope straight down the side of the window and tie it neatly onto the cleat.*

eight *When you reach the end of the curtain, take the rope through the last hook.*

CONTINUED OVER ➤

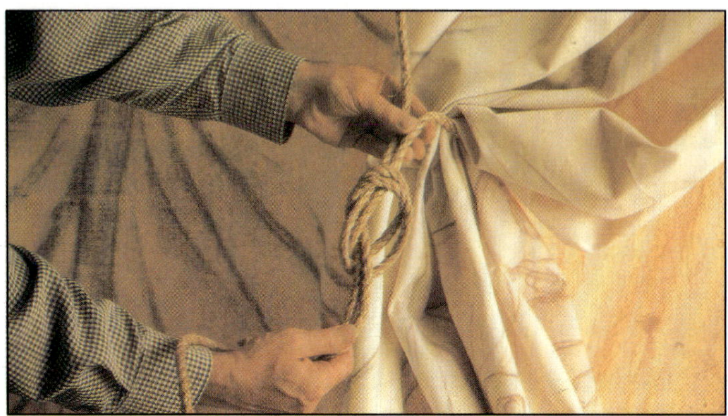

ten *Cut an extra length of rope and hook it over one of the top center hooks so that one length falls to the front and the other to the back of the canvas. Gather up the canvas and take hold of both ends of the rope. Tie these together in a knot and leave the ends dangling free.*

Above: The knot holding the curtain back from the window lets the light come through.

Above: Allow plenty of canvas so that it spills generously out onto the floor below the window.

Above: The knotted rope forms a decorative element in its own right.

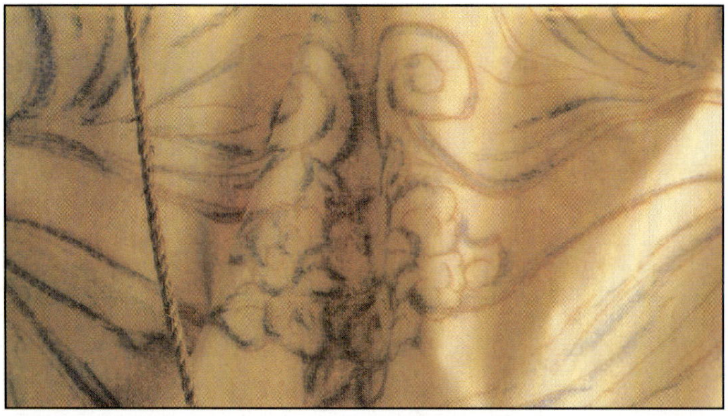

Above: The natural color of the canvas enhances the subtle colors of the design.

STANDARD PAINT CANS

NECESSITY REALLY IS THE mother of invention. This lamp was designed by a friend stuck in a remote village, who needed a good light to read by. The heavy lamp base is made from a large painted paint can filled with sand, while the shade is a smaller paint can drilled with a pattern of holes. The cord travels inside a curved copper plumbing pipe that is plunged into the sand. The graceful bend of the copper piping can be achieved only by using a special long spring used in the plumbing trade. If you know a friendly plumber, ask for help, otherwise a professional plumber should be able to bend the pipe for you. Ask an electrician to wire up the finished lamp.

YOU WILL NEED

½-gallon paint can
paint stripper (optional)
sandpaper
cardboard
scissors
felt-tipped pen
drill, with size 6 twist metal bit
hammer and nail (optional)
metal file
pendant lamp fitting
matte-black latex paint
paintbrush
1 gallon paint can
string
pipe-bending spring
3 yards copper pipe
hacksaw
rubber grommet
silver sand to fill larger can

one *Strip off the paint or remove the label from the ½-gallon can, then rub down the surface with sandpaper. This will be the shade. Cut a strip of cardboard the height of the can, then mark off three equal sections. Mark the other side in the same way but so the marks fall halfway between the others. Use the strip to mark the drilling points around the can.*

two *Drill holes through all the marked points. Drilling through metal is not difficult, but if the drill bit slips, dent each mark slightly with a hammer and nail before drilling. Find the center of the base of the can and drill four or five holes close together to make a larger hole. Use the end of a metal file to turn this into an even, circular hole that is the right size for a pendant lamp fitting.*

three *Roughen up the outside of the can with a file, smoothing the drilled-hole edges and scratching a texture into the surface. Paint the outside of the 1-gallon paint can matte black. Paint the lid separately. Drill a hole for the cord near the base of the can. The pipe-bending spring will not be as long as the copper pipe, so attach a piece of string to one end of the spring. Mark the string at intervals so that you will be able to tell how far down the copper pipe the string is.*

four *Insert the spring into the pipe and start to shape the top third of the pipe into a semi-circle. You will not be able to bend the pipe in one try, so make small bends, bringing the spring back up the pipe as you work. Saw off the straight section at the end, so that the curve will go into the can. Then attach the rubber grommet to the end of the copper pipe.*

five *At this stage you need an electrician to thread the cord through the copper pipe and wire the fitting to it. The two halves of the fitting hold the shade between them. Drill a centrally positioned hole in the lid of the large can to hold the copper pipe. Fit the lid over the base of the pipe and feed the cord out through the hole drilled near the base. Hold the lamp upright in the can and fill it with sand to ensure stability. Push the lid firmly onto the can.*

MINIMALIST CHAIR

SLEEK BEECH AND CHROME chairs abound in interiors magazines—with price tags to match. This makes renovating old chairs a very rewarding proposition. Most second-hand office-supply stores have lots of worn-out office chairs, often with torn upholstery or in hideous colors. Don't be drawn to a more modern chair that appears in a better state but has plastic-coated legs; metal legs look better when renovated.

YOU WILL NEED

old typist's chair
scissors
screwdriver or awl
pliers
industrial rubber gloves
chemical paint stripper
1–2-inch brush
steel wool
soap
medium-grade sandpaper
all-in-one stain and varnish
hammer
"domes of silence"
metal or chrome polish
soft, dry cloth

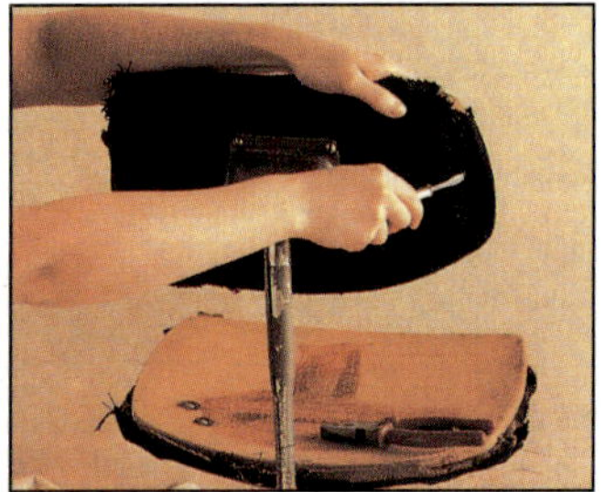

one *Start by cutting off excess fabric and foam. You need strong scissors with large plastic handles to avoid hurting your hands. Remove the fabric and upholstery staples from the back and underside of the chair. Use the screwdriver or awl for the hard-to-reach parts and the pliers to pull out the old staples.*

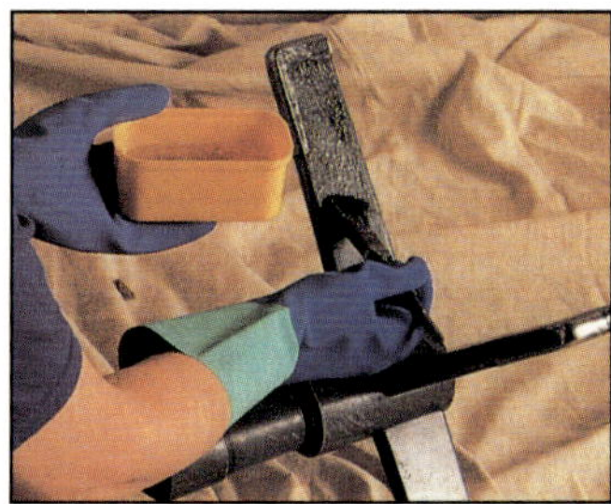

two *Remove the wheels and any other loose parts to prevent them from being damaged by the paint stripper. Wearing the industrial rubber gloves, brush the paint stripper onto the metal chair frame. Set aside for 5 minutes (or as long as the manufacturer recommends) and then wash off with steel wool and soapy water. Repeat until all the paint has been removed.*

three *Having removed the seat and back, make sure the surfaces are free of nails and staples. Sand the surfaces and edges of the seat and back until they are smooth and clean. Seal the wood with all-in-one stain and varnish, and let dry.*

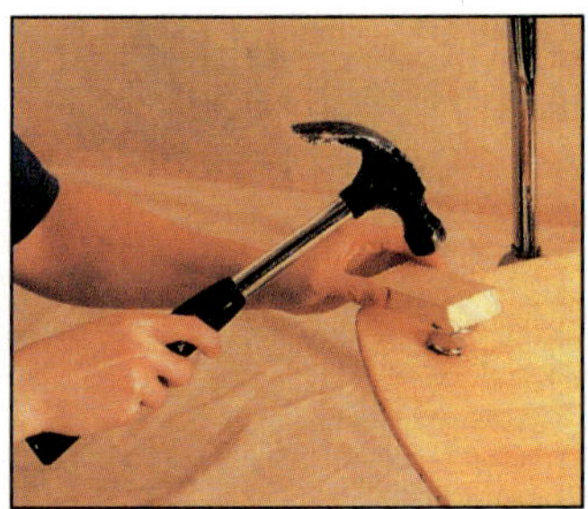

four *Reattach the seat, back and wheels. Use "domes of silence" to cover any sharp bolts that might rip your clothes. Finally, polish the metal using a soft, dry cloth.*

Magic Beads

TRANSPARENT BEADS DON'T block out the light or keep out the draft, but when the sun catches them, they sparkle like jewels, and using them full-length on a small square window can turn a light source into something bright and magical. Beads are available in brilliant, gem-like colors, softly coordinated pastels and clear colorless textures, and each has its own unique, light-enhancing quality.

YOU WILL NEED

2 narrow wooden strips, window width, plus 3–4 inches each side
wood glue
hammer
brads or small fine nails
ruler
latex paint: black and white
paintbrush
drill
colored bead curtain, with strip to attach it and screws
screwdriver
plastic anchors and screws
level
small jeweled drawer knob

one *Make the valance by sticking one edge of a wooden strip to the long edge of the other to form a right angle. Hammer in a few brads to secure it. Divide the length into sections and paint them alternately black and white.*

two *Drill, then screw through the holes in the strip to attach the bead curtain to secure it underneath the valance.*

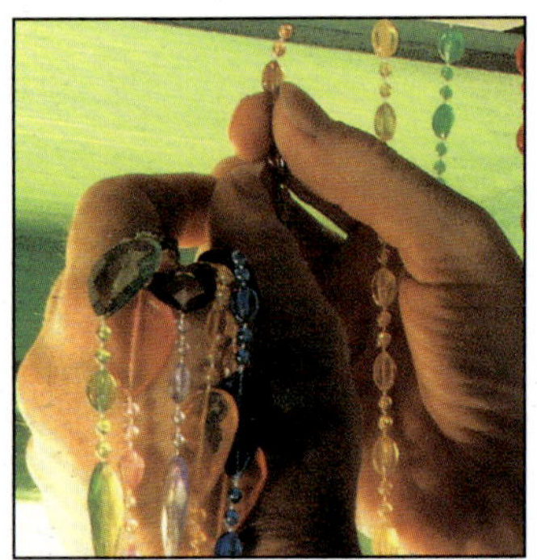

three *Drill, insert plastic anchors and screw the valance in place above the window. Use a level to check the position after attaching one side. Hang the lengths of beads in a pattern or at random along the strip.*

four *Drill a hole, insert a plastic anchor and screw the drawer knob into position—level with the base of the window if it is a small one, or halfway down if you have a larger window.*

ANTIQUE MAP

MAPS ARE BOTH FASCINATING to study and extremely decorative, and this makes them wonderful for covering walls. Choose an up-to-date map for a child's room to maximize the learning possibilities. Elsewhere in the house, "antique" or old Ordnance Survey local area maps will look terrific and create an eye-catching focal point. You can easily distress a new map to give it an aged appearance. You could even paper a whole wall in maps—perhaps of geographically adjoining areas.

YOU WILL NEED

tape measure
pencil
straightedge
level or plumb line
map
wallpaper paste
pasting brush
fine-grade sandpaper
tinted varnish
paintbrush

one *Measure and mark guidelines for positioning the map on the wall, using a straightedge and a level or plumb line. Paste the map to the wall as if it were wallpaper.*

two *Distress the map here and there by lightly rubbing it with sandpaper. Finish the aging process by applying a coat of tinted varnish.*

MATH MONTAGE

THIS IS A FUN idea for adding interest to a plain wall. The numbers and mathematical symbols have been enlarged on a photocopier. It doesn't matter if the black becomes streaked with white as the number is enlarged: This enhances the handcrafted look. It is most effective if you confine the montage to a set area, such as behind a desk, for maximum effect; just let the design fall away at the edges. You could also try musical notation behind a piano or shorthand characters in an office.

YOU WILL NEED

craft knife
self-healing cutting mat
masking tape
wallpaper paste
pasting brush
artist's paintbrush
clear varnish
varnish brush

one *Photocopy the numbers and symbols from the templates at the back of the book and enlarge them to various sizes. Cut them out carefully with the craft knife on the cutting mat.*

two *Try out the design first by attaching the shapes to the wall using small pieces of masking tape; move them around until you are satisfied. Alternatively, simply start and figure out the design as you go. Paste the shapes onto the wall using wallpaper paste. Use the artist's brush to paste small and delicate shapes. Give the whole design a coat of varnish, to protect it.*

3+5=8
(6)
90
L = 2π Ma / λT
4−3=1

PANELS AND STAMP MOTIF

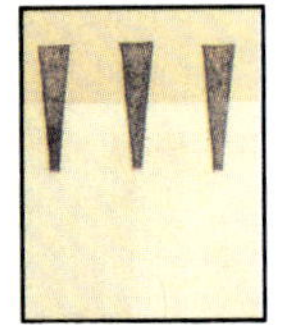

DECORATE LARGE AREAS OF a wall with these easy panels. Painting panels over a base coat quickly gives interest to large expanses of wall. It's a good idea to visually connect the panel and wall outside the panel with a simple recurring motif. This could be a strong modern shape, wavy lines or even flowers. By varying both the color of the walls and the style of the motif, you can create a wide range of different looks from the same basic treatment. Of course, you can also vary the size of the panels to fit the shape and dimensions of the room.

YOU WILL NEED

latex paint in cream, white and black
paint roller
paint-mixing tray
level
straightedge
pencil
masking tape
course brush
scrap paper
scissors
high-density foam rubber
glue
craft knife
tape measure
old plate
small roller

one *Give the wall a base coat of cream latex paint. Using the level and straightedge, draw the panels on the wall when it is dry.*

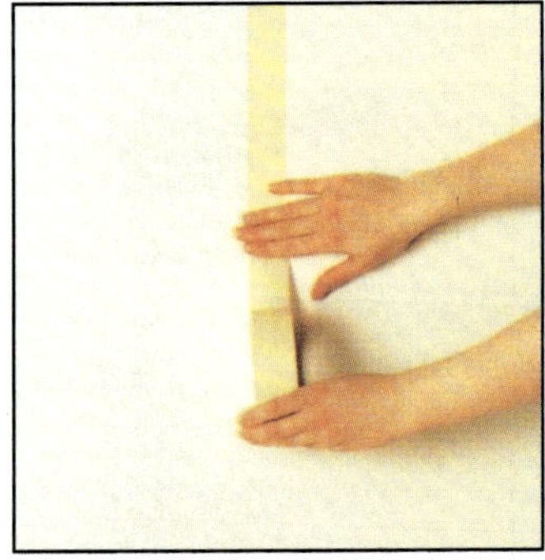

two *Mask off the outer edge of the panels with masking tape. Drag white latex paint over the base coat.*

three *Design the motif on paper. Stick the motif to the foam. With the craft knife, cut out the unwanted areas of the design to leave a raised stamp.*

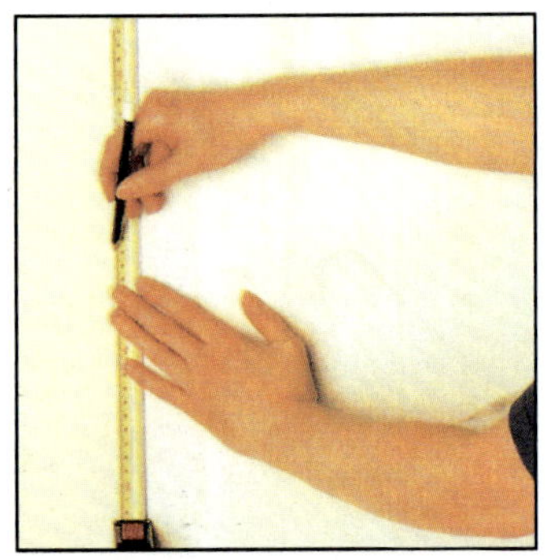

four *Decide on the spacing of the stamps and lightly mark the positions on the wall.*

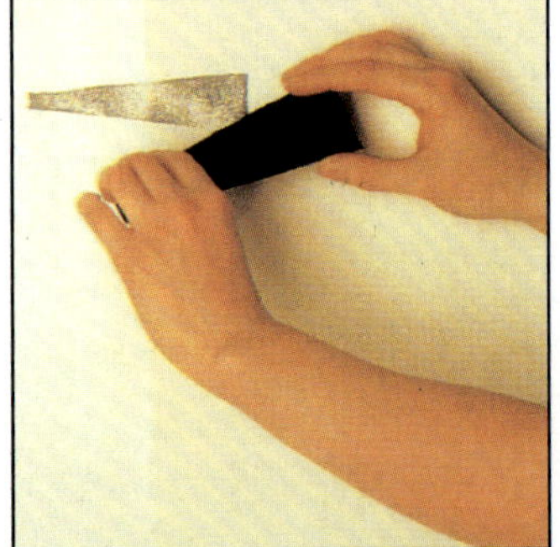

five *Put some black paint onto the plate and evenly coat the small roller. Roll the paint onto the stamp. Stamp the design in the marked positions.*

ARTS

ESCHER-STYLE WALL

INTRICATE "THREE-DIMENSIONAL" designs, inspired by the *trompe-l'œil* drawings of the artist M.C. Escher, look stunning on a wall on which you want to make a real impact. The instructions for how to construct the design sound complicated but, in fact, once you have begun cutting out and assembling it, it soon becomes obvious how the shapes fit together. The beauty of Escher's designs is that all the components relate logically to one another in proportion and shape so that, once you have begun construction, the design practically assembles itself.

YOU WILL NEED

scrap paper
pencil
metal ruler
paper: light gray, dark gray and black
craft knife
self-healing cutting mat
straightedge
level or plumb line
wallpaper paste
pasting brush
clear varnish
varnish brush

one *Plan and draw the whole pattern to scale on paper or refer to the diagram at the back of the book. Decide on the colors of paper you want to use; choose three tones of the same color to achieve a three-dimensional effect. Measure the paper. Divide a sheet of the light gray paper into thirds.*

two *Measure in from the edge to the depth of the large gray triangle shapes that form the border and mark the points of the triangles.*

three *Draw the diagonals to make the triangle shapes. Cut out the large light and dark gray triangles and then the diamond shapes, using the craft knife on a cutting mat. You will find that, once you have cut one shape, you will be able to use it as a template for others, because of the way the shapes relate to one another.*

four *Draw the smaller light and dark gray diamonds that make two "sides" of the small "boxes." Cut out the smaller diamonds. Cut out the large and small black shapes.*

five *Using a level or plumb line and straightedge, draw vertical lines on the wall the same width as the large gray shapes.*

six *Paste all the shapes into place using wallpaper paste and pasting brush. Smooth out any wrinkles with the palms of your hands. Give the design two coats of protective varnish.*

ESCHER'S DECKCHAIR

DECKCHAIRS ARE CHEAP and widely available in several styles. The slings are usually canvas, available at furniture stores in a variety of brightly colored plain and striped materials. Deckchair canvas comes in the correct width and with ready-sealed edges. To give an old deckchair a new lease on life, use a pattern of stencils, or turn checks into a "three-dimensional" puzzle. This design is based on M.C. Escher's work and is made from a combination of positive and negative motifs.

YOU WILL NEED

- deckchair
- deckchair canvas
- scissors
- spray adhesive
- high-density foam
- craft knife
- self-healing cutting mat
- ruler or triangle
- colored tape
- pencil
- fabric paint: black and white
- paintbrush
- needle
- matching thread

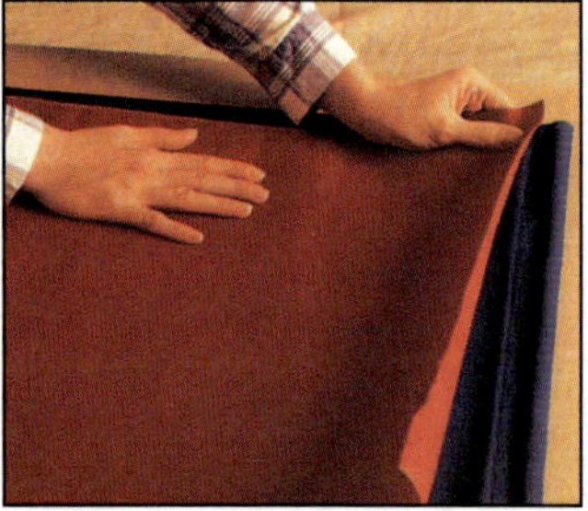

one *Remove the old sling, making a note of how it was fastened so that you can fasten it in the same way later. Using the old cover as a pattern, cut out the new fabric, allowing for hems along the top and bottom edges.*

two *To make the two stamps for printing, photocopy the motifs from the back of the book to the desired size. Stick to the foam with spray adhesive. Cut around the design with the craft knife.*

three *Using the knife, chip away the zigzag shape between the dotted lines to leave two elements of the design distinct. Remove all the foam that is not part of the "negative" design. It is helpful to mark the backs of the stamps with colored tape to indicate which color paint is used with which stamp. Repeat steps 2 and 3 to make the "positive" stamp.*

four *Using a ruler and pencil, draw parallel lines lengthwise on the canvas, the distance between them equalling the full width of the design when the two stamps are put together (see step 7).*

five *Apply the black paint to the raised portion of one of the stamps.*

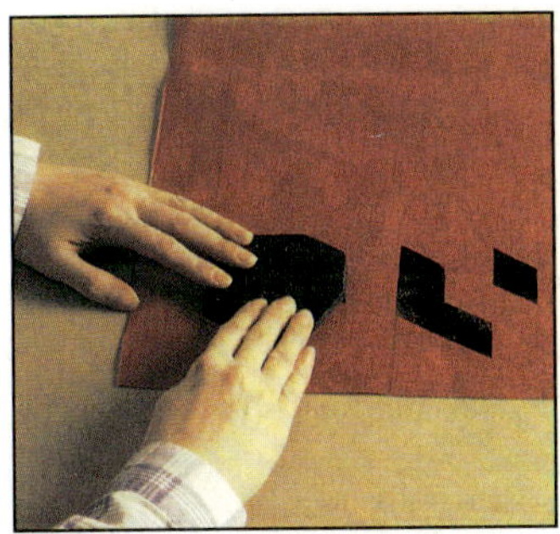

six *Applying light, even pressure, stamp the black design regularly within the grid lines.*

seven *Repeat with the white design. When dry, hem the top and bottom edges of the canvas, then fasten to the chair frame.*

Trellis Hanging Rack

A GARDEN TRELLIS MAKES AN effective hanging rack. Extend the trellis to make regular diamond shapes and then frame it with wood to give a finished look. You could confine this idea to a small area or attach a few pieces of trellis together to run the whole length of a wall. Put hooks on as many crossovers as you want, and collect decorative items, as well as more mundane utilitarian objects, to add to the display. Move things from time to time, so the display always offers something new to catch the eye.

YOU WILL NEED

tape measure
pencil
length of garden trellis
hacksaw
1 x 1 inch strips wood
miter block and saw or miter saw
dowel
wood screws
screwdriver
drill, with wood, metal and masonry bits
burnt-orange latex paint
paintbrush
plastic anchors
wood filler

one *Measure the area you want to cover and mark out the area on the trellis. Cut the trellis to size with a hacksaw. Measure and cut the lengths of wood to make the frame. Miter the corners using a miter block or miter saw. Screw the frame together.*

two *Mark the dowel into lengths and cut a notch in each length, for hanging hooks. Cut the dowel into lengths, using the miter block or miter saw.*

three *If the trellis is riveted at the crossovers, drill the rivets out. Position the dowel pegs on the trellis over the crossovers. Screw the pegs to the trellis. Paint the trellis and the frame with latex paint in your chosen color. Burnt-orange has been used here.*

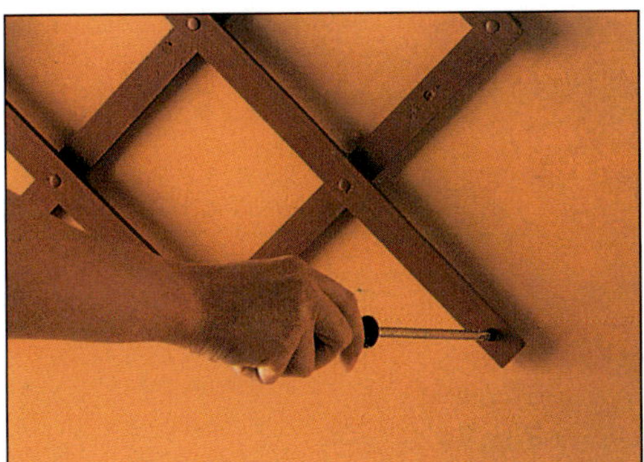

four *Drill holes in the wall with a masonry bit and insert plastic anchors. Drill pilot holes in the trellis slightly smaller than the screws, to prevent the wood from splitting, and then screw the trellis to the wall.*

five *Attach the frame around the trellis by screwing it onto the wall. Fill and paint over the tops of the screws and any gaps. When the trellis and frame are dry, give the whole hanging rack a second coat of paint.*

BROWN PAPER PANELING

BROWN PAPER has its own characteristic color and texture, which look quite wonderful on walls. You can buy it on large rolls, which make papering under a chair rail simplicity itself. Here, the brown paper has been combined with gum arabic tape for an unusual and elegant interpretation of a classic interior look. You could also add a simple baseboard, using 2 x 1 inch timber.

YOU WILL NEED

brown paper
wallpaper paste
pasting brush
plumb line
pencil
straightedge
paintbrush
gum arabic tape
level
black beading
glue gun and glue sticks

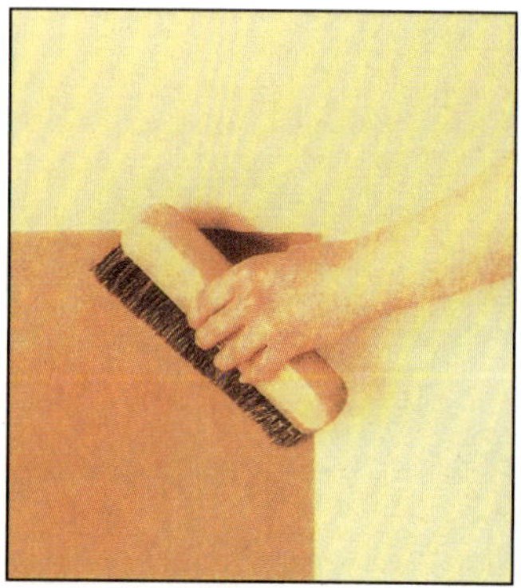

one *Stick the brown paper, matte side inward, to the wall. Use wallpaper paste, as if it were wallpaper.*

‹ two *Use a plumb line and straightedge to mark vertical guidelines for the stripes on the brown paper. With a paintbrush, wet the wall in a stripe the width of the gum arabic tape and stick the tape down. Make sure you cover up all the guidelines.*

three *Use a level and straightedge to draw a horizontal guideline for the under-the-chair-rail border. Stick the tape in place in the same way as before.*

four *Attach the beading along the top of the border, using the glue gun.*

DECORATIVE CIRCLES

THERE IS NO REASON why the papers used for the walls and roofs of dolls' houses cannot be used on a full-sized wall. You could confine them to a limited area, such as below a chair-rail or within paneling, or use them more extensively all over the wall. Here, the wall has been painted a complementary color to the paper's and then circles have been cut out of the paper to reveal the color behind.

YOU WILL NEED

- scrap paper
- pencil
- colored pencil
- doll's house paper
- latex paint for the base color
- paint roller
- paint-mixing tray
- round template
- craft knife
- self-healing cutting mat
- long metal ruler
- wallpaper paste
- pasting brush
- clear varnish
- varnish brush

one *Plan and draw the whole design to scale on paper. Choose a paper with a small repeat pattern for the circles. Choose your base-paint color to coordinate with the paper; it may help to paint swatches on scrap paper to see how well the colors work together.*

two *Paint the wall in the base color. Decide on the size of the circles; you may have a plate, saucer or other round object of the right size, which you can use as a template. Decide on the spacing of the circles.*

three *Trim the paper, ready for pasting, using a craft knife on a cutting mat. Cut out the circles. Paste the paper to the wall as if it were wallpaper. Be especially careful of the edges where you have cut out circles, as these are delicate. If you prefer, draw guidelines for positioning the cut-out circles; otherwise, position them by eye. When the paste is completely dry, apply two coats of clear varnish, letting it dry between coats.*

PULL-DOWN STOOL

RESTRICTED SPACE IN APARTMENTS is common; you need to use every inch of space, and it is not easy to fit in extra seating, by the telephone in the hall for example, or in any other small area. Folding chairs are an obvious solution, but the problem of where to store them still arises. One answer is to adapt the clever folding brackets and hinges available from do-it-yourself stores, which are usually used for tables and shelves, to make a folding stool. Instead of a solid piece of fiberboard, you could use dowel decking, such as that used in bathrooms. It is important that the stool is attached to a masonry wall and not to a partition wall, which will not be able to take the weight, resulting in damage to the wall and person on the stool. Check the manufacturer's recommendations for fitting the right kind of screws and plugs.

YOU WILL NEED

- pair of folding brackets with screws
- silver spray paint
- medium-density fiberboard
- saw
- pencil
- ruler
- compass or circular templates in three sizes
- clamp
- drill, with wood and masonry bits
- jigsaw (optional)
- medium-grade sandpaper
- paintbrush
- yellow paint
- clear varnish or lacquer
- screwdriver
- 2 long screws and plastic anchors
- level

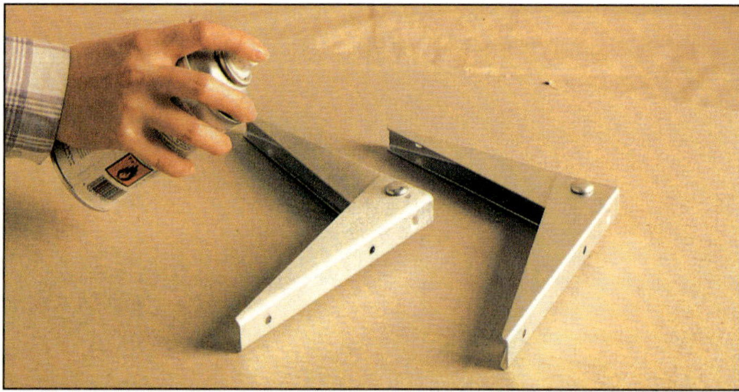

one *Spray the brackets silver on a protected work surface.*

two *Cut the fiberboard to the right size for the seat: 12–18 x 8 inches is normal. Draw a line down the center of the seat.*

three *Place the brackets on the seat and mark their positions in pencil.*

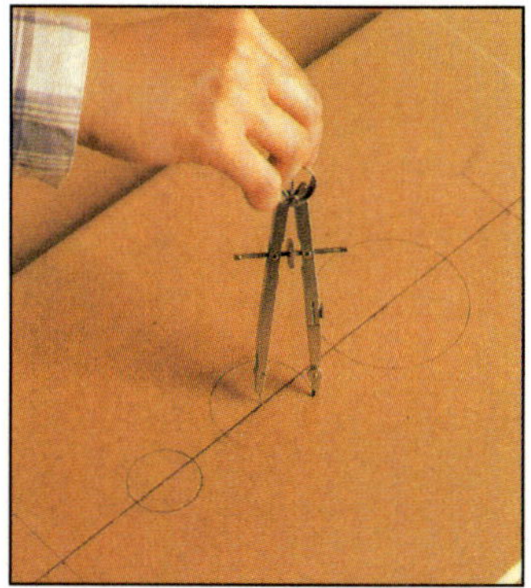

four *With the compass, draw three circles of increasing size. Alternatively, find three circular objects of suitable sizes to use as templates.*

five *Holding the seat firmly clamped to the work bench, drill a ring of holes just inside the pencil marks; this will allow you to cut out the circles with a jigsaw. If you are not confident with a jigsaw, take the seat to a hardware store or an employee at a lumberyard who will cut the holes for you.*

six *Sand the holes to a smooth finish, both inside and on the top and bottom.*

seven *Sand off any pencil marks or fingerprints to prepare the surfaces for painting.*

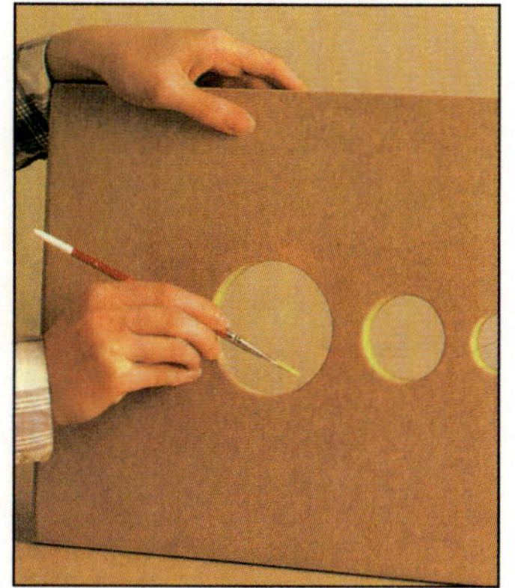

eight *Paint the inside of the holes yellow to highlight them.*

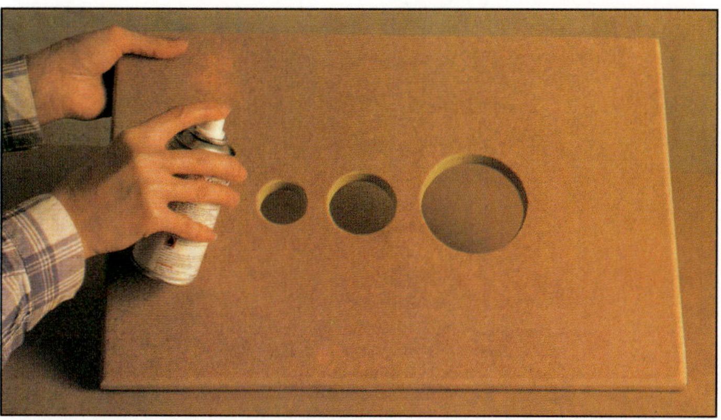

nine *Seal the seat with clear varnish or lacquer. A spray type is easy to use and will give a smooth finish.*

CONTINUED OVER ➤

ten *Screw the brackets to the seat. Hold the seat against the wall, which must be a masonry wall, and mark the position of the first hole with a pencil.*

eleven *Drill a hole using the masonry bit. Insert the plastic anchor and screw the seat loosely to the wall. Level the seat using a level and mark the position for the second hole on the wall. Drill the hole, insert the plastic anchor and screw the other side of the seat to the wall.*

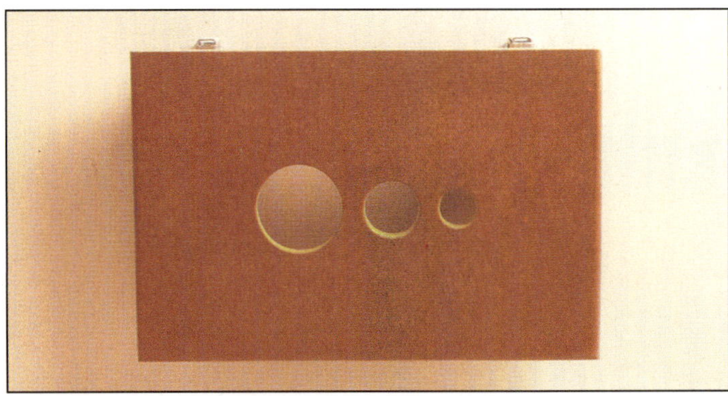

twelve *Check that the stool folds neatly against the wall.*

LOUNGE CHAIR

LOUNGE CHAIRS COME IN various heights and with all kinds of additional features, but the fabrics, which are mostly garish prints and stripes, seem at odds with the stylish tubular frames. Apart from the obvious solution of re-covering, using the existing fabric as a pattern, a clever alternative is to make a textural webbing cover. This fabric is long-lasting and overcomes the problem of sagging. Re-covered in this way, the lounge chair offers both comfort and durability.

YOU WILL NEED

lounge chair
chrome cleaner
soft cloth
tape measure
16 yards upholstery webbing rolls
masking tape
pencil
scissors
needle
matching thread
6 packets large eyelets
hammer
softwood block
6½ yards cord or rope

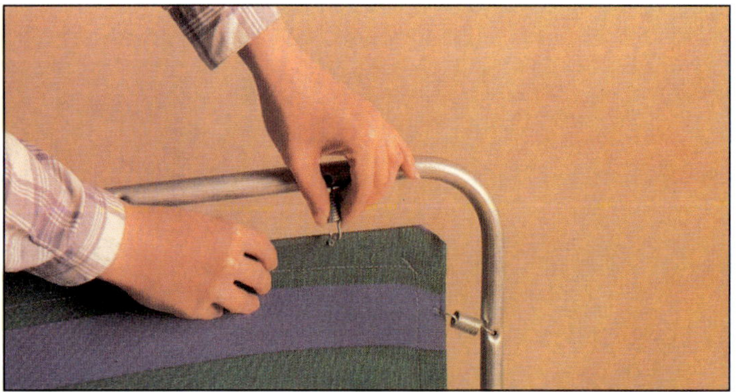

one *Remove and discard the old cover. Thoroughly clean the metal frame with chrome cleaner and a soft cloth. Measure the width of the frame for the horizontal straps, and almost double this measurement so that the ends of the straps will very nearly meet in the middle.*

two *Position a couple of webbing strips with masking tape and work out how many strips you will need in each section of the frame. Cut the webbing to length and hem the ends.*

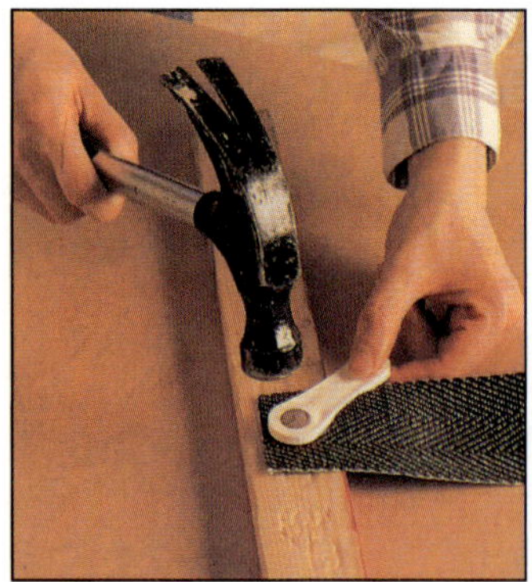

three *Follow the manufacturer's instructions for applying an eyelet to each end of the straps.*

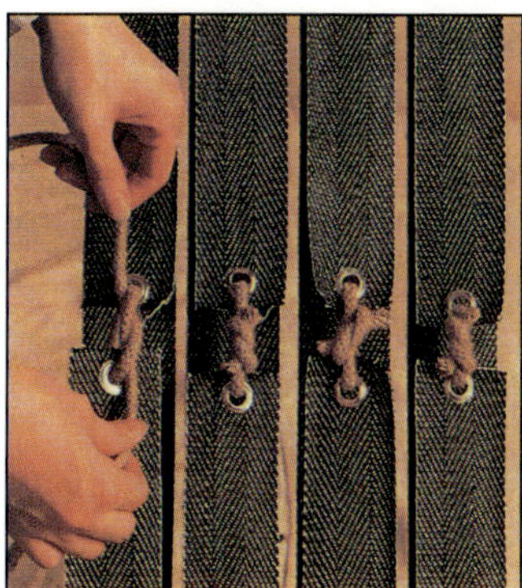

four *Turn the lounge chair upside down, wrap the straps around the frame and fasten the ends together with cord or rope where they meet in the middle. Leave a gap wide enough for another strap near the hinges of the lounge chair.*

five *Starting at the foot, secure a vertical strap with an eyelet. Weave the strap under and over the double thickness of the horizontal straps until you reach the top. Secure the end with another eyelet.*

six *Near the hinges, thread another horizontal strap through the vertical ones, but wrap the ends around the two outermost verticals instead of around the frame.*

KITCHENS

KITCHENS

KITCHENS ARE THE HEART of any home. So why not make yours look like it? You can, but remember—behind every outstanding kitchen is an outstanding decorator, for this is one room in the house where combining fun and function without breaking the bank requires ingenuity, and lots of it.

Look at what the kitchen has to be: work room, family room, storage room, dining room. Achieving all this in a functional, flexible, minimal-maintenance room AND making it a place where people like to be, depends on careful planning and lots of clever ideas.

The projects in this chapter present some of these ideas, many of which bring a new meaning to the word "recycling." The kitchen is where discarded objects come into their own—they not only look great but have a useful purpose as well.

The next time you visit a market collect some fruit crates—with a coat of paint and a piece of ribbon they make great stackable storage boxes. Transform a flea market window box into a striking and practical shelf for bottles, or suspend three metal garden sieves on lengths of chain to

In any kitchen it is essential to be able to find the cutlery, and a decorative cutlery box in a striking modern design is a real asset.

create a vegetable rack that's just ingenious.

There's also a horticultural solution for the windows. To flood the kitchen with warm, glowing light, yet avoid the stares of passers-by, try our wonderful blind made from a length of scrim edged with broad strips of burlap. With its cotton-reel pulleys it sounds a bit old fashioned, but that only adds to its appeal.

Once you've seen how much can be done with so little, your imagination will take over and no object, corner or surface will escape your attention. Your kitchen won't just be a better place to work, but bright and cheerful enough to make your whole day.

COUNTRY-STYLE SHELF

THE HEART HAS BEEN USED to convey a universal message in folklore for centuries. Here, a heart has been used to make a stamp that resembles a four-leafed clover. The smaller heart is a traditional solid shape that fits neatly along the edges of the shelf supports. The background color was applied in three separate coats and rubbed back slightly between coats; a final lighter color was applied over the top. When the shelf was dry, it was sanded with medium-grade sandpaper to reveal some of the grain and layers of color.

YOU WILL NEED

tracing paper
pencil
spray adhesive
high-density foam, such as uhholstery foam
scalpel
deep red latex paint
plate
paintbrush

one *Trace and transfer the pattern shapes from the template section. Lightly spray the shapes with adhesive and place them on the foam. Cut around the outline of the shapes with a scalpel. Cut out the single heart shape. First cut out the outline, then part the foam and cut all the way through.*

two *Use the stamp as a measuring guide to estimate the number of prints that will fit along the back of the shelf. Mark their position with a pencil. Spread an even coating of deep red paint on a plate.*

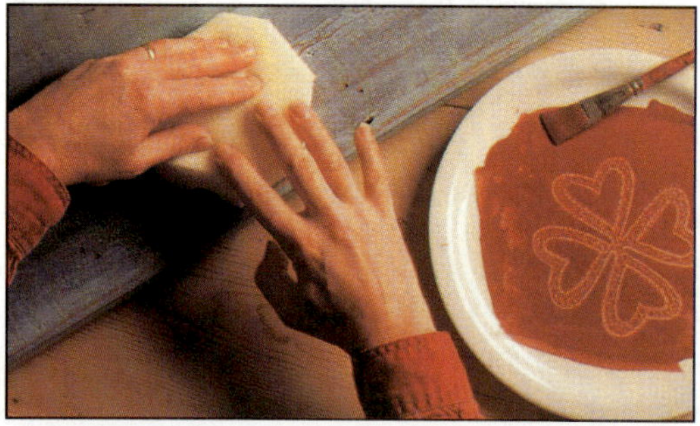

three *Make a test print of the clover-leaf stamp on a scrap of paper to ensure that the stamp is not overloaded with paint. Referring to the pencil guidelines, press the stamp into the paint and make the first print on the wood.*

four *Continue until you have completed all of the clover-leaf shapes. Try not to get the finish too even; this is a rustic piece of furniture. Finish off the shelf with a row of small hearts along the support edges, then add one between each large motif.*

Mediterranean Crates

Wooden fruit and vegetable crates are much too good to be thrown away once their original contents have been used up, so rescue them from your local market and dress them up with color and ribbon to make a great set of useful containers. The crates here work especially well, as they have a solid base that can be separated and used as a lid. These rustic Mediterranean crates look wonderful stacked with candles, tablecloths or other bright odds and ends.

YOU WILL NEED

3 wooden fruit or vegetable crates
sandpaper
pliers
wire cutters
staple gun (optional)
powder paint: red, blue and green
paintbrushes
40-inch piece checked ribbon
scissors

one *Rub off any rough edges on the crates with sandpaper. Detach the base from one of them to be the "lid." Remove and replace any protruding staples if necessary.*

two *Mix the powder paints according to the manufacturer's instructions. Paint one of the crates red on the inside, blue on the outside, and green along the top edges.*

three *Paint the other crate green on the inside, blue on the outside, and red along the top edges.*

four *Paint the lid blue. Bind the six center seams with crosses of checked ribbon, tied securely at the back.*

TACTILE TABLECLOTH

ALL SORTS OF WONDERFUL TRIMMINGS are now available, and a trip around the notions department will, with a little imagination, generate any number of ideas. Here, simple upholsterer's webbing was used to edge a plain and practical burlap cloth. The webbing was decorated with string in very loose loops. The charm of this simple design lies in its interesting textures, so it is probably best to use materials in shades of the same colors, as here. However, if you wish, you could make a bold statement in bright primaries or contrasting colors.

YOU WILL NEED

about 2½ yards burlap
dressmaker's scissors
dressmaker's pins
needle and basting thread
iron
sewing machine
matching sewing thread
8¾ yards webbing
brown string

one *Cut the burlap to the size required, allowing for hems. Turn under the hems and pin, baste, press and machine-stitch. Cut a length of webbing to go around all four sides. Pin and machine-stitch the webbing around the edge.*

two *Lay the string on the length of webbing and twist it to experiment with different designs—a repeating pattern will look more professional.*

three *Pin, baste and hand-stitch the string to the webbing, to hold it securely. It doesn't matter if there are gaps in the stitching; the looseness of the string is all part of the effect.*

WINDOW BOX SHELF

THIS ROUGH-HEWN RUSTIC box, stained dark brown, was found at an antique store, and was probably in a garden shed thirty years ago. It is a good reminder not to write anything off until you have assessed its potential, for here, painted and refurbished, it is both decorative and useful. Hang a window box on your kitchen wall to hold all the colorful bottles and jars that are usually hidden in a cupboard.

YOU WILL NEED

wooden window box
sandpaper
latex paint: red, blue, green and white
paintbrushes
fine-grade steel wool
shellac button polish
drill, with wood bit
2 plastic anchors and screws
screwdriver

one *Rub down the wooden surface of the window box with sandpaper. Paint it in bright colors, highlighting different parts in contrasting colors. Let dry.*

two *Mix white paint with water in equal parts and apply a coat of this all over the window box. Let dry. Rub back the white paint with fine-grade steel wool so that it just clings to the wood grain and imperfections.*

three *Apply a coat of button polish to protect the surface from stains and to improve the aged effect. Drill two holes in the back of the window box and attach it to the kitchen wall.*

EXPRESSLY FOR WILLIAMS-SONOMA INC.
SAN FRANCISCO, CA. 94120.

Hanging Jam Jars

THIS BRIGHT IDEA FOR getting double mileage out of kitchen shelves is borrowed from a tool shed. Woodworkers and gardeners line the undersides of their shelves with jam jar lids and then screw in jars filled with nuts, bolts, nails, screws and other useful things. Everything is kept neat, in view and within easy reach. Fill your jars with cookies, candy, rice or different types of beans and lentils. You could even use smaller jars to create an unusual and inexpensive herb and spice rack.

YOU WILL NEED

4 or more jam jars, with lids
kitchen shelf
pencil
awl
screws (no longer than the shelf depth)
screwdriver

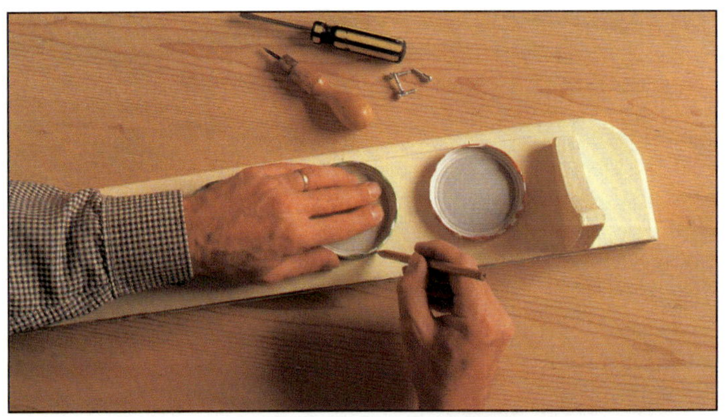

one *Arrange the jam jar lids along the underside of the shelf. There should be sufficient room between them for a hand to fit and sufficient depth for the jars to fit. Lightly mark the positions with a pencil.*

two *Use an awl to make two holes through each lid into the shelf.*

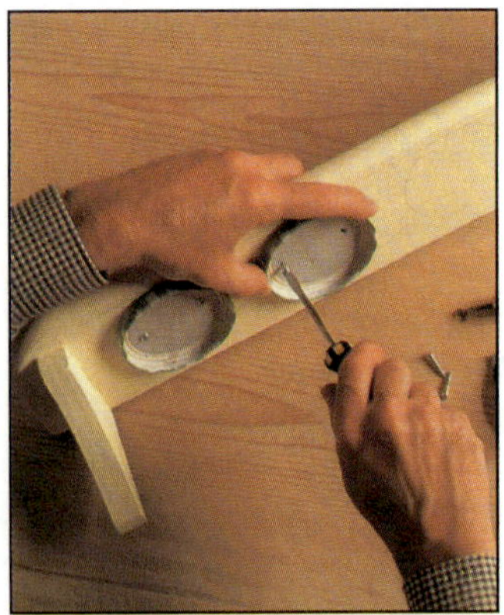

three *Screw the lids securely in place.*

four *Screw on the jars. It is easier to do this with the shelf on a work surface than with the shelf already hanging on the wall. Hang up the shelf.*

New Ways with Napkins

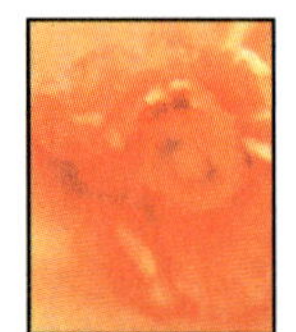

Napkins in jewel-bright colors add a wonderful and inexpensive splash of brilliance to any dining table and immediately conjure up visions of hotter climates and more exotic places. Choose tapestry yarn in strong colors to edge the napkins and trim each one in a different style, adding buttons and beads where appropriate. They will prove really eye-catching when used with a plain, boldly colored tablecloth, country-style china and chunky knives and forks.

YOU WILL NEED

colored linen napkins
colored tapestry yarn
tapestry needle
large button
about 50 tiny multicolored beads
tailor's chalk (optional)

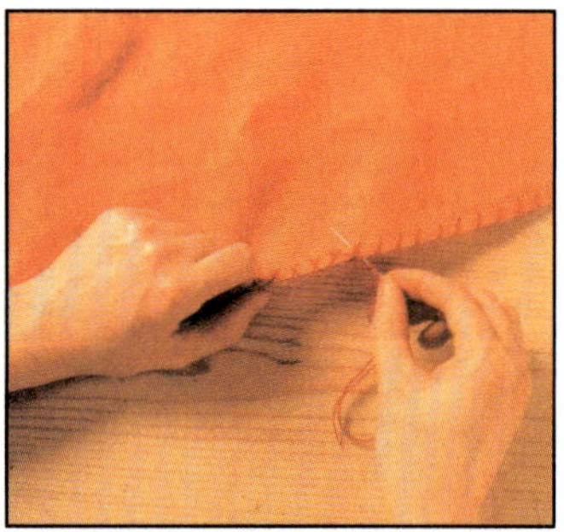

one *If your napkin has an openwork edging, work a cross-stitch following the decorative holes in the edge. If not, work an evenly spaced cross-stitch along the edge. Attach a button with tapestry yarn at one corner.*

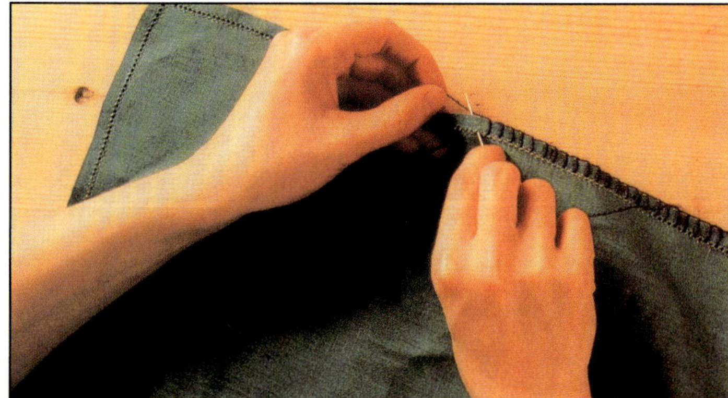

two *Work the edge of the second napkin in blanket-stitch by holding the thread under the needle and pulling the point of the needle through. Take a few strands of tapestry yarn, knot them in the center and stitch them to one corner.*

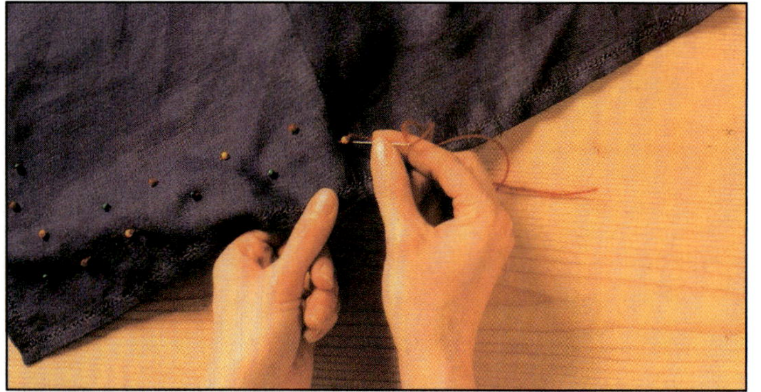

three *For the bead edging, work out a design by arranging the beads on a flat surface. You could mark these on the napkin first, by chalking tiny dots where you feel the beads should be. Sew the beads securely in place.*

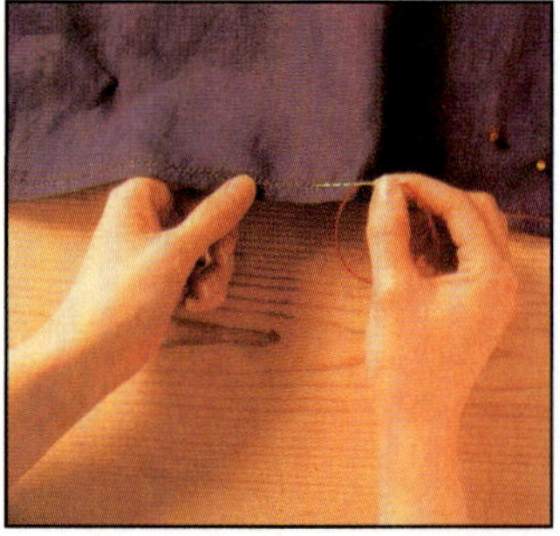

four *Complete the edging with running stitch. Simply take the thread and weave it in and out of the fabric at regular intervals, to form a pretty line of stitches about ½ inch from the edge.*

PUNCHED-TIN WALL

PUNCHED-TIN DESIGNS are surprisingly interesting and effective. They are a standard technique of folk-art interiors, but in this context, they are often kept to quite small areas. However, there's no reason why punched tin can't be used over a much larger area, where it will look much more dramatic and exciting. You will need to frame the tin in some way, so it makes sense to put it above a chair rail; it could be bordered at the top by a picture rail. Another idea would be to enclose it within moldings to form a series of matching panels on the wall.

YOU WILL NEED

scrap paper
pencil
metal file
thin tin sheet
long metal ruler
china marker
metal punch
tack hammer
wood scrap
drill, with metal and masonry bits
level
straightedge
plastic anchors
dome-headed screws
screwdriver
clear varnish or lacquer
varnish brush

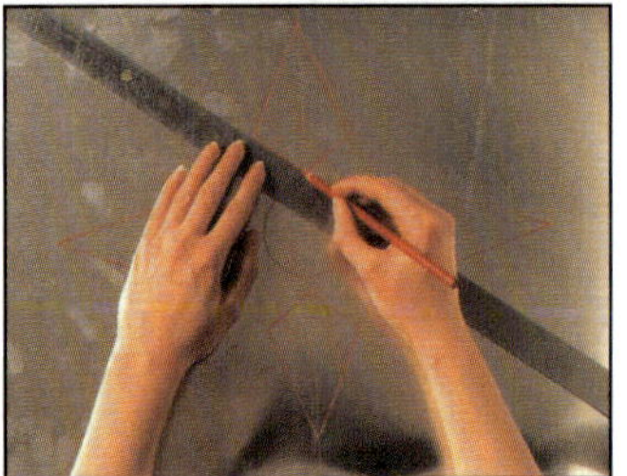

one *Design and draw the pattern to scale on paper first. Use a metal file to smooth any rough edges on the metal sheet. Draw the pattern to size on the reverse side of the metal sheet using a china marker.*

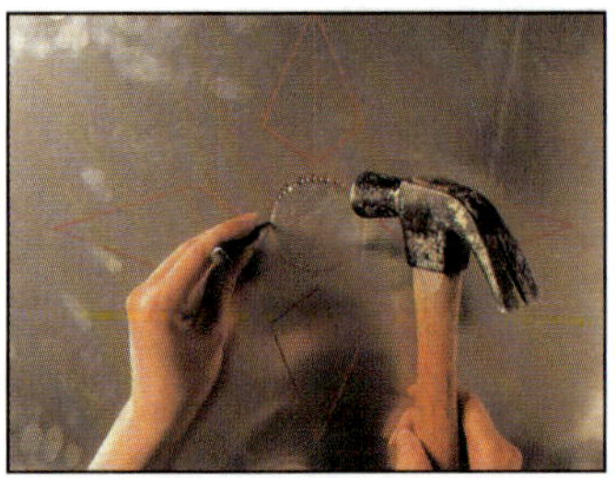

two *Practice on a spare scrap of metal to get a feel for how hard you need to punch. Punch out the pattern. Put a piece of wood behind the tin to protect your work surface. Drill holes in the corners of the metal sheet.*

three *Using a level and straightedge, draw accurate horizontal guidelines on the wall to indicate the position of the metal sheet. Drill holes in the wall where the corners will be. Insert plastic anchors in the holes. Screw the metal sheet securely in position on the wall.*

four *Finish with a protective coat of varnish or lacquer.*

MEUBLES DE JARDIN

VEGETABLE RACK

MOST KITCHEN ACCESSORIES seem to be made from practical but unattractive plastic, or high-tech and expensive chrome or stainless steel. This modern black vegetable rack is not the product of a design team from Tokyo, Milan or Paris—although it looks as if it could be—but is, in fact, three garden sieves (made from either wood and wire or galvanized iron) and a length of gatepost chain. Vegetables look enticing on display at the market, so why not store them in a place where they can be seen and appreciated? Hang this rack in a kitchen corner so you can reach the vegetables easily when you need them for cooking.

YOU WILL NEED

3 yards chain, plus length to hang the rack from the ceiling
hacksaw
pliers
string
3 metal garden sieves
felt-tipped pen
scissors
masking tape
kitchen cloth
center punch
hammer
drill, with metal and wood bits
15 "S" hooks (optional)
combine hook
ceiling hook and fixings (or long wall bracket)

one *Saw the chain into nine sets of twelve links, only sawing through one half of each link. Pry the links apart with pliers to separate the nine sections.*

two *Wrap a piece of string around one of the sieves to measure the circumference. Mark the measurement on the string. Cut the string to length.*

three *Fold the string into three equal lengths, marking it with the felt-tipped pen as you do so.*

four *Place the marked string around one of the sieves and stick masking tape on each third around the edge. The other two sieves need six marks—three around the top edge and three around the base edge. It is important to do this accurately so that the rack hangs level.*

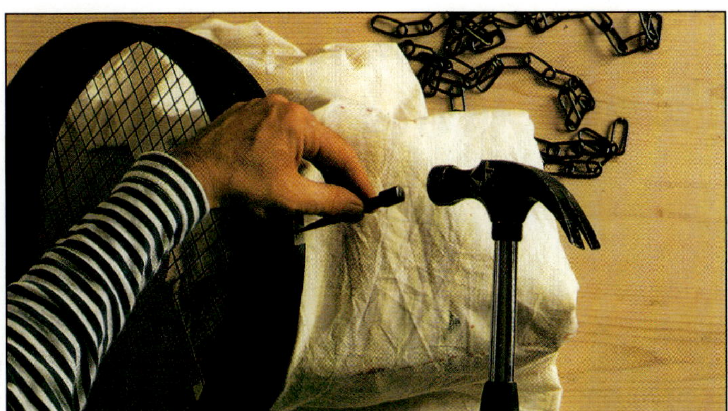

five *Place the sieves on a hard surface covered by a kitchen cloth. Use a center punch with a hammer to dent the metal at each marked point.*

six *Using the dent marks as guides, drill holes on all three sieves. The dent mark should prevent the drill bit from slipping on the metal.*

seven *Insert "S" hooks into all the holes. Arrange the sieves in the order in which they will hang—the sieve with only three drilled holes goes on the bottom tier. Starting with the three-holed sieve, attach a length of chain to each "S" hook, adjusting the level to suit your needs by attaching the hooks at different links. To save money, you could dispense with the "S" hooks completely and simply pry apart and then rejoin the chain links to attach the sieves directly.*

CONTINUED OVER ➤

eight *Clip the three top chain lengths together with a combine hook and add an additional length to suspend the rack from the ceiling. Find a beam for the ceiling hook, as it needs to be strong to support the weight of vegetables.*

Above: The vegetable rack will look equally at home in a rustic interior or a stark, modern one.

COLORFUL KITCHEN CHAIR

INTRODUCE PROVENÇAL CHECKS and stripes to the kitchen with soft furnishings; many kitchen chairs have detachable pads or padded seats, and the informality of the kitchen perfectly suits a mix of frills, ties and prints. Consider the colors and patterns of your tablecloths and then, using bright colors, simple ginghams or stripes, mix and match. As an alternative, smart ticking stripes or pale pastels would give this old-fashioned chair a sophisticated air.

YOU WILL NEED

kitchen chair
tissue or pattern-cutting paper
pencil
thin foam
scissors
3 yards of 54-inch fabric
fabric marker
tape measure
ruler or triangle
dressmaker's pins
sewing machine
matching thread
iron
ribbons or ties (optional)

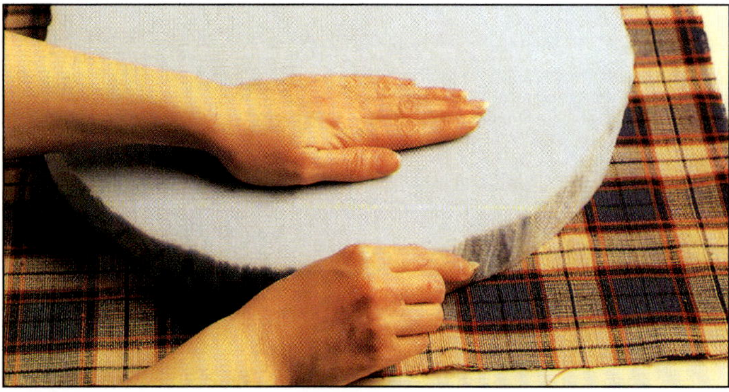

one *Using the thin paper, draw the shape of the chair seat and cut it out of foam to form a cushion. On the wrong side of the fabric, draw the cushion shape again, adding a ¾-inch seam allowance all around. Measure the depth and the circumference of the foam.*

two *Cut a bias strip of fabric to these measurements, with a 1½-inch seam allowance all around. Attach the strip to the seat cover, by pinning and machine-stitching the pieces together all around the edge, with right sides together.*

three *Decide how deep you want the skirt to be. The length is three times the circumference of the seat.*

four *From straight-grain fabric, cut one continuous panel or join two together. Hem the bottom edge and the two ends. Fold, pin and press the fabric into box pleats. When pleated, the skirt should be the same length as the sides and front of the cushion pad. Sew along the top edge to secure the pleats. Attach the pleats to the bias-cut strip of the chair cover, with right sides together. Leave the back edge of the chair cover free of pleats, but turn up the hem allowance on the bias strip.*

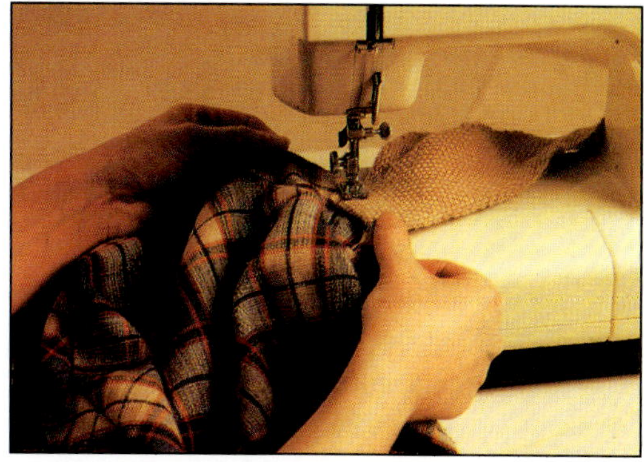

five *Stitch ribbons or ties to the unfrilled edge and tie them around the backrest to hold the cover in place. Alternatively, cut ties from leftover fabric. Machine-stitch them with right sides together, leaving a small gap. Trim the seam allowances and clip the corners. Turn the ties right side out through the gap and slip-stitch the gap closed. Attach the self-ties in the same way as the ribbons.*

FOLK MOTIF CHAIR

OLD KITCHEN CHAIRS ARE functional and comfortable but often very plain. This particular chair was just begging for a makeover and is now the center of attention. This modular style of decoration lets you unite a non-matching set of chairs by stamping them with a similar design in the same colors. They will look much more interesting than a new set, and will cost only a fraction of the price. All you need to do is to cut out the five pattern elements with a scalpel, and you are ready to start redecorating.

YOU WILL NEED

latex paint: light blue-gray, dark blue-gray, red and white

paintbrushes

ruler and pencil

plate

medium-density sponge cut into the pattern shapes

clear matte varnish

one *Paint the chair with two coats of light gray-blue latex. Rub back the paint between coats. Find and mark the center of the backrest with a ruler.*

two *Spread out the three paint colors evenly on a plate, press the diamond shape into the paint, make a test print, then stamp it in red in the center of the backrest.*

three *Stamp a white circle on either side of the diamond.*

four *Stamp a dark blue-gray triangle and then a red half moon as shown.*

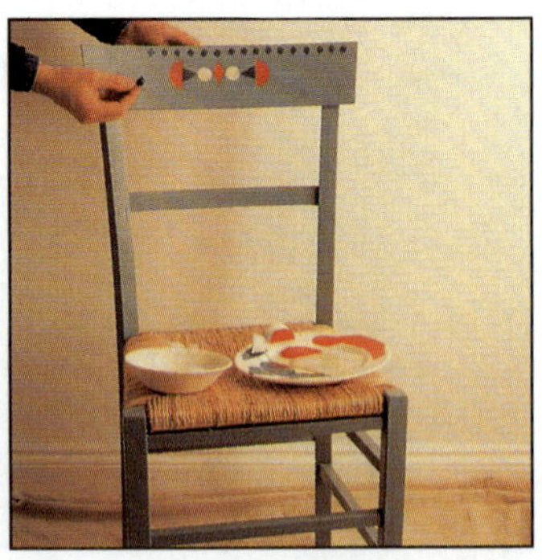

five *Stamp dark blue-gray diamonds around the edge of the backrest.*

six *Stamp dark squares on the cross-bar, then fill in the borders with white.*

seven *Stamp dark blue-gray triangles with the point outwards to make a "sawtooth" border.*

eight *Stamp red circles on the front legs where the lower crossbars meet them. Stamp dark blue-gray triangles above and below the circles, pointing outward. Add some dark blue-gray and white diamonds to the centers of the lower crossbars. Finally, when the paint is dry, give the chair a coat of clear matte varnish to protect the design.*

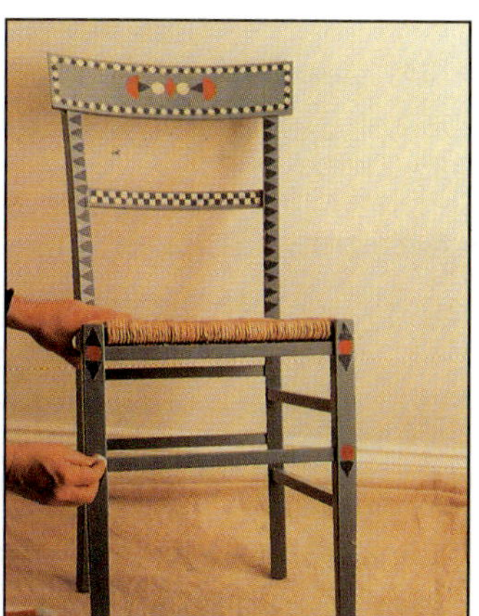

STENCILED HARDBOARD

DAMAGED OR IRREGULAR FLOORS are frequently covered in hardboard, and you may feel that this smooth, hard surface is especially appropriate if you have adopted a modernist, minimalist approach to decorating. If you discover hardboard in mint condition, in most instances it is not wise to lift it, as it is probably hiding some horror below. However, with several coats of varnish, hardboard has a natural patina of its own, which is very appealing, and works as a neutral background as well as a wooden floor does. Introduce additional interest by using stencils, which here mimic a fifties-style rug, although the brown hardboard would suit different colors. The contrast of black or white works well; choose a bold, non-figurative pattern.

YOU WILL NEED

pencil
paper
black water-based paint
paintbrushes
metal ruler or straight edge
masking tape
self-healing cutting mat
sheet of acetate
craft knife
pin
stencil brush
lint-free cloth or fine-grade sandpaper (optional)
eraser
gloss varnish

one *Draw the border motif to the desired size on paper, either copying this pattern or designing your own.*

two *Photocopy the design and make sure that the pattern works, by placing several sheets together.*

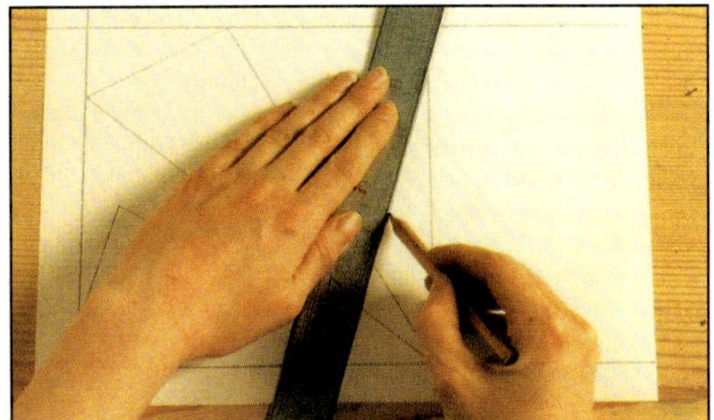

three *Work out a right-angled section for the corners. Make sure it ties in neatly with the repeat on both sides.*

four *Black in the design and photocopy it. Lay the copies around the floor, to ensure that your design will look good, and experiment until you have an effect you are happy with.*

five *With pencil, mark the outer edge of your border on the floor (in the photograph, this is about 5½ inches from the edge of the room).*

six *Draw out pencil guidelines for your border all around the room.*

seven *With masking tape, stick one of the photocopies, to the cutting mat. Tape the sheet of acetate over it.*

eight *Using the steel ruler and holding the knife at an angle, carefully cut out the stencil. To help get neat, sharp corners, make a pin prick just at the corner first; this also helps to prevent you from cutting too far.*

nine *With masking tape, attach the stencil to the hardboard, lining it up carefully with your guidelines.*

ten *Using a stencil brush, stipple in the neat black triangles, making sure that the paint is very dry so that it does not seep under the stencil.*

CONTINUED OVER ➤

eleven *Lift up the stencil and reposition it for the next section. Remember to make sure the underside of the stencil is free of paint. If you need to mask certain areas of the stencil so that you continue the pattern when working the corners, do this with a piece of paper held firmly in place with masking tape.*

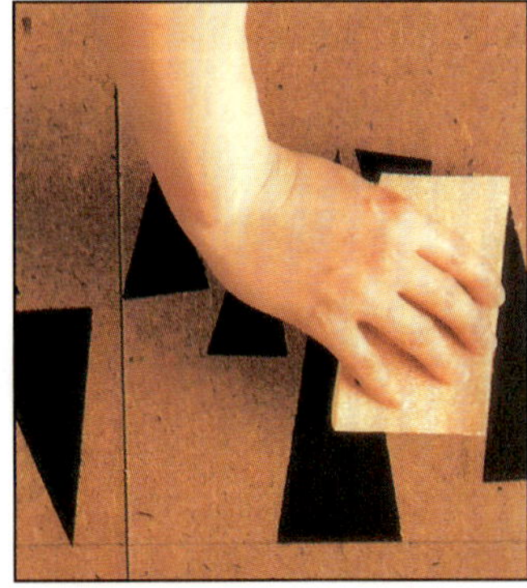

twelve *If you make a mistake or smudge the stenciling, rub it clean with a damp cloth or, if the surface is more porous, very gently sand away the paint when dry. Finally, remove the guidelines with an eraser and seal the floor with at least two coats of varnish.*

Cut-above tiles

If you'd like to retile your kitchen but are short on funds, this is the cheapest way of achieving the effect: simple photocopies cut into tile shapes, pasted to the wall and then varnished for protection. Find an appropriate motif that will fit neatly into a tile shape. Then you just need enough patience to cut out and paste the copies onto the wall. You could adapt the idea to other areas of the house: just change the motif to fit.

YOU WILL NEED

cutlery motifs
pencil
metal ruler
craft knife
self-healing cutting mat
straightedge
level
wallpaper paste
pasting brush
clear varnish
varnish brush

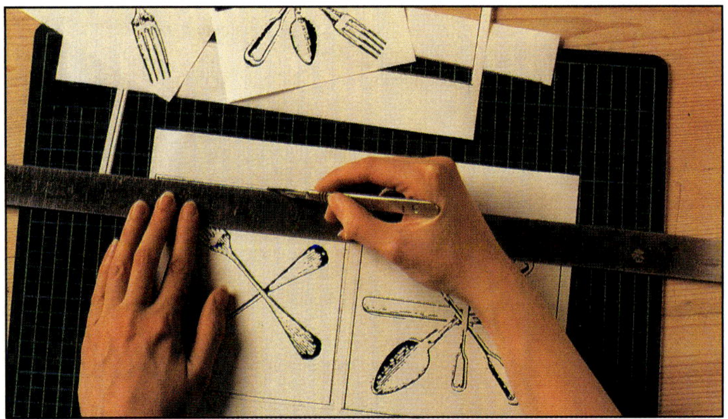

one *Photocopy the motif as many times as necessary. Draw a tile-shaped outline around the photocopies. Carefully cut the photocopies to the shape and size of a tile using the craft knife and cutting mat.*

two *Using a straightedge and level, draw guidelines for positioning the tiles on the wall to make sure you put the photocopies on straight. Paste the photocopies onto the wall, making sure you cover all the guidelines. Let dry.*

three *Several coats of varnish will protect the wall and create a wipeable finish. Let dry between coats.*

CUTLERY BOX

THIS PROJECT FUSES THE clarity of high-tech design with the starkness of surrealist sculpture—and provides an ideal place to keep your cutlery at the same time. The stylish boxes look especially good in a modern kitchen, where chrome and stainless steel keep the lines crisp and the surfaces reflective. Make separate boxes for knives, forks and spoons and say goodbye forever to rummaging in the kitchen drawer.

YOU WILL NEED

small silver-plated knife, fork and spoon, polished

3 metal boxes with lids

felt-tipped pen

coarse-grade sandpaper

metal file

metal-bonding compound (Chemical Metal)

craft knife

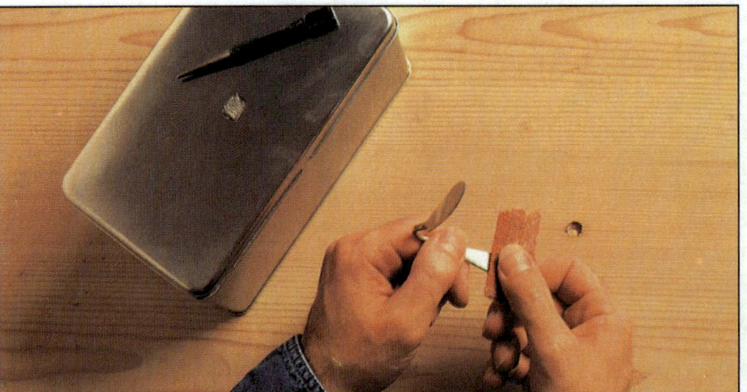

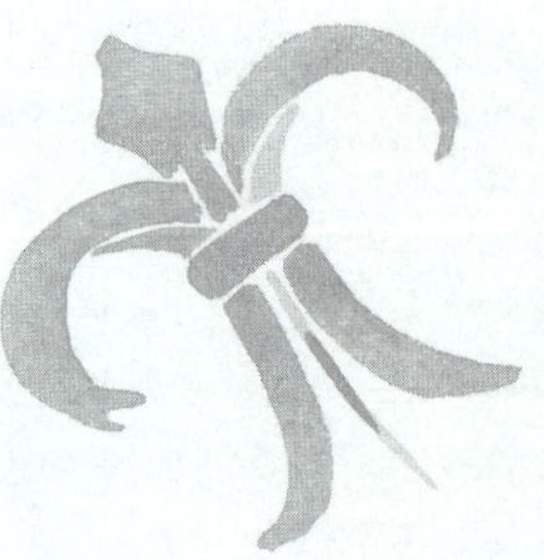

one *Bend the knife to a right angle halfway along the handle, over the edge of a table if necessary. Mark the position of the knife on the box. Roughen the parts of the knife and the box that will touch, with sandpaper and a file respectively.*

two *Mix the metal-bonding compound. Follow the manufacturer's instructions. Apply to the roughened area on the lid. The knife will be attached at this point, so the bond must be strong.*

three *Press the knife handle into position on the bonding. Use a fine instrument, such as a craft knife, to remove any excess bonding. Repeat these steps for the fork and spoon and their two metal boxes.*

RAINBOWS

THIS REALLY MUST BE THE QUICKEST, cheapest and brightest way to deal with a bare kitchen window. It would also work well in a hallway or on a small staircase window. All you need to do is buy an insect blind—a stretch of door-length, multicolored plastic strips. Then, screw two cup hooks either side of the window frame to hold the blind, and get your scissors out for a trim. The one in this project is V-shaped, but zigzags, rippling waves or even asymmetrical designs are equally possible.

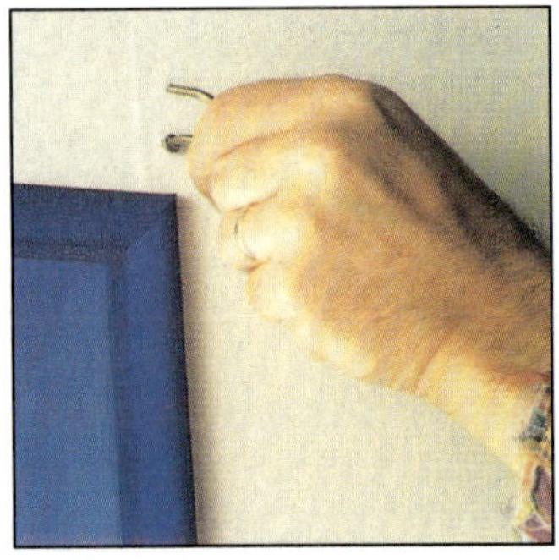

YOU WILL NEED

wooden rod
2 cup hooks
ruler
pencil
door-size insect blind
scissors

one *Place the rod along the top of the window and position the cup hooks so that the strips will hang over the whole width of the window.*

two *Measure the windowsill to find the center and make a small mark. This is where the blind will touch.*

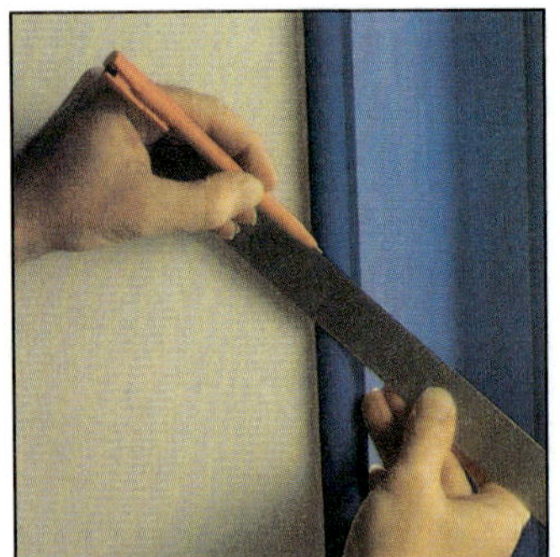

three *Place the ruler on a slant between the mark and the point you want the side drop to reach. Measure and mark the same point on the other side of the window frame.*

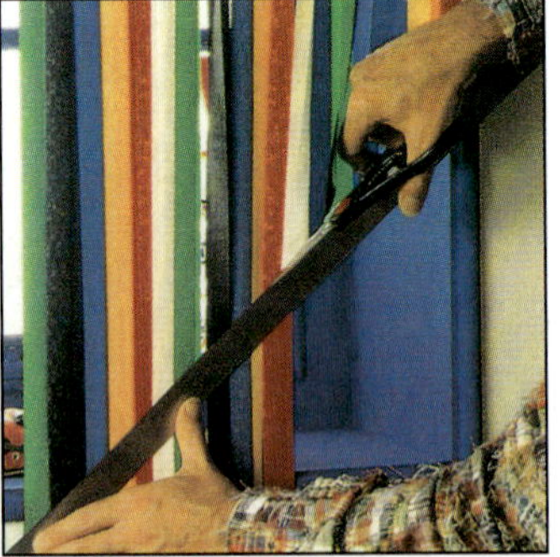

four *Hang the insect blind on the rod and position it on the hooks, then hold the ruler up against it, between the two pencil marks. Cut the strips along the top of the ruler.*

TROMPE-L'OEIL LINOLEUM

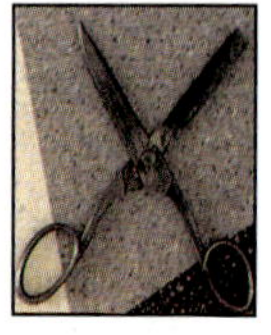

LINOLEUM NOW COMES in many thicknesses, colors and patterns, and while it doesn't quite have the appeal of a beautiful classical floor, by cutting it into "three-dimensional" patterns and playing with slight color variations you can create stunning effects. Aside from the fact that linoleum is durable, water-resistant and probably one of the least expensive floor coverings, given this dramatic treatment, it can become the centerpiece of any kitchen. Rolls of linoleum and floor adhesive were used in this project, but you could also use self-glued tiles to make a floor reminiscent of a Venetian palazzo.

YOU WILL NEED

power sander, with fine-grade sandpaper
tape measure
pencil
paper
ruler
long metal ruler or straightedge
hardboard sheet
saw
linoleum rolls in different colors
craft knife
contact floor adhesive

one *You need a smooth, flat surface. If necessary, lay a marine-plywood or hardwood floor. Make sure that no nail heads are exposed, then lightly sand the floor.*

two *Measure the floor. To ensure a good fit, it's very important to work out the pattern on paper first, using the template.*

three *Draw grid lines on the floor as a guide for laying the linoleum shapes. Draw each of the pattern shapes on a piece of hardboard and cut them out with a saw.*

four *Cut out the linoleum around the templates. Accuracy is important.*

five *Try out your pattern in pieces of linoleum and see if any need trimming. Number them on the back to fit them together more easily. Use contact adhesive to glue the tiles to the floor.*

Stool with Wood

THIS IS A VERY SIMPLE and yet effective look, which does not involve any complicated techniques. A variety of wood moldings is available at your local lumberyard or hardware store, intended for embellishing doors and paneling. However, like the paneling used here, it also gives instant texture to otherwise plain objects, lending them unexpected style.

YOU WILL NEED

- wooden stool
- white undercoat paint, if necessary
- paintbrushes
- ruler
- pencil
- wooden moldings
- glue gun
- oil-based brown paint, mixed with 2 parts matte glaze (scumble)
- creamy white oil paint
- dry brush

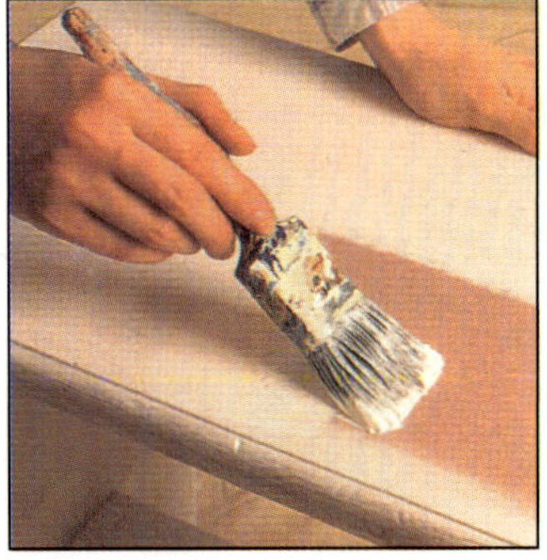

one *If your stool is already painted in strong colors, paint it white to give a neutral base color.*

‹ two *Draw a central grid in pencil on the sides of the stool and decide on the positioning of the moldings. Stick them onto the surface. Both curves and angles are suitable.*

three *Using the brown glaze and working continuously in one direction (to simulate the grain of the wood), paint the whole stool.*

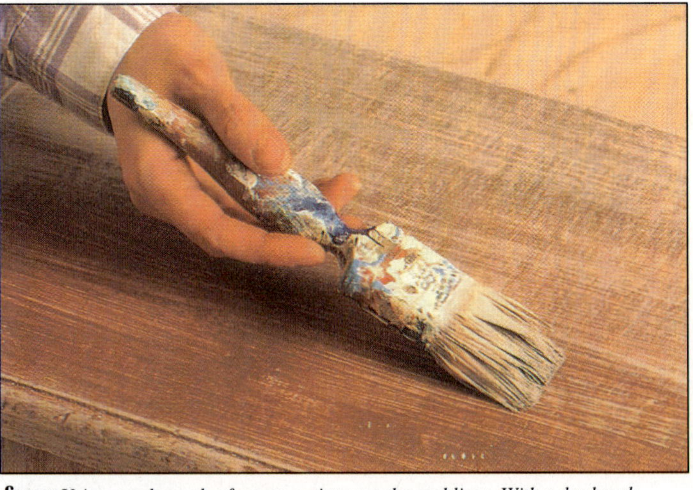

four *Using a pale wash of cream, paint over the moldings. With a dry brush, remove some of the glaze while still wet to give it a limed appearance.*

Vermeer-style Marble

You may be faced with a hardboard floor and long for the grandeur and impact of a marble one. Marbling is relatively easy to do. A wonderfully strong pattern is used here, taken from Vermeer's Old Master paintings. You may choose to do a simple checkerboard or even pretend you have a huge slab of marble. Find a small piece of marble as reference (from the great variety of marbles to choose from) to create a realistic effect. This technique is not suitable for anywhere where there is a lot of moisture, but in the right place it can look amazing.

YOU WILL NEED

- tape measure
- paper
- pencil
- ruler
- black felt-tipped pen
- white undercoat paint
- paint roller
- long straightedge, e.g. skirting length
- artist's oil colors: black, light gray, dark gray, and silver
- oil-based glaze
- paintbrushes
- lint-free cloth
- bird's feather or quill
- softening brush
- dry cloth
- fine artist's brush
- turpentine
- black oil-based eggshell paint
- matte varnish

one *Measure your room, then draw a scale plan and a grid on it, using the template at the back of the book.*

two *Fill in your design, starting from the middle point of the floor plan and working out to the edges.*

three *You need a very flat surface, such as hardboard or marine-plywood. Undercoat the floor with a couple of coats of white paint.*

four *Draw the design on the floor in pencil. Put a small dab of black paint in each square that is going to be painted black.*

five *Add a little light gray oil paint to the oil-based glaze and apply it very thinly with a brush to all the squares that do not have black dots and will therefore be white "marble."*

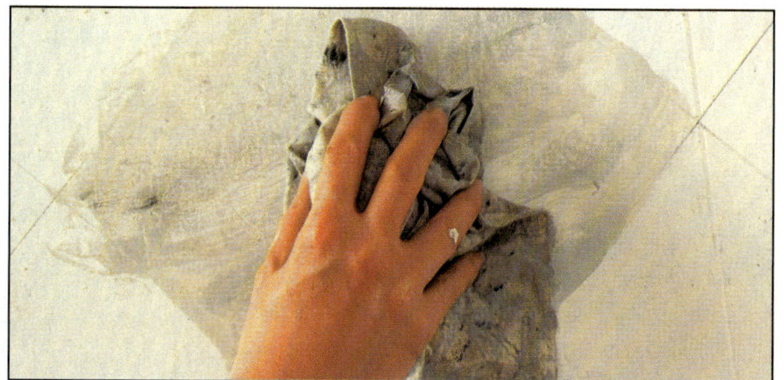

six *With a lint-free cloth, soften the glaze while it is still wet to blend it and remove all traces of brush marks.*

seven *Dip a bird's feather or quill into a mixture of black paint thinned with a little oil-based glaze, and gently draw across the surface, to simulate the veins of the marble.*

eight *Use the softening brush to blur the outlines of the veining and blend them with the background. Wipe the brush regularly on a dry cloth to avoid smudges.*

nine *With a fine artist's brush, further soften the effect by adding turpentine, which will dissipate the lines. You can also add more of the same color or a second color, but remember to soften it again.*

CONTINUED OVER ➤

ten *Clean up the edges of the pencil squares with the corner of a dry cloth.*

eleven *Carefully fill in the black squares indicated by the black dots.*

twelve *Using a little dark gray or silver paint, applied directly onto a brush dampened with turpentine, soften the black in swirling motions so that it looks like slate. Finally, give the floor several coats of varnish.*

WOODEN MESSAGE BOARD

A MESSAGE BOARD IS AN essential piece of equipment in a family kitchen and can also be an attractive display unit. This one makes a pleasant change from the utilitarian and unappealing cork type. Using a darker shade on the wooden strips and a lighter tone of the same color on the wall produces a coordinated look. The slats used here are 1 x 1 inch, but you could use a different size if desired.

YOU WILL NEED

tape measure
wooden slats
pencil
saw
blue-green latex paint
paintbrush
level
straightedge
drill, with masonry and wood bits
plastic anchors
wood screws and screwdriver
small nails
hammer
bulldog clips

one *Measure the wood to the correct length and cut as many pieces as you will need. Paint the wood with latex paint.*

two *Mark guidelines for attaching the slats using the level and straightedge. Drill holes and insert plastic anchors. Drill holes in the slats and screw them to the wall.*

three *Tap in nails at intervals along the slats. Hang the clips from the nails.*

On the Shelf

EVERYONE HAS SHELVES somewhere in the home, but how many of us have thought of decorating them with different styles of edging? This project includes three different designs using natural materials that would be suitable for a kitchen. Experiment with anything and everything around the home, and you'll be surprised at just how innovative and exciting shelf edging can be. If you attach your trimmings with double-sided tape, they can be removed in an instant so, with very little effort, you can change the designs as often as you like.

YOU WILL NEED

tape measure
string
scissors
tape
red raffia
Chinese-language newspaper
pencil
double-sided tape or pins

one *Measure the length of your shelf. Cut a piece of string about 2 inches longer than the shelf, so it can turn around the corners. Cut more lengths of string, approximately 6–8 inches long.*

two *Gather together bunches of about three lengths of string. Fold the bunches into loops and then pass the ends over the string and through the center of the loop. Pull the loops taut to secure them. You can tape the string to the work surface if it makes it easier to work on it. Cut small pieces of red raffia and tie them into small knots between every two or three strands of looped string. Cut the raffia close to the knot.*

three *For the newspaper edging, measure the shelf. Cut strips the length of the shelf, and the depth you require. Fold each strip, accordion-fashion.*

four *Experiment by drawing different designs onto each folded strip. Cut out the edging shapes. Open them out and smooth them flat. Choose the shape that co-ordinates best with the style of decoration in the kitchen or reflects the shapes of the contents of the shelves.*

five *For the raffia edging, cut a piece of raffia the length of the shelf. Cut many short lengths of raffia.*

six *Loop them singly onto the main piece, as for the string edging. Tighten the loops and fill in any gaps. Trim the ends to one length to make an even fringe. Use double-sided tape or pins to attach the trimmings to the edge of each shelf.*

AFRICAN DAYS

KENYAN CLOTHS ARE GORGEOUSLY rich and vibrant. The patterns and colors are bold and brilliant, and there is no need to hem, stitch or gather them. Just run a clothesline across the window and pin the cloth onto it—use color coordinated clothespins and line to pull this easy and exotic window treatment together.

You won't be able to draw this curtain, but keep an extra clothespin or two handy so you can use them to hold the cloth back and let the outdoors in—even on a rainy day!

YOU WILL NEED

2 cup hooks or eyelets
plastic-coated clothesline
multicolored plastic clothespins
African cloth panel

one *Screw the hooks into the wall (or window frame) at an equal distance from the window.*

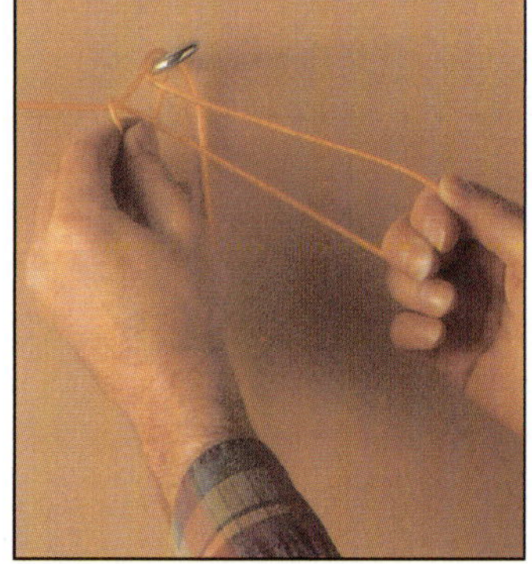

two *Loop the clothesline around the hooks and tie a knot.*

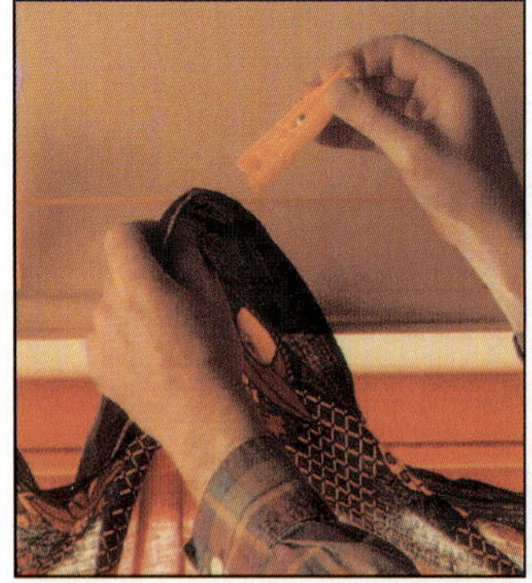

three *Clothespin the cloth to the line, gathering it up a bit for the first and last pins to add weight around the edges.*

four *Bundle up the excess line on one side and tie it in a knot. Let this hang down instead of cutting it off.*

TUSCAN DOORWAY

WITH PATIENCE AND A little confidence, you can attempt a simple *trompe-l'oeil* wall decoration to create the atmosphere of a Tuscan country house in your own kitchen. The key to this rustic look is to layer the colors and then rub the layers back to reveal those underneath. The rest of the effect is created by masking off successive areas and finally adding simple, freehand "coach lines," so called because they are similar to the decorative lines on the liveries on horse-drawn coaches. It doesn't matter if your lines aren't perfect; it adds to the look. A final wash of watery ocher enhances the aged look.

YOU WILL NEED

- latex paint: cream, yellow, terra-cotta and green
- paintbrushes in different sizes
- paint roller
- paint-mixing tray
- pencil
- scrap paper
- triangle or ruler
- level
- straightedge
- string
- masking tape
- hand-sander
- brown pencil

one *Experiment with colors. You can pick quite strong shades, as they will soften when they are sanded back. Apply the cream base coat.*

two *Wash over the base coat with a warm yellow paint.*

three *Draw your design to scale on paper using a triangle or ruler.*

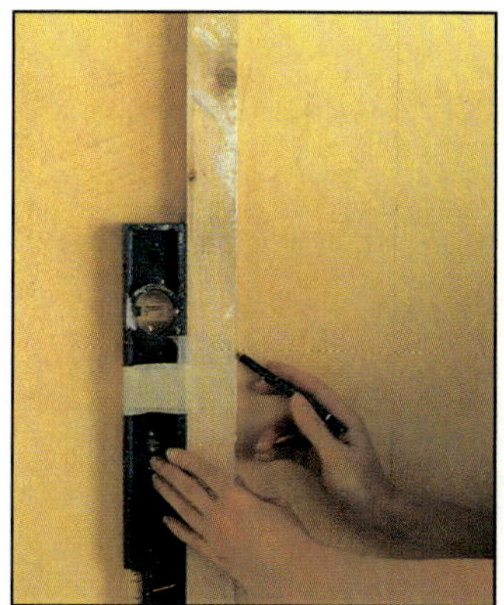

four *Measure and draw the straight lines on the wall, using the level and straightedge.*

five *Draw the curve, using a pencil tied to a length of string in the same way as you would use a compass.*

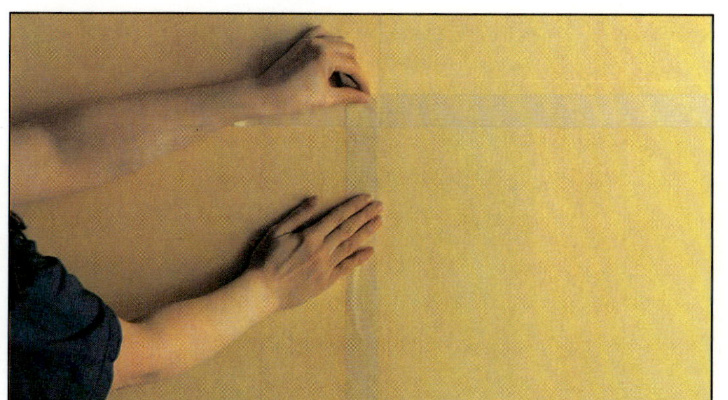

six *Mask off the areas to be painted in terra-cotta with tape.*

seven *Paint in the terra-cotta areas and immediately remove the tape.*

eight *Paint the other areas green, masking off if necessary.*

nine *Paint a thin cream outline around all the edges by hand.*

CONTINUED OVER ➤

ten *Lightly sand over the design, going back to the base coat in some areas and leaving others untouched.*

eleven *Wash over everything again with the warm yellow paint. Mask off the squares in the border. Paint the outlines and immediately remove the tape.*

twelve *Paint in all the outlines and immediately remove the tape.*

thirteen *Use the brown pencil to draw in extra-fine lines in the semi-circular "fan-light."*

PAINTED BRICK "TILES"

THIN BRICK TILES ARE widely available and take on a new character when painted an interesting color. You can arrange them in traditional brick-fashion or one above the other. Herringbone and basketweave patterns are also possible. As the right side is rough and the back is smooth, you can also have fun making patterns with the textures. Halved and quartered bricks make interesting borders and more complex variations on whole-brick designs. The color you paint the bricks is all-important; the same design in white looks very different from ocher, for example.

YOU WILL NEED

straightedge
level
pencil
thin bricks
brick adhesive
hacksaw
pale yellow latex paint
paintbrush
grout (optional)

one *Use the straightedge and level to draw guidelines for the positions of the bricks on the wall. Then, using adhesive and following the brick manufacturer's instructions, stick the bricks in place. Cut some bricks in half or in quarters with the hacksaw. Use the smaller pieces to make a border at chair-rail height.*

two *Give the bricks a first coat of latex paint.*

three *If you wish, grout the bricks and then paint over them and grout again. Otherwise, just give the bricks a second coat of paint.*

BURLAP & SCRIM BLINDS

THE NATURAL MATERIALS OF burlap and linen scrim are teamed up with bamboo canes to make this unusual Roman blind. The blind obscures the window effectively at night, and by day the sunlight streams through the scrim, making it appear almost transparent. The bamboo canes give the window a "potting shed" effect, and the ingenious pulley adds a distinctive touch—not only does it look interesting, it is also practical.

YOU WILL NEED

burlap, to fit window
scissors
scrim, same size as burlap
stapler
6 bamboo canes
iron
tape measure
saw
iron-on hem tape (optional)
needle
matching sewing thread
¾-inch brass rings
¾-inch hinged rings
coat hangers
pliers
pencil
thin cardboard
4 empty wooden spools
4 screws
screwdriver
washers (optional)
string

one *Cut the burlap into four strips. Working on the sides first, fold a strip of burlap down the length of either side of the scrim to form a border, and staple the burlap and scrim together.*

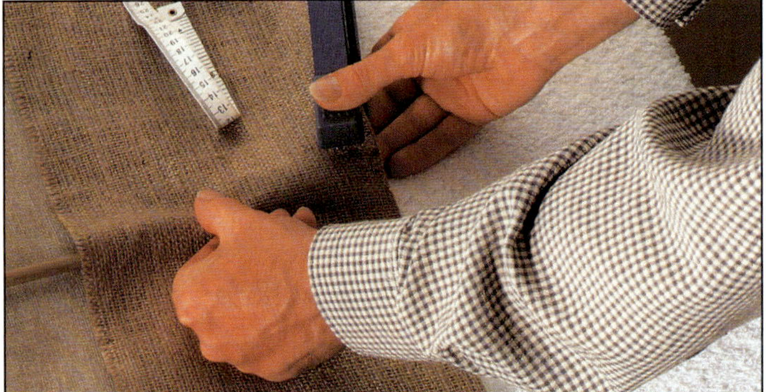

two *Divide the length of the drop by six to calculate the position of the bamboo canes. Saw the bamboo canes to fit the width of the window. Insert the first cane in position by holding it with the ends pushed up into the burlap border and stapling either side of it to make a channel. Repeat this process on the other side. Position the remaining canes in the same way, at equal intervals.*

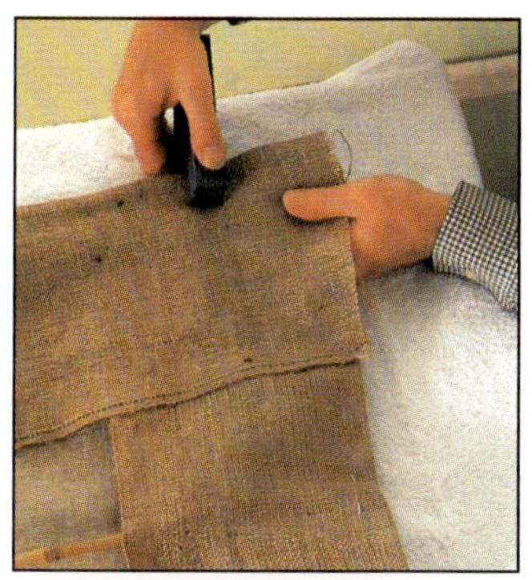

three *Fold the burlap over the scrim at the bottom, as you did with the side, with a bamboo cane along its bottom fold. Staple this in place. Repeat this process with the top edge.*

four *If you are using iron-on hem tape, place it under the seam between the scrim and burlap and press it with a hot iron.*

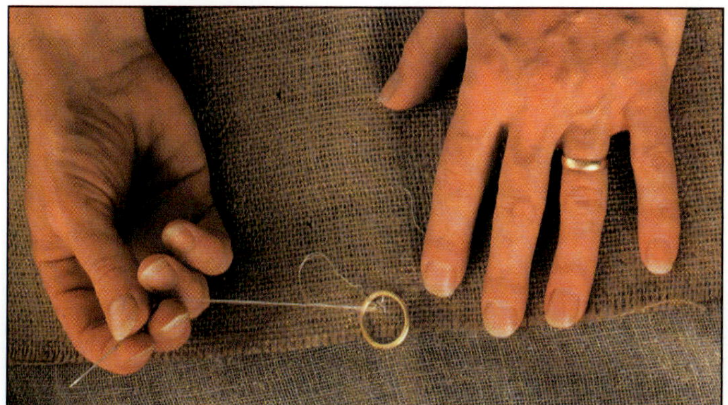

five *Stitch a brass ring to every point at which the burlap and scrim meet on a bamboo strut, including the bottom strut. Take the needle right through the fabric so that the thread goes around the bamboo each time for a strong attachment. Sew the two hinged rings, in line with the others, on either side of the blind top.*

six *Trim off overlapping burlap. If the fabric frays, insert some iron-on hem tape.*

seven *Cut five lengths of coat hanger wire from the longest part of the hanger—three lengths at 6¼ inches and two lengths at 10 inches.*

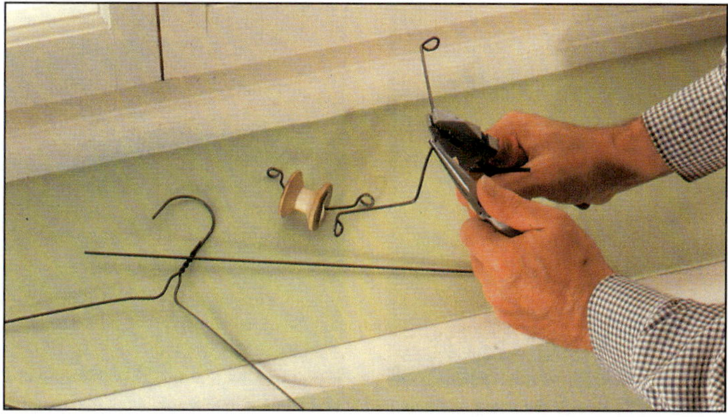

eight *Using the photograph as a guide, draw the shape to hold the spools onto a piece of cardboard. Then bend the shorter pieces of wire to that shape so that they will hold the spools.*

CONTINUED OVER ➤

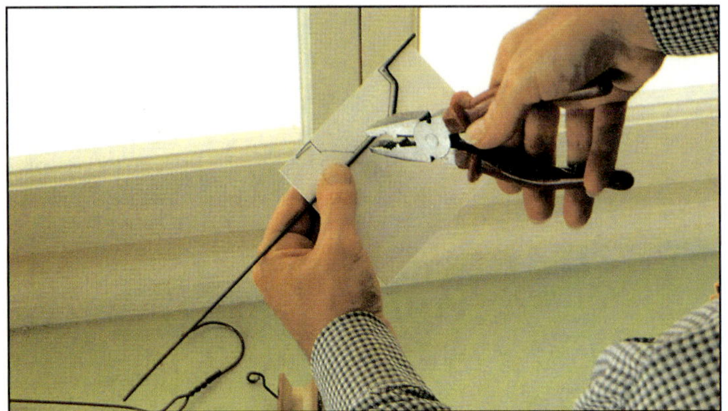

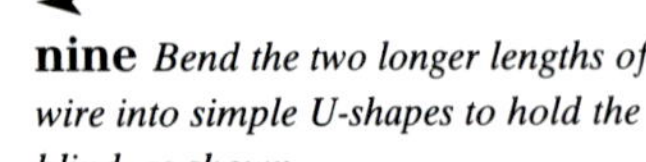

nine *Bend the two longer lengths of wire into simple U-shapes to hold the blind, as shown.*

ten *Screw the first spool into the top right corner. Ensure that the screw heads are big enough, or add a washer to get a firm attachment. Align the loops of a pulley and a longer wire and attach both gadgets in place with the same screws. Screw the other spool and wire on the other side of the window, the same distance from the edge.*

eleven *Open out the hinged ring and use it to clip the blind up in position in the window.*

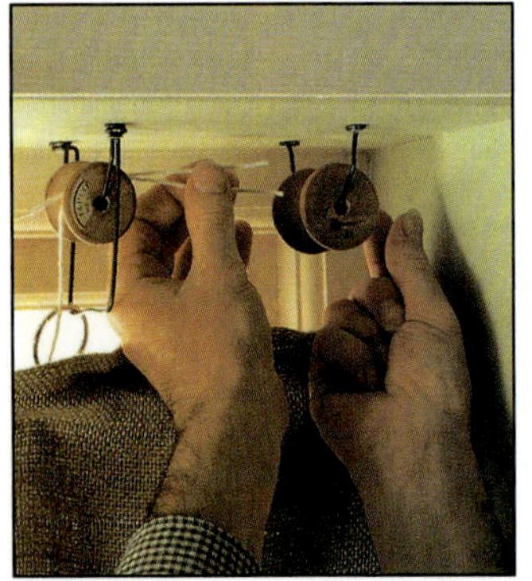

twelve *To thread the blind, start at the bottom and tie the string to the lowest ring. Thread up through the rings and over the pulleys. Do the same for both sets of rings.*

thirteen *Tie the two strings together about 6 inches down from the corner pulley to prevent the blind from pulling up unevenly. Screw the last cotton spool into the wall for tying the string when you pull the blind.*

SHEET-METAL TREAD MATS

SHEET-METAL TREAD PLATES are a versatile and long-lasting floor covering and will give a room a unique look. They may be painted—either plain or patterned—but also look absolutely dazzling left in their natural state. The sheets come in a wide range of metals, including copper, zinc and stainless steel, and can be cut to size by the store. Lay the sheets on concrete or a subfloor of hardboard, chipboard or marine-plywood.

YOU WILL NEED

sheet metal tread mats
wood scrap
metal file
drill, with metal pilot drill bit, and wood drill bit (optional)
wood screws (optional)
screwdriver
floor adhesive (optional)
metal or wooden quadrant beading

one *Use a metal file to file away any rough edges, but be careful not to create file marks on the visible top surface of the sheets. Use a small piece of wood as a rest and a metal pilot drill bit to drill holes in every corner of the mats and at intervals of 8 inches along all the sides, depending on the size of the sheets.*

two *If you are laying the metal sheets over wooden floor boards, you can screw through the holes in the metal directly into the wood surface with wood screws.*

three *Butt up the sheets together and continue screwing them to the floor. If you have a concrete floor, the metal sheets can be glued directly in place. To finish, place metal or wooden quadrant beading around the edges.*

BEDROOMS

Bedrooms

IT DOESN'T MATTER WHETHER your fantasies run to the exotic, the minimal or the regal, the bedroom is one room in the house where you can indulge yourself to your heart's content. After all, it's your room so you can do what you like.

Whatever your tastes, our ideas rely more on imagination than money, more on practical inspiration than complicated tools. And with our short cuts and great tips, decorating your bedroom won't put you to sleep. A good place to start is with the curtains. Tip number one: Forget about curtain and fabric stores. Instead, try a specialty sari shop. As soon as you enter you will be enveloped in colors you've only dreamed about. Imagine sunlight filtering through a window dressed with gossamer-light, deep-hued saris, the lightest breeze creating shivers of movement among the golden threads.

Or perhaps you dream of a bedroom of cool serenity and creative order. This calls for Japanese inspiration: simple, uncluttered lines, plain fabrics and pale colors. A garden trellis covered with heavy tracing paper becomes a translucent screen, providing privacy with the softest light—the perfect solution for windows that open onto a blank wall.

A canopy bed draped in cool white cotton adds romance and grandeur to any bedroom. It is simple and easy to create.

Once again, side-step traditional stores and head straight to a painter's supplier—decorator's dustsheets are incredibly inexpensive and make a perfect covering for a futon mattress. Making the base is easier than you think. To cast a subtle light on your Asian dreams, make a bedside lamp from corrugated cardboard and bamboo skewers.

Sleep like a king or queen under a canopy. Store-bought decorative wooden and plaster moldings provide the fanciful trimmings and the gilded finishing touches, and the effect of filigree wall paneling can be created by using nothing more than simple radiator cover panels.

WHITE MISCHIEF

SMALL DETAILS SUCH AS the curtain clips in this project make the important difference between an obvious and an elegant solution to curtain hanging. The white muslin lawn is a generously long piece, folded in half, allowing a drop 1½ times the length of the window—it really is a very simple, yet elegant example of window dressing. Small brass curtain clips fit over the rod and catch the muslin along the fold.

YOU WILL NEED

dowel, window width
woodstain
dish cloth
drill
plastic anchors and nails
hammer
curtain clips
white muslin lawn
long thin wooden stake

one *Stain the length of dowel by shaking woodstain onto a soft cloth and rubbing the dowel with it until you achieve the desired effect.*

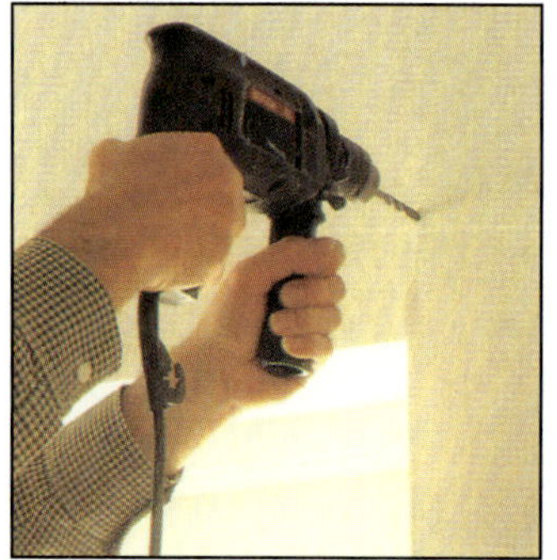

two *Drill two holes on either side of the window in the wall and insert the plastic anchors. Hammer in the nails.*

three *Clip the muslin along the fold, leaving an equal distance between the clips. Thread the rings onto the dowel and place the dowel over the nails.*

four *Spread the rings along the dowel so that the muslin falls in even drapes.*

five *Knot the front drop of muslin onto the end of the stake and prop this across the window.*

LOVELY LINENS

PRETTY UP PERFECTLY PLAIN LINENS with splashes of vibrant color. To add definition, border with strips of rickrack edging; for frilliness, buy eyelet lace and sew it onto the pillowcase. You could then weave ribbon or tapestry yarn through the lace to add color. Alternatively, look for linens that have a fine-holed edging and thread through the holes with fine tapestry yarn. To complement the edges, add tiny decorative crosses to buttons sewn onto the pillowcase. A more time-consuming, but extremely effective decoration is made by scalloping the edge of a sheet and decorating with tapestry yarn.

YOU WILL NEED

paper
pencil
cardboard
scissors
single or double white sheet
sewing machine
white sewing thread
small, sharp-pointed scissors
red tapestry yarn
tapestry needle
plain pillowcase
3 yards eyelet lace
dressmaker's pins
needle and basting thread
buttoned pillowcase, with fine-holed decorative edge
glue gun and glue sticks
decorative red buttons
small cushion, with frilled-edge and center-opening cover

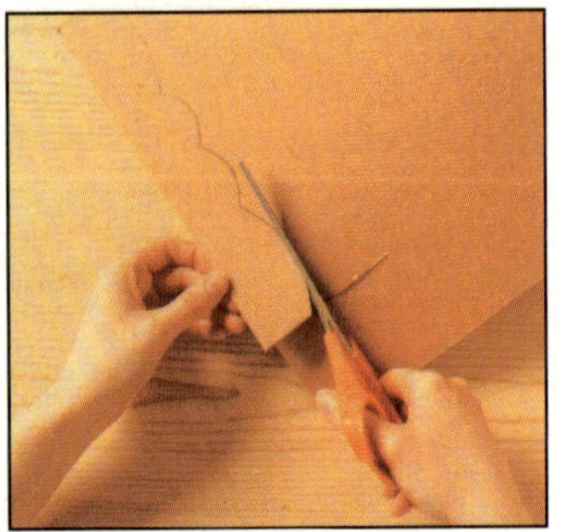

one *Cut out a cardboard template for the sheet edging. Draw around it, then machine satin-stitch over the line. Cut along outside the sewn line.*

two *Cut lengths of colored tapestry yarn and knot the ends. Sew the lengths of yarn through the sheet, leaving the long ends as decoration.*

three *Edge the plain pillowcase with eyelet lace. Then use a tapestry needle to thread colored yarn through the holes in the lace. You can also use this technique to decorate pillowcases with fine-holed decorative edging.*

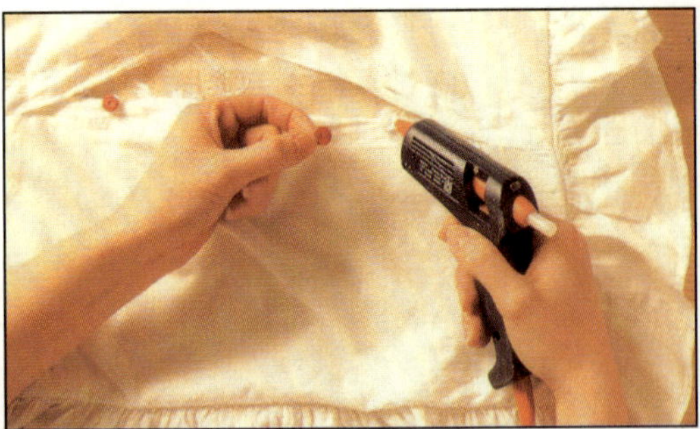

four *You can liven up plain buttons on a pillowcase by using a glue gun to apply decorative colored buttons on top. Decorate around cloth buttons by making neat cross-stitches over them with tapestry yarn.*

JAPANESE SCREEN

THIS SCREEN IS THE perfect treatment for a minimalist room scheme. It lets you hide from the outside world, yet you still benefit from the light filtering through. The screen is made from a simple wooden garden trellis, painted matte black, with heavyweight tracing paper stapled behind it. You can cut the trellis to fit your window recess, but always do it to the nearest square so it looks balanced.

YOU WILL NEED

garden trellis
blackboard paint
paintbrush
heavyweight tracing paper
staple gun
craft knife
red latex paint
drill, with wood bit
2 eyelets
tape measure
wire coat hanger
wire cutters
pliers
2 picture hooks

one *Paint the trellis black and let dry. Blackboard paint creates a perfectly matte finish, but other matte or gloss paints can be used. Staple sheets of tracing paper onto the back of the trellis. If necessary, trim the tracing paper with a craft knife so that no overlaps or seams are visible from the front. It must look like a single sheet.*

two *For added interest, paint one square red and let dry. Drill a very fine hole in the top of the trellis, at the first strut in from each end.*

three *Screw an eyelet into each hole. Measure the length of the window to determine how long the hooks for hanging should be. The base of the screen should touch the window frame below. Cut two pieces of coat-hanger wire to the correct length for the hooks, then hang the screen on these from picture-rail hooks.*

JAPANESE FUTON

THIS STYLISH AND UNCLUTTERED bedroom exudes a typically Japanese sense of simplicity, order and tranquility. Wooden pallets were used to make the bed base. These come in different sizes, but they can be sawn down and stacked to get the right size. The beautiful cream cotton bedcover is, unbelievably, a decorator's dust-sheet, decorated with knotted cords. Dust-sheets like this are incredibly cheap, so you can have the minimalist look for a minimal outlay. Just add a pillow and a cushion—and sleep well!

YOU WILL NEED

wooden pallets
medium- and fine-grade sandpaper
light-colored wood stain
paintbrush
2 yards black cotton cord
scissors
needle
thread
decorator's dust-sheet
2 black tassels
square cream-colored cushion

one *Rub down the wooden pallets, using first medium-grade, then fine-grade sandpaper. Apply a coat of light-colored wood stain to seal and color the wood. Lay the pallets on the floor to make a bed base.*

two *Cut six 12-inch lengths of black cotton cord. Make each length into a loop tied with a reef knot.*

three *Slip-stitch the knotted cords onto the dust-sheet to make three rows of two cords down the center of the bed. Spread the dust-sheet on the bed and fold it neatly over the pillows. Sew two black tassels onto the cushion and place it on the pillows. Tuck the dust-sheet under the mattress all the way around the bed.*

Trimmed Cushions

DRESS UP A PILE OF PLAIN CUSHIONS and transform the atmosphere of your bedroom in an afternoon. The embellishments used here are dressmaker's trimmings, which are available in a wide range of materials, shapes, colors and sizes. Upholstery trimmings tend to be more expensive and the range is limited, so it is well worth looking out for a dressmaking specialty store. Craft or sewing stores often carry notions and scraps, with short lengths of fringe, beading, braids and lace, which are ideal for embellishing cushions. Tie tassels and cord around the ends of a bolster cushion, for example, or embellish a plain black cushion with an unusual motif.

YOU WILL NEED

3 cushions: 2 velvet and 1 silk
fringe
needle and matching threads
pencil
compass
thin cardboard
scissors
pins
black lace and fringe
black bobble trimming
tape measure

one *For the first cushion, slip-stitch the ends of a length of fringe, so that it doesn't unravel.*

‹ **two** *Cut a quarter circle from thin cardboard and place it on the cushion as a guide for the curve of the fringe. Slip-stitch along the edge of the fringe using matching thread.*

three *For the second cushion, pin three or four parallel rows of black lace and fringe onto a yellow-ocher velvet cushion.*

four *Slip-stitch the trimmings in place with matching thread.*

five *For the third cushion, stitch two rows of black bobble trim onto an orange silk cushion. Pin one row, then use a tape measure to line up the second.*

EGYPTIAN DREAM

A PAIR OF COTTON SHEETS makes the most wonderful drapes, and all the seams are perfectly finished. The bigger the sheets, the more luxurious and elegant the window will look—drapes should always be generous. Wooden pegs can be wedged into a piece of old wooden floorboard or driftwood—if you drill the holes at an angle, the attachment will be stronger as well as more decorative.

YOU WILL NEED

scissors
cotton tape, 2½ yards
2 flat king-size cotton sheets
needle
white sewing thread
drill
length of floorboard or driftwood, window width plus 6 inches either side
6 old-fashioned wooden pegs
level
plastic anchors and screws
screwdriver

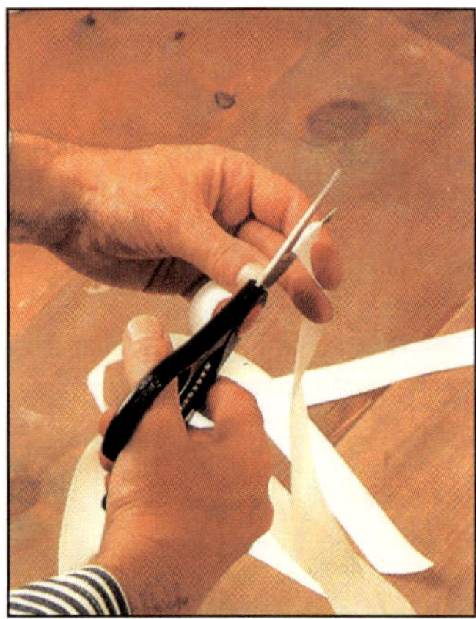

one *With scissors, cut the cotton tape into six strips of equal length.*

two *Divide the width of each sheet top by three and use the divisions as points to attach the tapes. Fold each tape in half and use small stitches to sew them to the top of the sheet.*

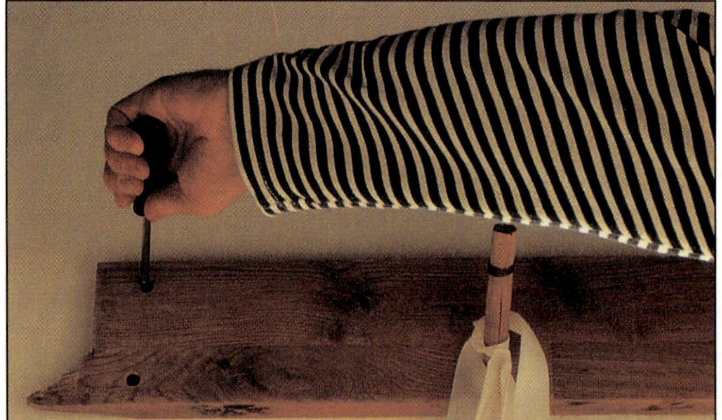

three *Drill six holes at equal distances along the floorboard and wedge in the pegs. Drill a hole at either end of the floorboard and screw it into the wall, using a level to check that it is straight and appropriate hardware to secure it.*

four *Tie the tapes securely and neatly to the pegs and arrange the drapes.*

CURTAIN CALL

THIS IS AN EXTREMELY QUICK and effective way to trim the top edge of a loop-headed curtain. Tie ribbons around the loops and hang a selection of beautiful decorations from them. Here we have used pieces of potpourri, but you can also use earrings, bells, tin stars, buttons and other decorative odds and ends. If you have a pinch-pleated or a simple gathered curtain heading, a small bow or knot with ribbon left hanging would look effective.

YOU WILL NEED

tape measure
½-inch-wide burlap or linen ribbon or tape
dressmaker's scissors
needle and matching sewing thread (optional)
potpourri
glue gun and glue sticks

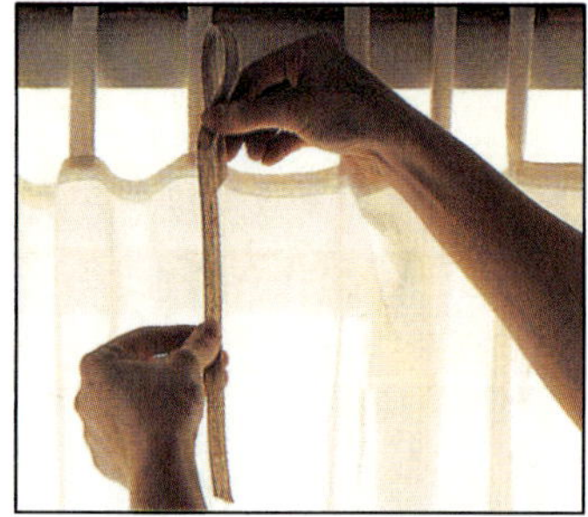

one *Decide the appropriate length or lengths of ribbon or tape needed in relation to the drop of the curtain, so that they will look in proportion.*

two *Cut the ribbon or tape to length and cut the ends at an angle, so they look neat. If you are using a ribbon that frays, hem the ends. Select the pieces of potpourri that most complement one another. Using a glue gun, attach the pieces of potpourri to the ends of the ribbon or tape.*

three *Tie the ribbon or tape to the curtain loops. It is best not to attach them permanently, so you can change the design when you want to and take them off when you wash the curtains.*

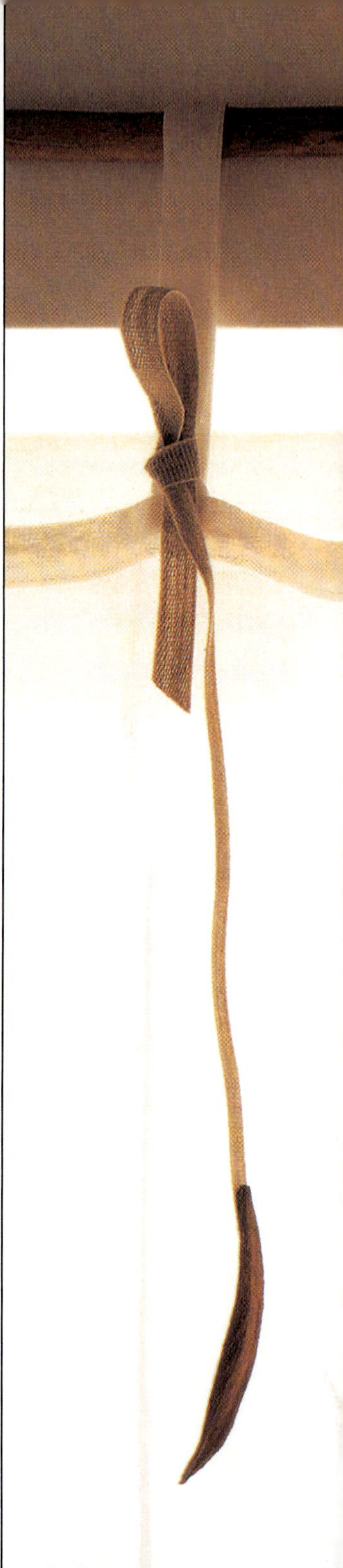

Victorian Lace

Nothing looks more romantic and feminine than a brass bed covered with snowy white, lace-trimmed bed linen. Make layers of scallops and frills on sheets, bolsters, pillows and bedcovers. Start by buying a good cotton duvet (or comforter) cover with a scalloped edge. Search second-hand stores and flea markets for lace-edged tablecloths, dressing-table runners, tray cloths and curtain panels. Look for old white cotton sheets with embroidered edges to add interest.

YOU WILL NEED

plain white bed linen
selection of lacy tablecloths, tray cloths, mats, chair backs or dressing-table runners
pins
iron
iron-on hemming tape or needle and white thread
bolster
rubber bands
white ribbon or raffia

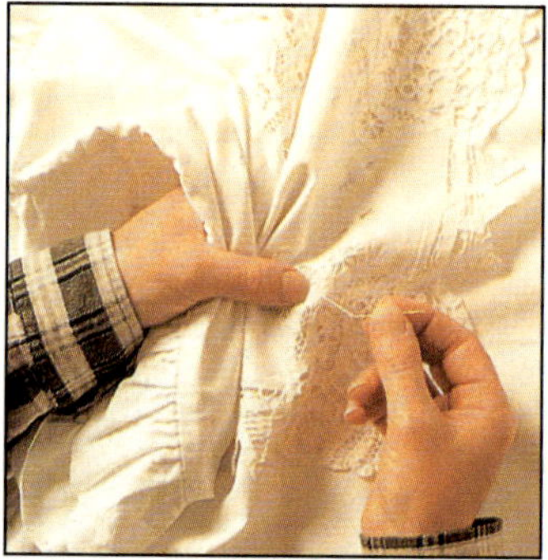

one *Select suitably sized lace additions to make central panels or corner details on the pillowcases and duvet cover. Pin them in position.*

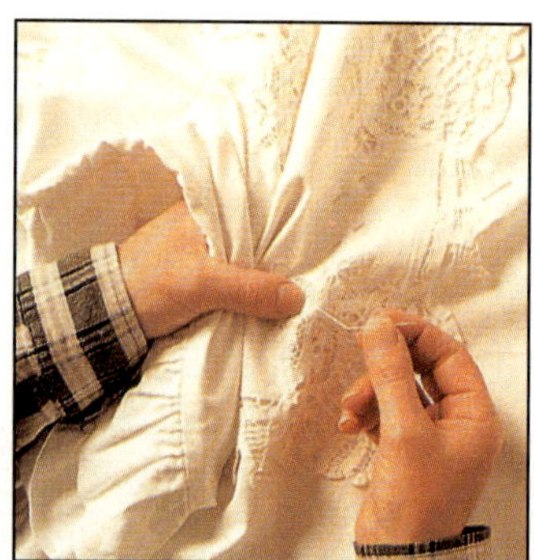

two *Use iron-on hemming tape and an iron to bond the two layers together, or slip-stitch them in place.*

three *Roll the bolster up in a lace-edged tablecloth and bunch up the ends, securing them with rubber bands. Tie ribbon or raffia over the gathered ends and drape the lace edging.*

BUTTONED BLANKETS

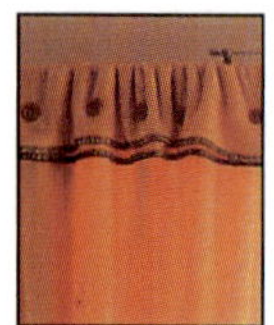

THESE BLANKETS WERE too striking to hide away in the bedroom, so they were transformed into an attractive window treatment. They're excellent at keeping out the draft and are simply rigged up on a couple of towel rods. You need a solid wall, as the blankets are heavy. The blankets are doubled over and held together with a row of large safety pins.

YOU WILL NEED

2 chrome towel rods
drill
plastic anchors and extra-long screws
screwdriver
2 colorful wool blankets
10 large colored buttons, to contrast with blanket colors
dressmaker's pins or double-sided tape
needle and thread or yarn
large safety pins or diaper pins

one *Attach the towel rods to the wall above the window by drilling holes and inserting plastic anchors. As towel rods are not long enough to cover the whole width, hang them at different heights.*

two *Fold both the blankets in half lengthwise. Drape them over the curtain rods to create a 12-inch valance, as shown. Take down the blankets. Decide upon the position of the buttons, trying them out by attaching them to the blankets with dressmaker's pins or with double-sided tape.* ›

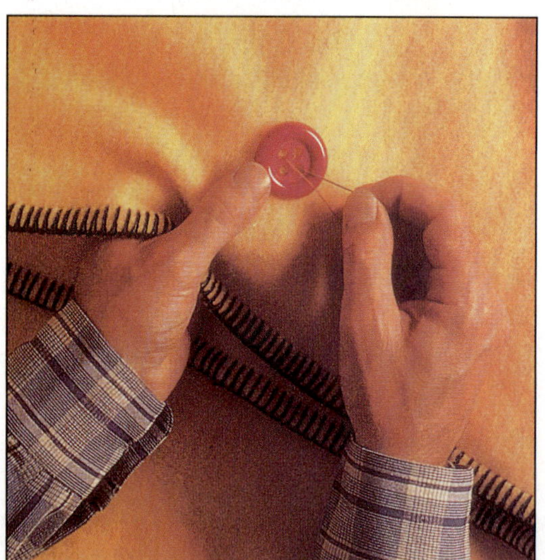

three *Stitch the buttons along the valance, just catching the first layer with a few stitches to secure the buttons, but without damaging the blanket.*

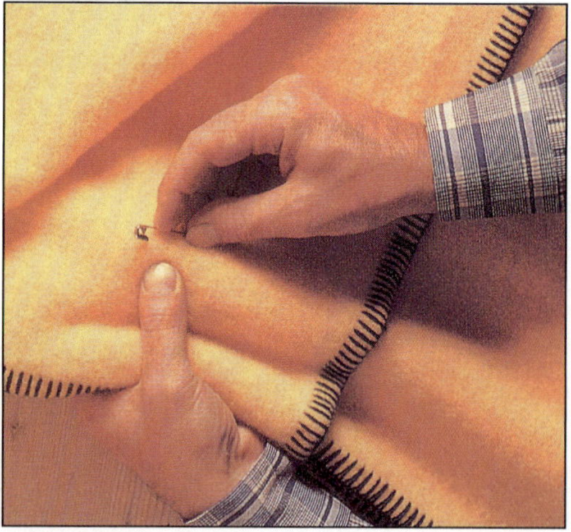

four *Pin a row of safety pins about halfway down the valance, on the underside where they won't show. Hang the blankets back in position. Re-pin carefully, so that each safety pin goes through the inside layer of the valance and the outer layer of the curtain.*

Canopied Bed

A SIMPLE DRAPED CANOPY is a great way to define and decorate a sleeping area without completely enclosing it. The muslin is draped over a wooden trellis. The natural rustic character of the twigs combines very well with the unfussy appearance of unbleached muslin. Muslin is inexpensive, so buy more than you need—any extra will make a pretty cascade at the end of the bed.

YOU WILL NEED

at least 12 yards unbleached muslin
iron-on hemming tape
iron
trellis
rubber bands
twine
scissors
ceiling hook

one *Turn up a hem at each end of the fabric and use iron-on hemming tape to make a neat hem. Find the middle of the fabric length and bunch and wrap the muslin around the narrow end of the trellis at this point.*

two *Pull the fabric into a pleasing shape, then secure it with rubber bands. Wind the twine to cover the rubber bands and decorate the fabric.*

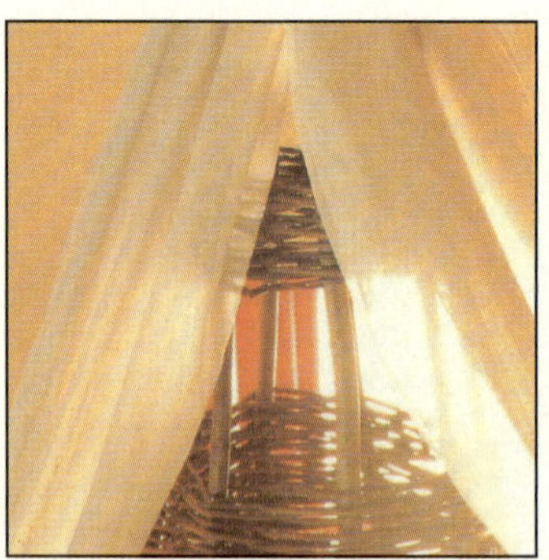

three *Attach a ceiling hook centrally above the bed. Hang the trellis from it. Drape the muslin on either side of the trellis and over the bed ends.*

STAMPS AND DRY BRUSH

SOMETIMES, WITH A ROOM that has unusual furnishings, it is worthwhile giving it even more of a distinctive style, by making a design statement on the walls or floor. Here, the busy look of dry brushstrokes combines with the elegant simplicity of Japanese calligraphic characters. The result is a warm and uniquely stylish look that makes a memorable room.

YOU WILL NEED

calligraphy brush
ink: black and rust
white paper
scissors
paper glue
foam block
craft knife
hammer
masking tape
latex paint: cream, rust and white
large and small paint rollers
dry paintbrush
matte varnish

one *Paint your Japanese characters with the calligraphy brush first, following the examples shown in this project. Make photocopies of each design. Cut the characters out roughly and glue one of each character to the foam. Keeping the knife at an angle, cut off all the white paper and the foam underneath it, to make a raised stamp.*

two *Prepare the floor, hammering in any protruding nails. Ensure that it is clean and dry. Tape off both edges of alternate boards. Apply a base coat of cream latex and let dry.*

three *Draw a dry brush, dipped into a little neat rust paint, across the unmasked boards in a series of parallel strokes, letting the base coat show through in places. Repeat this exercise with white paint, which softens the whole effect. Let dry, then repeat the procedure with both colors on the remaining boards.*

four *Plan your design of Japanese characters, using spare photocopies of the characters, roughly cut out. Using a small roller, ink some of the stamps with black ink. Replace some of the photocopies with black stamped characters.*

five *Repeat, using the rust-colored ink. Seal well with matte varnish and let dry.*

CRYSTAL TIES

TIE AN EXQUISITE SILK curtain with crystal drops for an elegant look. The use of a very rough burlap tassel, bound loosely and casually, makes this interesting and unusual. The crystal drops were bought at an antique shop; search around for interesting examples. Or, use crystal drops from a bead store or colored stones from earrings or a cheap necklace, all of which will look equally lovely.

YOU WILL NEED

burlap tassel tie-back
scissors
crystal chandelier drops
gold beading wire or very fine gold string
wire cutters

one *You need only one tassel tie-back for two curtains. Split the tassel in half, then unravel the rope. Re-bind the tassel to make it look less formal.*

two *Thread the crystal drops onto gold wire or fine string to make several strands of various lengths.*

three *Fasten the lengths of crystal drops onto the tie-backs. Some will simply hook on; others should be wired. Loop the tie-backs around the curtains and onto the wall.*

CANOPY BED

THIS POSITIVELY REGAL CANOPY BED, draped with cool white cotton, will add majestic splendor to your bedroom. This sort of bed was popular around the second half of the nineteenth century, when fully draped four-posters became less fashionable. The style imitates the ornate four-poster, but is actually a box made to fit against the wall with a canopy that extends no more than a third of the length of the bed. This canopy is made out of a wood and picture-frame molding and adorned with plaster scrolls bought at a do-it-yourself store. The wall plaque is not strictly a part of the canopy, but it adds the finishing touch. Use a fine white fabric, such as voile, muslin or cotton sheeting, for the drapes.

YOU WILL NEED

- plaster-cast head wall hanging
- backing paper
- shellac
- paintbrushes
- gold spray paint
- black latex or poster paint
- cloth
- steel wool
- 2 scrolled plaster decorations
- larger scrolled plaster decoration
- 62-inch fancy picture-frame molding
- wood stain (optional)
- 2 x 1 inch strip wood, 46 inches long
- 62-inch door-frame molding
- saw
- mitering block
- glue gun and glue sticks
- ¾-inch wooden dowel, 4 inches long
- curtain rings with clips
- heavy-duty staple gun or eyelet screws
- at least 11 yards fine white fabric
- scissors
- drill, with appropriate drill bit
- plastic anchors
- screwdriver and long screws

one *Place the plaster-cast head on a piece of backing paper to protect your work surface. Apply a coat of shellac to seal the surface. Let the first coat dry (for about 20 minutes), then apply a second coat of shellac. Let dry.*

two *Spray the head with gold spray paint. Let dry. Paint over the gold with black latex or poster paint. Cover the gold completely.*

three *Before the paint dries, rub most of it off using a slightly damp cloth. The black will have dulled the brassiness of the gold beneath.*

four *Burnish the high spots, such as the cheekbones, nose and brows, using steel wool. Give the scrolled decorations and picture-frame molding the same treatment, or stain them with your chosen color of wood stain. Cut the length of wood into one 30-inch and one 16-inch length. Cut the door-frame and picture-frame moldings into one 30-inch and two 16-inch lengths.*

five *Using a mitering block, saw the corners on the door-frame and picture-frame moldings that are to meet to make up the box shape. These will be both ends of the longest pieces and one end of each of the shorter ones.*

six *Glue the mitered door moldings at the edges and put the box shape together, placing the longest piece of wood at the back. Surround the front three sides with the fancy molding. Then glue the short piece of wood in the center of the piece as a reinforcement.*

seven *Cut the dowel into two 2-inch lengths and glue one piece into each top corner of the canopy at the back of the molding. They will act as supports for the scrolls.*

CONTINUED OVER ➤

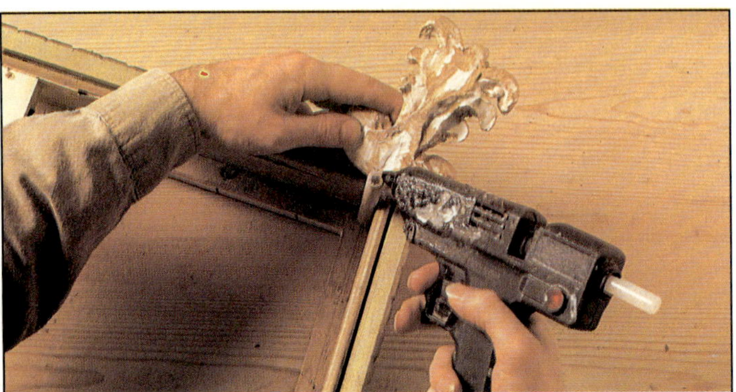

eight *Apply hot glue to each length of dowel, and then stick the corner scroll decorations in place.*

nine *Attach the curtain rings with clips at equal distances around the inside of the moldings, using a heavy-duty staple gun or eyelet screws.*

ten *Cut the fabric in half along its length. Before putting up the canopy, clip one length of fabric around one side to see how much fabric falls between each pair of clips. It will be easier to hang the drapes once the canopy is in place if you have worked out the spacing in advance. Remove the fabric. Attach the canopy to the wall near the ceiling, using appropriate attachments, and attach the plaster head to the wall. Clip the drapes in place and drape the fabric around the bed.*

Beach Mat Bed

A simple four-poster frame can be built to fit around an existing base and mattress. This requires only basic carpentry skills, as the timber can be cut to size when you buy it and just needs drilling and screwing together. The wood used here is basic construction timber that has been left in its natural state, but you could color it with woodstain or paint it to coordinate with the decor of the bedroom.

Grass beach mats are perfect for hanging around the four-poster, especially if your room is decorated with natural fabrics and earth colors. The loosely stitched grass mats let a soothing, soft golden light filter through and allow the air to circulate.

YOU WILL NEED

grass beach mats

package of brass paper fasteners

rough twine

scissors

odd-shaped shells, pebbles and driftwood

one *Fold one short edge of each beach mat over the top rail of the four-poster frame. Push paper fasteners through the mats just below the rail and open out the prongs. Use four fasteners along the top of each beach mat.*

two *The mats are edged with different colored tape that makes fine stripes around the bed. Arrange the mats to make the most of this striping.* ›

three *Decide how many blinds you want to tie up—maybe all, or just a select few. You will need about 1 yard of rough twine for each mat to be rolled up. Cut the lengths required, and tie some shells, pebbles and bits of driftwood randomly along the length and at each end of the twine.*

four *Dangle the ropes with shells and stones over the top rail and use them to tie back the rolled-up blinds.*

GILDED CHAIR

MANY A BEAUTIFUL BENTWOOD chair is relegated to the attic because its cane seat is damaged. Re-caning is expensive and it is hard to find skilled craftsmen; it often seems easier and cheaper to buy a new chair. This is a shame because a bentwood chair can become the star of a room, with some effort but little expense, by setting in a solid seat. Once the cane has been removed, the chair looks wonderful with gold-leaf decoration.

YOU WILL NEED

wooden chair
craft knife
small screwdriver or awl
4 wooden blocks
pencil
saw
drill, with wood bit
8 wood screws
screwdriver
sheet of paper
scissors
sheet of plywood
masking tape
jigsaw (optional)
medium-grade sandpaper
size
paintbrush
gold leaf or two 25-sheet packages gold Dutch metal
clean, dry paintbrush
clean, dry cloth
varnish

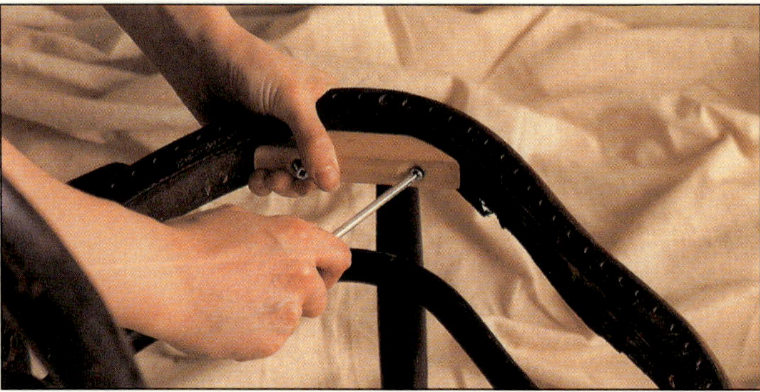

one *If the seat needs repairing, cut out the cane with a craft knife and pick out the remaining strands with a screwdriver or awl. To make the supporting corner blocks, hold the pieces of wood inside each corner, mark the shape on the wood and then cut the pieces to shape. Hold a corner block in position and drill through it into the chair. Screw the block into position. Repeat for all four corners.*

two *Lay the paper over the seat and trace the shape. Cut out to create the template. Tape the template to the plywood and draw around it.*

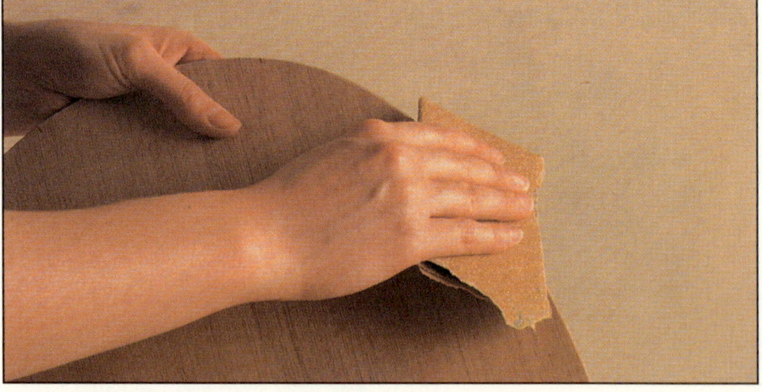

three *Cut around the pencil line. (A lumberyard can do this for you if you do not have a jigsaw.) Sand the edges of the wooden seat to fit and drop it into place. Prepare the chair for gilding by sanding all the surfaces lightly. Roughening the wood helps the size to adhere.*

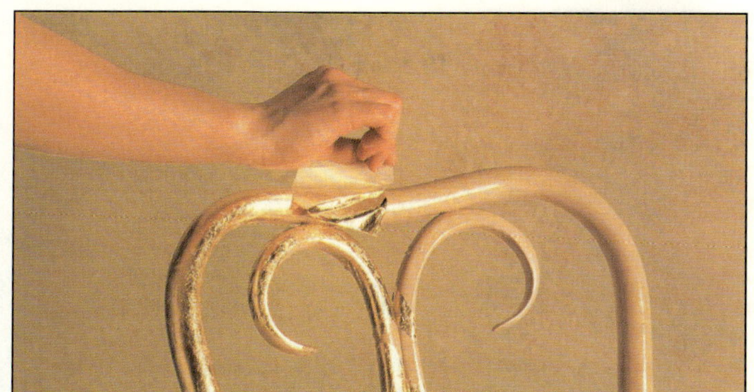

four *Paint the chair with size and let it dry. Follow the manufacturer's recommendations. Holding the gold leaf by the backing paper, lay a sheet on the chair. With a clean, dry brush, rub the gold leaf onto the chair. Continue until the chair is covered. It is very important that both the brush and your hands are clean and dry.*

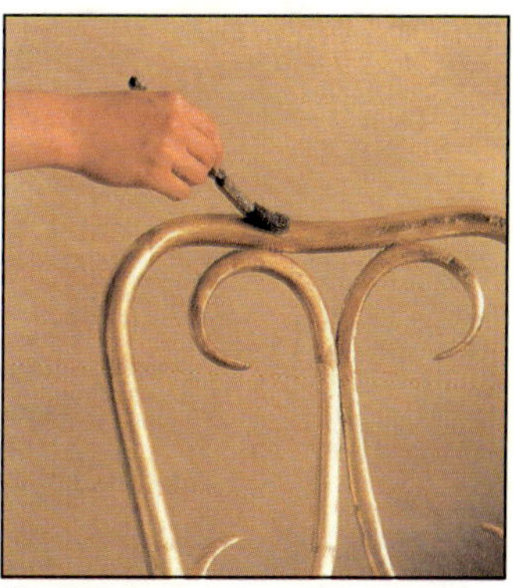

five *Rub the chair with a clean, dry cloth to remove any loose flakes. Finally, to protect the gold leaf, seal the whole chair with varnish.*

Gustavian Chair

Pretty Gustavian painted chairs give a lightness and elegance to bedroom furniture. They are expensive because few are available outside Scandinavia, where they originated. Create your own by painting a wooden chair of classic shape. It should have a padded seat, pretty outlines and enough space on the back rest for a motif. Traditional colors are grays, dark blues, aquamarine, honey yellow and red, as well as white.

YOU WILL NEED

- classic wooden chair
- medium- and fine-grade sandpaper
- latex paint: white, blue-gray and black
- household paintbrush
- fine and medium paintbrushes
- monogram motif
- tracing paper
- soft and hard pencils
- masking tape
- clear matte varnish
- typeface or script samples (e.g. from a calligraphy book)
- large sheet of paper
- scissors
- 1 yard of 54-inch (or twice seat-cover width) white cotton fabric
- indelible laundry or fabric marker
- staple gun
- needle
- matching thread
- gold and silver spray paint

one *Lightly sand the chair with medium-grade sandpaper to make a key for the paintwork. Paint the chair with an undercoat of white latex. Mix blue-gray latex then, using the fine paintbrush, carefully outline the shape of the back of the chair. Add similar detailing to the seat and legs. Let dry. Trace your chosen letters and scrolls. Turn the tracing paper over, and rub all over the back with the soft pencil. Turn it over, position it on the chair back and tape it in place. Go over the outlines with a hard pencil to transfer them to the chair.*

two *Fill in the outlines in blue-gray with the medium paintbrush. Refer to your original reference for where the brushstrokes should be thicker.*

three *Let dry. Apply a coat of matte varnish (water-based varnishes have very short drying times). Cut a piece of paper roughly the size of the chair seat pad, to give you an idea of the area to which you need to apply lettering. Photocopy type alphabets or sections of script, enlarging them, if necessary.*

four *Cut up the script and arrange the pieces on the paper. Put the paper against a brightly lit window, and smooth the fabric over the design. Attach to the glass with masking tape. Using the fabric marker, carefully trace over the letters. Cover the seat pad with the fabric, securing it on the back with staples. Take a second piece of fabric, just smaller than the underside of the seat, turn under the edges and sew in place to cover the staples.*

five *Lightly spray over the whole seat with gold paint. Repeat with silver. Replace the seat pad in the chair. Lightly sand the paint with fine-grade sandpaper to give it a charming, slightly aged effect.*

ROMANTIC NETTING

EVEN IF YOU HAVE NO practical need for mosquito netting, the light and airy beauty of this project makes it ideal for the bedrooms of urban romantics who dream of being in the Punjab or on the Serengeti plains. Netting like this can be bought at camping stores and comes complete with a spoked wooden coronet that opens like a fan to support it. Here, the spokes have then been decorated with dangling glass ornaments to make the netting look more exotic than utilitarian. Plain white netting is very appealing, but it can also be dyed to any pale color.

YOU WILL NEED

mosquito netting, with coronet and fixings

dangling glass ornaments and earrings

fine wire

long-nosed pliers

ceiling hook

one *Fan out the spokes of the wooden coronet and fit them into the channels of the netting.*

two *Thread assorted glass ornaments, beads and earrings onto lengths of fine wire to make decorative pendants.*

three *Thread the wire ends through the netting at the bottom of the spokes. Use long-nosed pliers to twist the ends together to secure them.*

four *Attach the ring and rope provided to the center of the coronet. Hang the net from a ceiling hook above the bed.*

Copycats

Create a truly beautiful setting by mixing fine, snowy-white linens, soft, filmy voile and crunchy tissue paper with gold lettering and initials. It looks extremely impressive and, although quite time-consuming, is easy to execute. Use any kind of calligraphy that appeals to you. (Here, the frontispiece from some sheet music was used.) Photocopy and enlarge your choice and trace it on to the voile, linen and tissue paper.

YOU WILL NEED

typeface or script samples (e.g. from a calligraphy book)

voile for curtain

masking tape

gold fabric paint

fine paintbrushes

iron

tissue paper

gold acrylic paint

organza ribbon

linen hand towel

carbon paper or soft pencil (optional)

hard pencil (optional)

one *Select different types of script samples. You may not find everything you need from one source, so look out for individual details. Photocopy the script samples, enlarging them to size. Experiment by moving the pieces of script around to create pleasing combinations and arrangements. Position the photocopies on the voile for the curtain, devising a pattern along its length.*

two *Tape your photocopy to a table or work surface, ensuring that it is flat. Tape the fabric on top, so you can see the script through it. Using gold fabric paint and a fine paintbrush, trace the lettering onto the voile. Press the fabric, following the manufacturer's instructions, to set the color.*

three *To decorate wrapping paper, trace different types of writing onto tissue paper, using gold acrylic paint. Complement the wrapping paper with a bow of white or gold-trimmed organza ribbon.*

four *For the monogrammed hand towel, use paper cutouts to plan your design. Tape the chosen letter flat onto a work surface. Lay the towel over the alphabet, and tape flat. Trace over the letter onto the towel with the fabric paint.*

five *If you wish to apply an initial to a chair or other piece of furniture, put carbon paper onto the back of the photocopied lettering or rub all over the back with a soft pencil. Then transfer this to the furniture by going over the outline with a harder pencil. Paint over the outline and let dry.*

Bijou Boudoir

Ballroom dancers, punk rockers, brides and prima ballerinas all love it—netting has that special star quality that windows sometimes need. You can cut, pleat, layer, scrunch and bunch it—there is nothing to sew, and it is so light that many filmy lengths can hang from a single strand of plastic-coated sprung wire.

Netting comes in a wide variety of colors, and the idea from this project could easily be translated into a stunning party window in dramatic purple or scarlet and black. Tie the lengths of netting back with feather boas, strings of pearls or even kitschy diamanté dog collars to make the most glamorous window this side of Cannes.

YOU WILL NEED

- pliers
- 4 eyelet hooks
- 2 lengths of plastic-coated sprung wire, window width
- 4 yards each pink and white netting (tulle)
- scissors
- fine wire
- feather boa
- fake-pearl strands

one *Screw in an eyelet hook at the same height on either side of the window recess.*

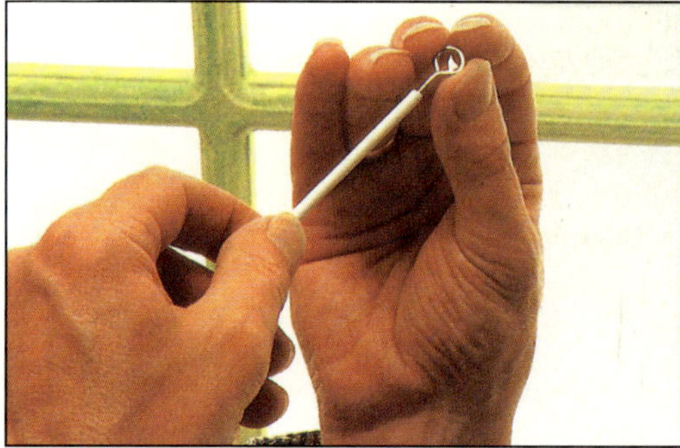

two *Loop the eyelet on the wire through the hooks and stretch the wire taut across the window.*

three *Repeat the process, positioning the second wire about 3 inches in front of the first (of course, this distance will be dictated by the depth of your window recess).*

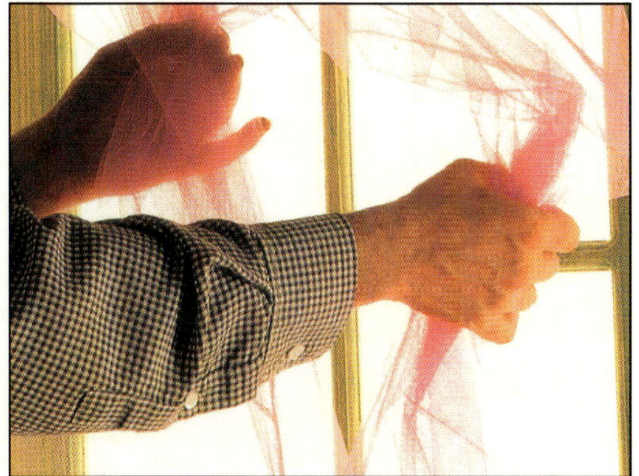

four *Cut the netting in half. Feed half the length of the pink netting over the back wire. Set aside the rest of the pink netting.*

five *Feed the length of the white netting over the back wire, next to the pink netting. Pull both lengths of netting into shape, making a double layer with each.*

six *Hang the other layer of pink netting over the front wire, trimming if required.*

seven *Cut out a large circle of pink netting to make the pelmet and fold this over the front wire to create a semi-circle.*

eight *Cut long strips of netting and scrunch them into rosettes. Tuck them between the wires. You will find that the netting is very easy to scrunch into good shapes. Pleat the semi-circular valance, adding folds and creases along the wire as you go.*

CONTINUED OVER ➤

nine *Make big white rosettes to go into the corners by scrunching up the white netting. Tuck them into the wire to secure them, then smooth them out to make a pleasing shape.*

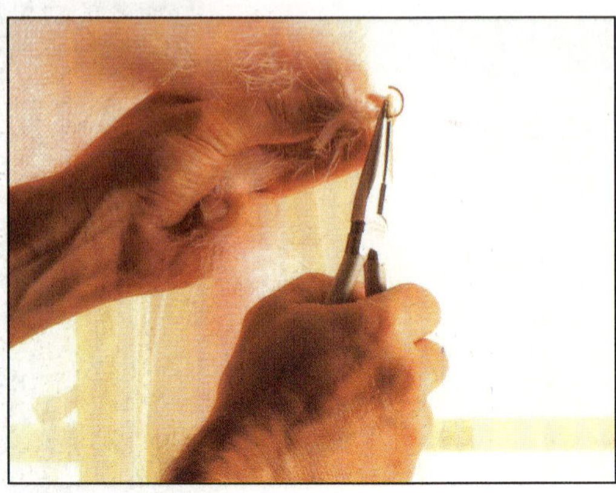

ten *Twist the fine wire into connecting rings and use them to attach the feather boa along the curve of the netting valance.*

eleven *Drape the strands of fake pearls from the center of the front wire and tie up the ends.*

Right: One of the great advantages of netting is that it is easy to handle, and is quite forgiving. If you don't like the first shape you have made, smooth it out and scrunch it up again. These rosettes are simply tucked between the front and back.

INDIAN SUMMER

THIS WINDOW SEAT RECESS was given a touch of glamorous Eastern mystery by layering fine, silky sari lengths behind each other to build up to a gloriously rich color. The sunlight picks up the gold embroidered flecks and braids, and the star lantern between the curtains casts its own magic spell. If you have never been in a sari shop, you will be amazed by the vast range of exquisitely patterned silks and voiles you can buy.

YOU WILL NEED

7 red and yellow sari lengths (or fewer)
braid, 7 yards plus width of each sari for braid edging
iron-on hem tape
iron
needle
matching sewing thread
wooden curtain rod
drill
plastic anchors and hooks
wrought-iron curtain rod

one *If the saris do not have braid edges, add them with iron-on hem tape. Cut the remaining braid into 5½-inch lengths to make seven loops for each sari. Space them at equal distances along the tops, and slip-stitch. Put the wooden curtain rod through all the loops of three saris and fix it into the recess with hooks. Hang the iron rod on the outer frame, and hang two saris on the left by threading their loops alternately so that one hangs in front. Hang the two other saris on the right.*

two *Separate the red and yellow saris, holding one in each hand about halfway down their length.*

three *Wrap the yellow one around the red one and knot them together. Arrange the folds of the knot so that the fabric tumbles away and spills to the floor.*

BLACK-AND-WHITE PRINTS

IMAGINE BEING ABLE to decorate soft furnishings with any image or picture of your choice. There is now a special transparent gel available that enables you to transfer black-and-white or color images onto fabric. The image can then be sealed to make it resistant to wear and tear. By enlarging or reducing the images on a photocopier, you can obtain a selection of prints that will fit perfectly onto any item that you would like to decorate, such as cushions, pillows or even a quilt. You can use the same process to monogram your bed linen in royal style. However, because the image will be reversed once it is transferred, you will have to photocopy any lettering onto acetate first.

YOU WILL NEED

- photocopies of chosen images
- scissors
- plain-colored cotton cushion cover
- iron
- plastic trash bag
- image-transfer gel
- paintbrush
- soft cloth
- sheet of acetate (optional)

one *Choose your images and make the required number of copies. Here, several copies of the same image are used to form a frame around the portrait.*

two *Cut away all the excess paper, leaving only the images that you want to transfer.*

three *To design the cushion cover, arrange the images on a flat surface. Experiment with spacing until you are happy with the design.*

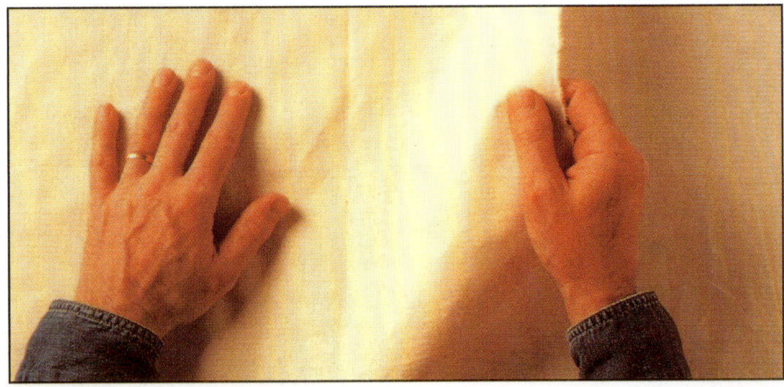

four *Pre-wash and iron the cushion cover. This is important because glazes used to stiffen fabrics may adversely affect the transfer process. Place the cover on a plastic trash bag to protect your work surface.*

five *Paint a thick layer of transfer gel onto the first photocopy, making sure that you have covered it completely.*

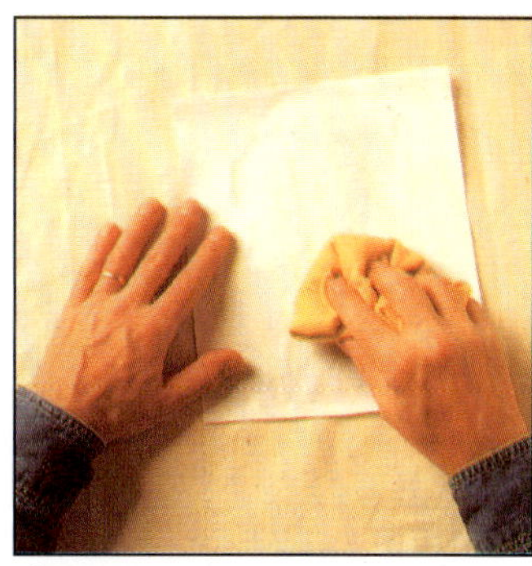

six *Place the image face-down in position on the cushion cover and gently rub all over the back with a soft cloth. Leave the image in position.*

seven *Repeat steps 5 and 6 with all the images, ensuring that they are positioned accurately before you make contact with the fabric. Let transfer overnight.*

eight *Soak the cloth with clean water and then use the wet cloth to saturate the photocopy paper.*

nine *Keep the cloth wet and begin to rub away the paper, working from the center outward. The images will have transferred onto the fabric. When all the paper has been removed, let the fabric dry.*

ten *Apply a final setting coat of the transfer gel to the prints and let dry completely.*

CONTINUED OVER ➤

eleven *You can use the same process to monogram your bed linen. Photocopy the initials onto a sheet of acetate. Then turn the acetate over and photocopy from the acetate onto paper to reverse. Cut out the print.*

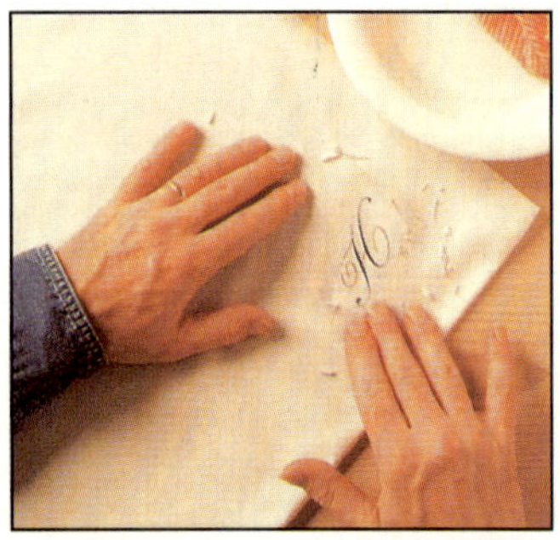

twelve *Transfer the initials as described in steps 5 to 10. The transfer process will reverse the initials once more, so that they are now the right way around.*

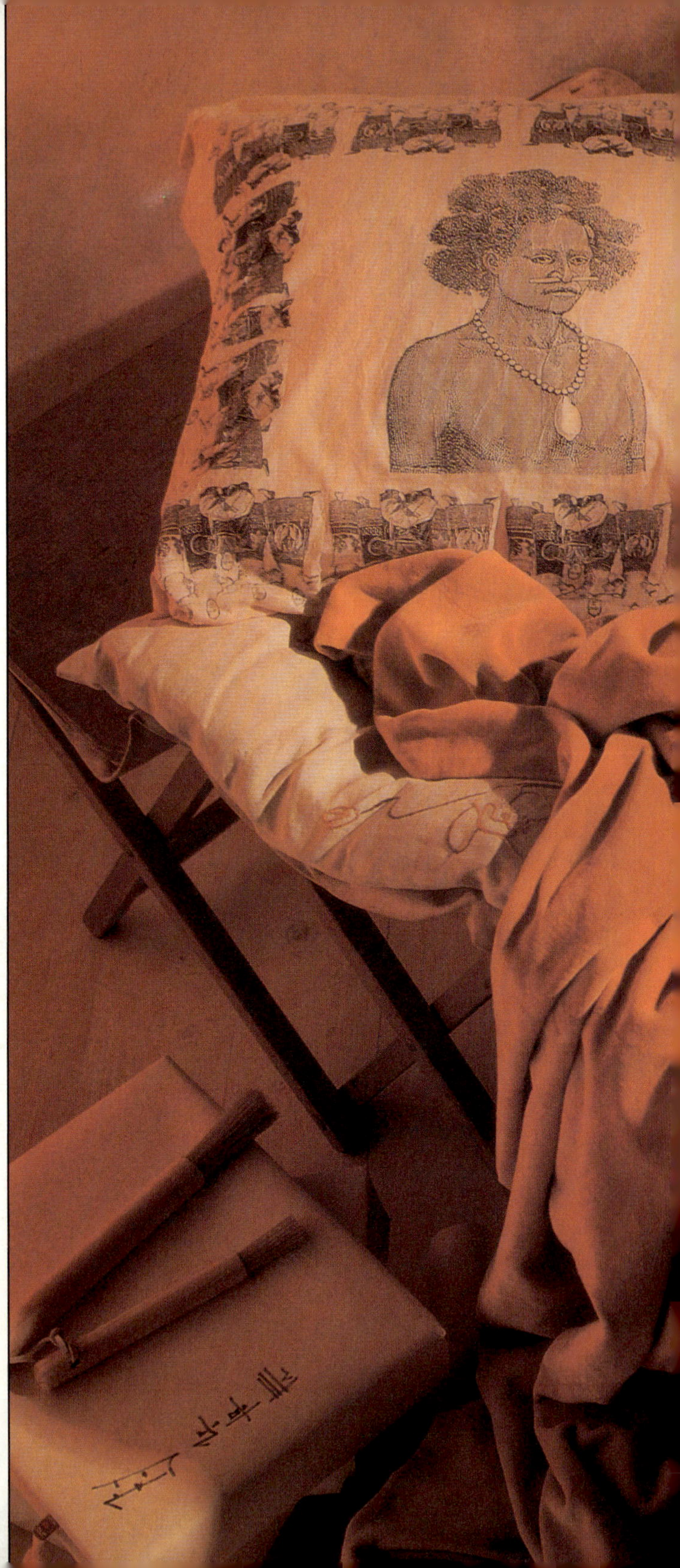

INDIAN TEMPLE BED

Indian temple wall paintings are the inspiration for this arch-shaped headboard. The bedroom feels as if it has been magically transported thousands of miles, but the real magic here comes in a simple can of paint. Before painting the headboard, set the mood with a deep rust-colored wash on the walls. If you can, use a water-based limewash for an authentic powdery bloom. If you are using latex, thin it with water.

YOU WILL NEED

- large roll of brown packing paper
- felt-tipped pen
- masking tape (optional)
- scissors
- spray adhesive
- chalk
- water-based paint: dark blue, bright blue and red
- plate
- kitchen sponge
- sandy cream latex paint
- medium and fine paintbrushes
- fine-grade sandpaper

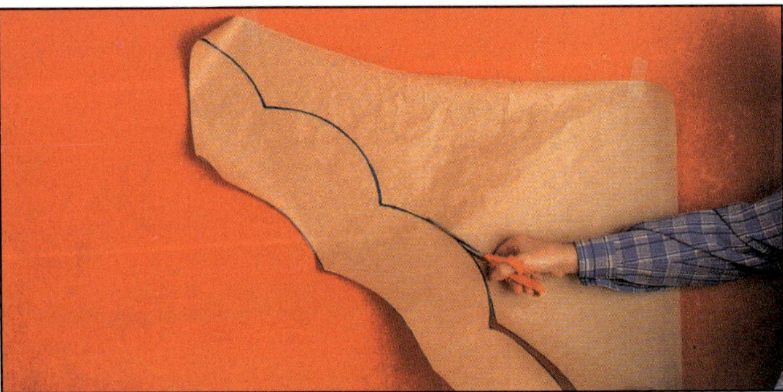

one *Refer to the diagram on the right that shows the shape of the arch. Transfer a half-arch onto brown packing paper, enlarging it as required using a grid system. Alternatively, tape a sheet of brown packing paper on the wall and draw the half-arch directly onto it, following the pattern shape. Cut out using a pair of scissors.*

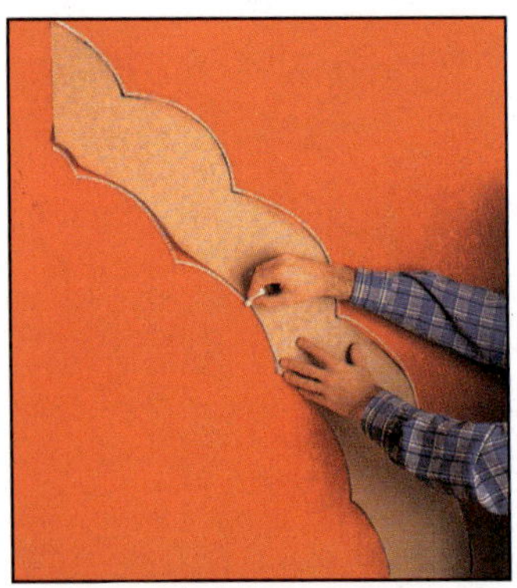

two *Position the paper pattern on the wall with spray adhesive and draw around the edges with chalk.*

three *Flip the pattern and draw around it to produce the second half of the arch. Spread some dark blue paint onto a plate and use a damp sponge to dab it onto the central panel. Don't cover the background completely, but let some of the wall color show through. When the paint is dry, apply the bright blue paint over the dark blue in the same way.*

four *When the paint is dry, paint the arch in sandy cream latex, using a medium-sized paintbrush. When the latex paint is dry, rub it back in places with fine-grade sandpaper to give a faded effect. Outline the inside and outside of the arch with the red paint, using a fine paintbrush. Support your painting hand with your free hand and use the width of the brush to make a single line. Outline the outer red stripe with a thinner dark blue line.*

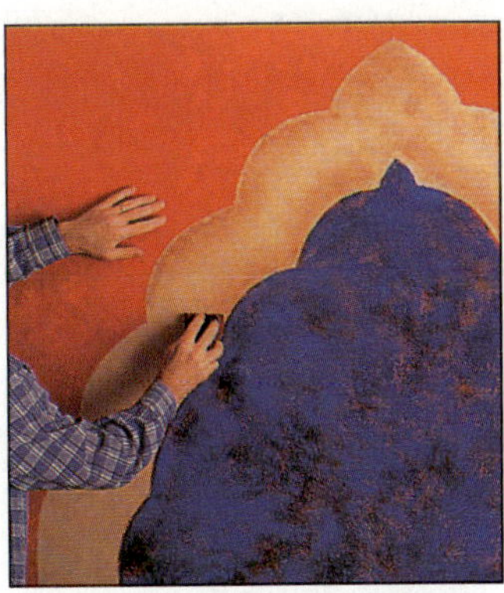

five *Let dry, then use fine-grade sandpaper to soften any hard edges and give the arch the naturally faded appearance of an old temple wall.*

Dream Trellis

Dress up a plain wall behind a simple bed with a most unusual trellis headboard made from woven twigs and branches. The trellis is very lightweight and is easily set in place. Continue the theme with twig accessories, such as chairs, and complement the decor with crisply starched white sheets and pretty cushion covers.

Country garden centers are always worth a visit, because trellis-work like this is handmade, and producers often use local garden centers as outlets. Alternatively, you might like to try making a trellis yourself.

You Will Need

garden raffia
scissors
handmade twig trellis
masonry nails or cavity wall fixtures
hammer

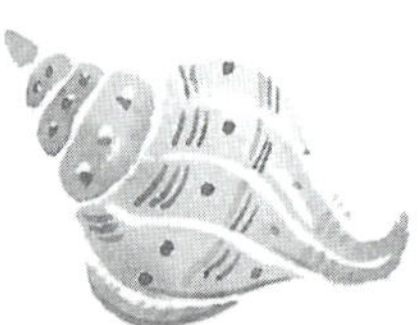

one *Divide the raffia into two bunches of approximately twelve strands each. Knot one end of each bunch.*

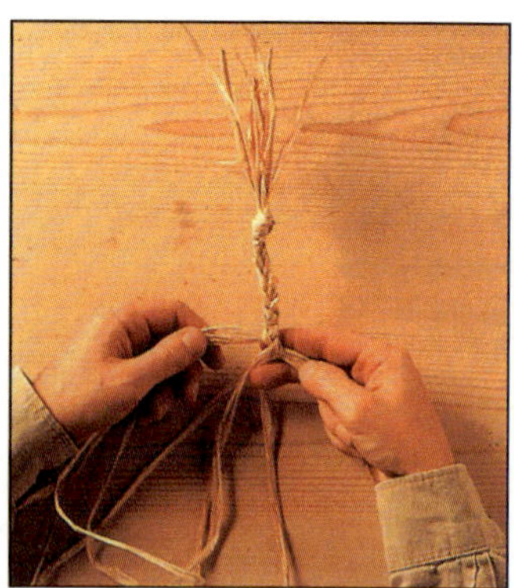

two *Braid the strands to make two braids about 4 inches long.*

three *Tie the braids onto the trellis 10 inches from each end. Attach the braids to the wall above the bed, suspending the trellis behind the bed.*

FOUR-POSTER SARI

THE DRAPES FOR THIS four-poster bed have been made from lengths of beautifully colored traditional sari fabric and ribbons. Whether wrapped, folded or tucked, they do not appear at all bulky. Most saris have border designs and end pieces, with quite plain central areas. The saris used here are made from organza, and the yellow and orange panels have been hung alternately around three sides of the bed.

YOU WILL NEED

8 sari lengths
pins
needle
matching sewing threads
$16^1/_2$ yards ribbon or braid
scissors
tape measure
self-adhesive Velcro dots (optional)
cushion pad
1 yard silk fabric
square cushion tassels (optional)

one *Pin and sew a length of ribbon or braid along the top of each sari to reinforce the fabric. Cut six 12-inch lengths of ribbon or braid per sari for loops. Pin the ribbon lengths along the top of each sari, about $11^1/_2$ inches apart. Turn under one end of each ribbon and slip-stitch to the sari, leaving the other end loose.*

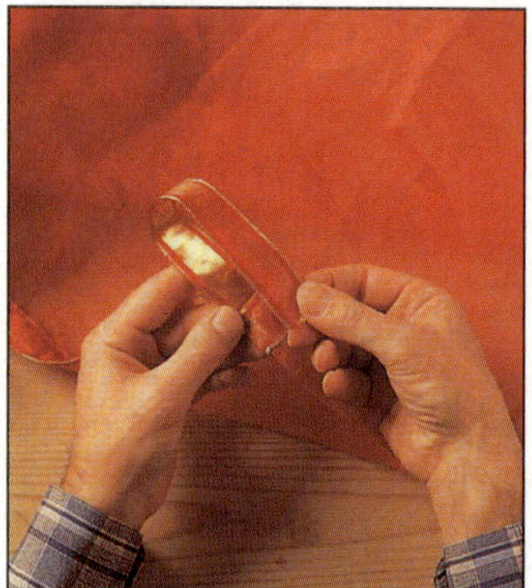

two *Hang the saris from the four-poster. Loop the ribbons around the rail. Sew the loose ends with a few small slip-stitches, or use self-adhesive Velcro dots.*

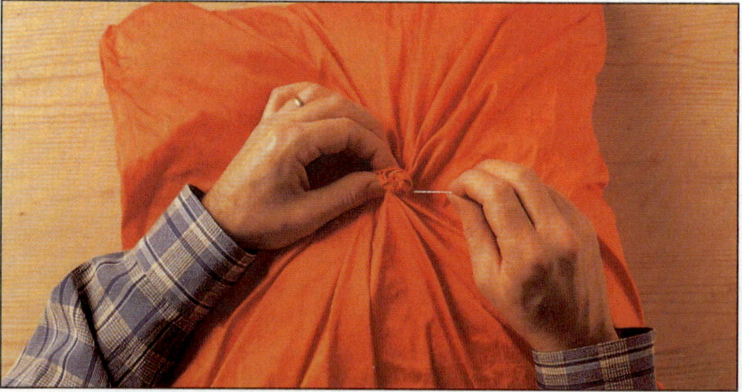

three *Place the cushion pad in the center of the fabric. Loosely fold two sides of the fabric over it, then fold the other two sides over them. Slip-stitch the back seam, but do not pull the fabric tightly around the cushion pad. Turn the cushion over. Pull up the fabric in the center and twist into a decorative knot. Hold the knot in place with a few stitches. Decorate with tassels in a shade of the same color, if desired.*

Fabric Swathed Chair

THIS EFFECT IS STYLISH and practical and yet needs no sewing skills. None of the usual difficulties caused by the need for washing fitted covers apply, so you can capitalize on the sheer drama that is created by brilliant white. A generous quantity of fabric is the only essential; this project uses a king-size, pure cotton sheet, which is ready-hemmed, but you can use any wide, preferably washable, fabric that is soft enough to knot and tie. Why not consider this a stunning addition to your Christmas decor, by wrapping the dining chairs in red silk?

YOU WILL NEED

chair
fabric
sewing machine (optional)

one *You need at least twice, and preferably three times, as much fabric as the width of your chair. Hem the fabric, if necessary. Throw the fabric over the chair and center it.*

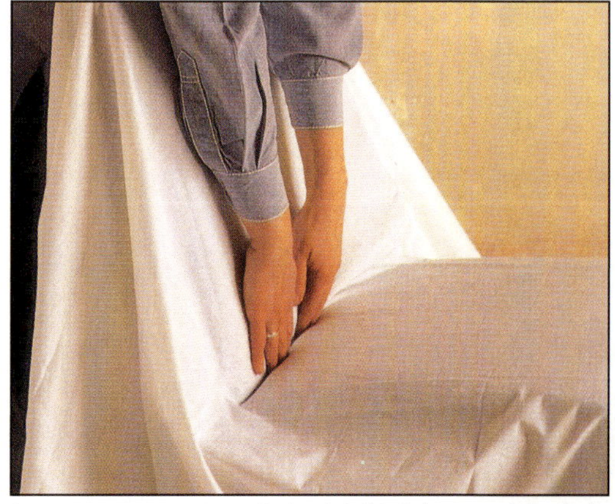

two *Tuck fabric down the back behind the seat of the chair. If the chair has arms, do this all around the seat, so that the cover doesn't pull when you sit on the chair.*

three *Sweep the fabric around to the back of the chair, letting it drape.*

four *Tie a knot, making sure that the fabric is an even length on both sides and that you have attractive folds and drapes at the sides. Try to tie the knot confidently the first time; otherwise the fabric can look tortured and may be crumpled. Remember that the fabric should cascade down from the knot.*

Sheer Fabric Chair

A beautiful chair with wonderful curved legs, a ladder back and cane seat might not seem to need further treatment; yet sometimes, for a change, or for a special occasion, such as a wedding party or a Valentine's Day dinner, you might want to decorate a chair without masking its integral beauty. A wistful, romantic appeal can be given by swathing the chair in translucent fabric to give it a softness that looks very special. The transparent fabric could be colored, or use one of the metallic fabrics in gold or silver, as long as the elements of the chair show through. Use the extra fabric to tie a sash in a knot or a big, soft bow and leave it either at the back or on the seat, like a cushion.

YOU WILL NEED

wooden chair

tissue or pattern-cutting paper

pencil

dressmaker's pins

3 yards of 54-inch transparent silk, voile or organza

fabric marker

dressmaker's scissors

measuring tape

sewing machine, matching thread and iron

one *On the paper, carefully trace the shape of the backrest of the chair. Use this as a template for cutting the back and front of the backrest cover, adding ¾ inch all around for seams. Pin the template to the fabric, draw around it and cut out the pieces. Trace the shape of the seat in the same way. Don't worry too much about getting an exact fit; the sash will take up any fullness. Transfer onto fabric, adding ¾ inch all around for seams.* ›

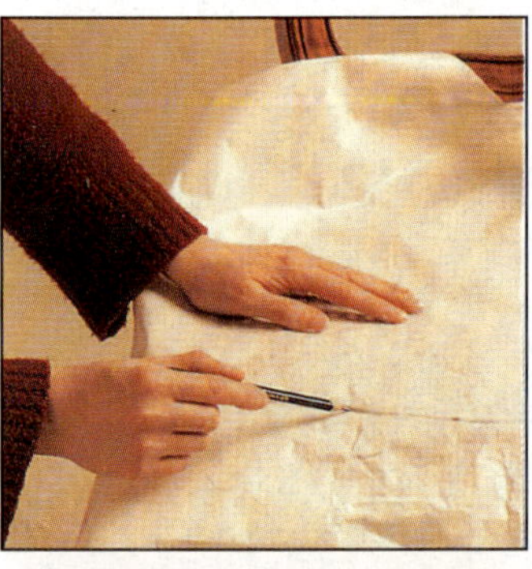

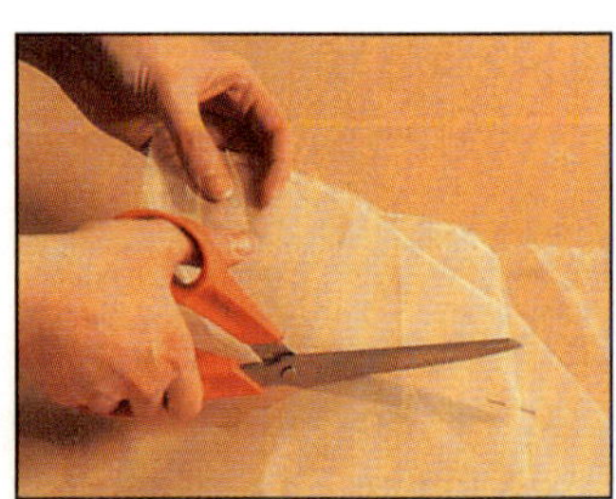

two *For the depth of the skirt, measure from the seat edge to the floor, then add ¾ inch for a seam allowance.*

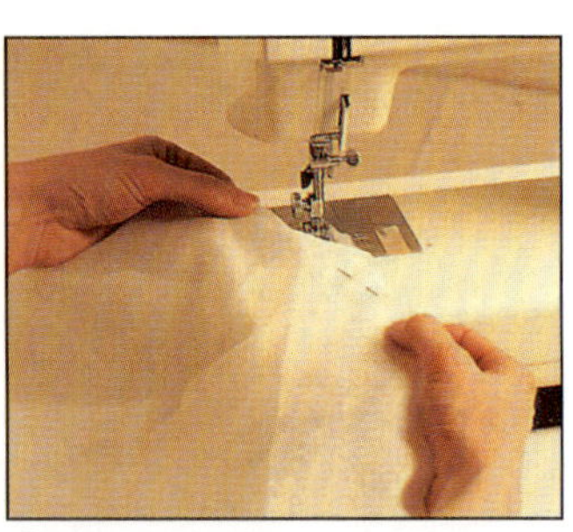

three *For the skirt, add 48 inches to the circumference of the chair seat. Cut as one panel. For the sash, allow 2 yards x 16 inches. Right sides facing, stitch the bottom of the front backrest panel to the top of the seat panel.*

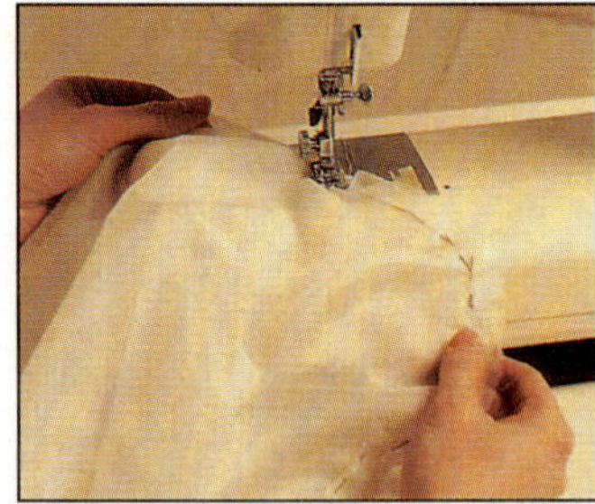

four *Press open all the seams as you go. With right sides together, stitch the front backrest panel to the back.*

five *Hem bottom of skirt. Press, pin pleats. Hem top of skirt. Sew to seat panel at sides and front and to back panel at back. Fold sash in half, right sides together. Sew seams. Turn right sides out, stitch open end. Tie to chair.*

PISTACHIO-SHELL BORDER

IN INDIA, THE DECORATION on floors and walls is as varied as the materials available. The floors of temples and shrines are often intricately patterned with natural objects, such as seeds, shells and stones. Restrict your decoration to places where you don't normally wear shoes. You can fill in just a small area or a whole border. A corner about 4 x 4 feet takes about 7 pounds of unshelled pistachio nuts.

YOU WILL NEED

cream latex paint
paint roller
paint-mixing tray
ruler
pencil
masking tape
blue acrylic eggshell paint
paintbrushes
white glue
pistachio shells
natural sponge
eggshell latex paint: peach, cream and pale blue

one *Make sure your floor surface is sound, dry and level; cover with hardboard or marine-plywood if necessary. Apply a base coat of cream latex. Measure and draw out your straight borders and edge them with masking tape. Draw your curved shapes straight on to the floor free-hand or using a traced shape. Fill in the lines with blue paint.*

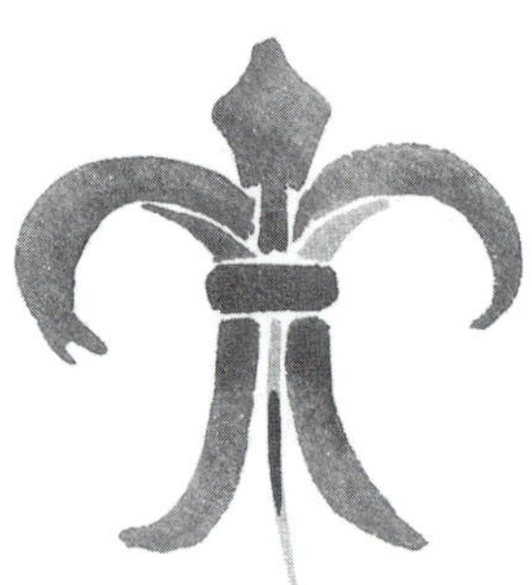

two *Apply plenty of thick white glue to a small blue area. Apply the shells, working on the fine areas first. You may find you need to grade the shells by size, in advance.*

three *When the glue is dry, paint blue over the shells and touch up any cream areas that need it. Randomly sponge the area inside the border, with the darkest color first.*

four *Let dry completely and then repeat, using a softer shade of the same color (in the photograph, peach mixed with cream). Let dry and then use the same technique to apply a new color (in the photograph, pale blue) over it.*

five *Seal the floor with watered-down glue, as recommended by the manufacturer; it should be applied thickly over the shells. The whiteness will disappear as it dries, leaving a clear surface. Let dry completely.*

Filigree Wooden Panel

RADIATOR PANELING NEED not be used only for its original purpose; it can also be used to create an unusual wall covering. It often comes in a variety of interesting designs that make it worth using over a much larger area. Turn it on its side and attach it above a skirting board to bring it up to chair-rail height. When choosing the colors, bear in mind that the background must be strong enough to show through the paneling.

YOU WILL NEED

- scrap paper
- pencil
- ruler
- radiator paneling
- white china pencil
- jigsaw or hacksaw
- latex paint in 2 colors
- paintbrushes
- paint roller
- paint-mixing tray
- level
- straightedge
- drill, with masonry and wood bits
- plastic anchors
- hammer
- wood screws
- glue gun and glue sticks

one *Plan the pattern on paper and decide where cuts in the radiator paneling are necessary. Mark off the sections to be cut out with a china pencil. Use a jig-saw or hacksaw to remove them. Choose the color.*

two *Paint the wall and let dry. Meanwhile, paint the paneling. Using a level and straightedge, mark a horizontal guideline for attaching the paneling to the wall.*

three *Drill holes in the wall for the paneling. Hammer plastic anchors into the holes. Drill holes in the paneling to correspond with the plastic anchors. Screw the paneling in position on the wall. Glue the paneling to the wall here and there, with the glue gun, to hold it flat against the wall. Then attach the border above. You can place a chair-rail between the two, if desired.*

RIBBONS AND LACE

MAKE THE MOST OF A BEAUTIFUL PIECE of sari fabric or a superb lace panel by displaying it in a window so that the light shines through. A few hand-stitched lengths of ribbon will let you tie back the fabric to reveal as much or as little of the window and the view as you like.

As the main fabric is very light and translucent, hang a length of white muslin behind it for extra privacy.

YOU WILL NEED

muslin, 1½ x window width
iron-on hem tape
iron
white fabric tape
thread
dowel, window width
2 cup hooks
scissors
white or cream linen or satin ribbon
sari fabric or antique lace panel

one *Finish the hems on the muslin with iron-on hem tape, then sew white fabric tape along the top to tie the muslin to the dowel. Screw the hooks into the window frame and hang up the dowel. Tie the muslin onto the dowel.*

two *Cut the ribbon into eight 10-inch lengths and stitch four along the top edge of the sari fabric or lace panel. Stitch the others at intervals along the sides—their positions will depend on the size of the panel and the parts that you want to show off. You can also hide any defects when you tie them up in this way.* ›

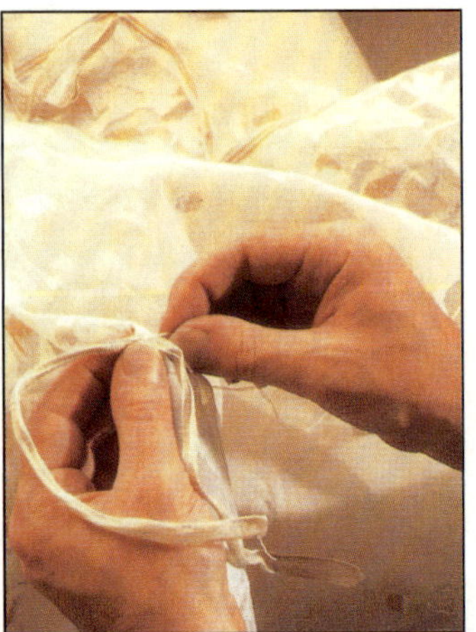

three *Tie the top ribbons to the dowel using simple bows. Arrange them along the dowel so that the fabric drapes over the window in the most appealing way.*

four *Tie up sections of the panel using the side ribbons. Experiment with combinations, standing back from the window to check your adjustments until you are happy with them.*

TEXTURED GOLD FLOOR

EXOTIC SOUVENIRS FROM far-flung places sometimes require a dramatic backdrop to set them off. Gold and copper are suitably flamboyant, but texture is also needed. Builders' scrim, used to reinforce plaster, fits the bill. It gives a surface that traps different amounts of gold and copper, creating the effect of beaten metal. As with all exotic finishes, the delight is more in the instant transformation than in practicality.

YOU WILL NEED

tape measure
pencil
paper
ruler
power sander, with fine-grade sandpaper
builders' scrim
scissors
white glue
oil-based gold paint
wide paintbrush
copper powder paint
heavy-duty floor varnish

one *Measure the floor. Take into account the width of the scrim, plan your design on paper first to make sure that your pattern doesn't leave awkward half lines at the edges. You may need to lay marine-plywood or hardboard to ensure a smooth, flat surface. Lightly sand the floor to make sure it's perfectly flat.*

two *Cut the lengths of scrim, starting with the longest, and lay it to your pattern. Conceal seams where two lengths cross underneath, overlapping the ends by at least 6 inches.*

three *Stick the scrim down with white glue. Brush out any glue that soaks through to the top to hold the scrim firmly. Don't worry if you spread glue outside the area of the scrim. Pencil in a few guidelines and put a weight on the other end of the scrim to keep it straight. Dilute the glue with water and coat the whole floor.*

four *Paint on the gold paint, covering the whole floor. If using an oil-based paint, ensure that you have plenty of ventilation in the room.*

five *When the paint is dry, dust the copper powder paint over the scrim, letting it be trapped by the mesh surface. Apply at least two coats of heavy-duty floor varnish to seal.*

Love Pillows

Make sure the right message gets across by stenciling the word "love" on your pillows in both English and French, the archetypal language of romance. The typeface used is the graphic designer's favorite, Gill (bold), chosen for its stylish simplicity and clarity. There is no doubt what is meant here. The word has been enlarged on a photocopier to 7 inches long. You can adapt this idea for other messages that are completely personal and private, but if you have children, discretion may be a good idea. Choose colors that match your bedroom's overall scheme or that are your favorites. Fabric paints are available in a wide range of colors. Always wash and iron the fabric before stenciling to rid it of any glazes that could block the color absorption.

YOU WILL NEED

photocopied enlargement of the words
spray adhesive
2 pieces of stencil cardboard
scalpel or craft knife
cutting mat or thick cardboard
sheet of thin cardboard
white cotton pillowcases
fabric paint
plate
stencil brush
iron

one *Enlarge the templates to the required size. Spray the backs of the photocopies with spray adhesive and stick them onto the stencil cardboard.*

two *Cut out the letters on a cutting mat. The O, A and R need ties to retain the internal letter features, so draw in "bridges" before you cut them out.*

three *Place a sheet of thin cardboard inside the pillow case, so that the color does not bleed through to the other side.*

four *Apply paint sparingly to letters. You can always build up color later, but too much paint can cause problems. When dry, seal with a hot iron.*

A E O L

M R U V

AMOUR
LOVE

AMERICAN DREAM

LIE IN STATE EVERY NIGHT, draped in the stars and stripes or any brightly colored flag that takes your fancy. This is a great bed-covering idea, and different rooms can have different flags to complement different color schemes. The timber-clad walls and peg-rail above the bed give the room a ranch-house feel that looks great alongside brilliant red, white and blue.

YOU WILL NEED

2 large flags
pillow
package of safety pins
wooden buttons
needle and thread
quilt

one *Fold one of the flags around the pillow and use safety pins to close the long seam.*

two *Sew three wooden buttons along one pillow edge to hold the seam closed. Leave the other edge open so the pillow can be removed.*

three *Select an assortment of wooden buttons to attach around the edge and across the center of the second flag.*

four *Lay the flag over the quilt. Sew on the buttons, stitching through both the flag and the quilt, so that the layers are held together.*

GINGHAM HEADBOARD

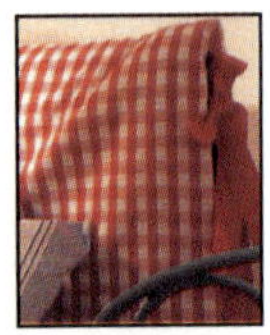

THIS HEADBOARD CONVERSION creates a fresh new style with added comfort. Gingham always looks crisp and clean, so you will wake up bright-eyed and ready to face the day. It is available in both small and large checked patterns and in a wide variety of both bright and pastel colors. The gingham is backed with quilter's batting. Alternatively, you could use other fabrics to create a different sort of mood—a small floral print for a feminine, country cottage decor or a vibrant primary color for a teenager's room, for example. The headboard should be rectangular in shape and can be solid or of a slatted or spindled type. Measure the width and height of the headboard, then double the height measurement so that the gingham folds in half over the top.

YOU WILL NEED

iron-on quilter's batting
tape measure
dressmaker's scissors
iron
gingham, width of the headboard x twice the height, plus seam allowance on all edges
iron-on hemming tape
needle and matching sewing thread
2 yards red ribbon
pins

one *Cut the batting to the size of the headboard. Press one end of the gingham onto the batting. The other end of the gingham will fold over the headboard back. Leave a large seam allowance all around the edge.*

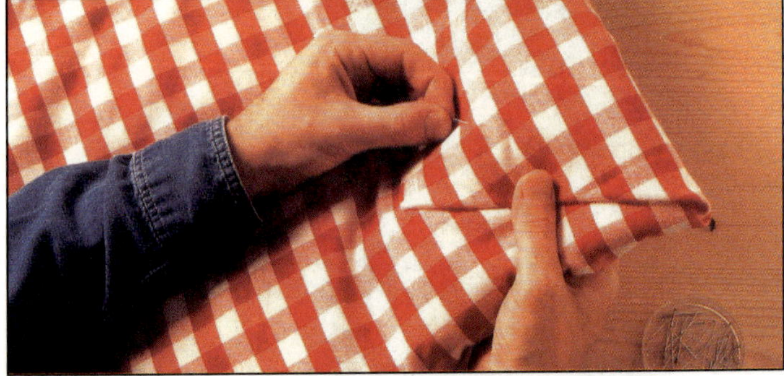

two *Fold the seams over and tuck the corners in neatly. Use iron-on hemming tape or a needle and thread to secure the edges. As the hems will be on the inside of the cover, they will not be visible.*

three *To make the ties, cut the ribbon into 16 equal lengths.*

four *Pin, then sew four ribbons, equally spaced, along the inside edges of each side of the cover. Fold the cover over the headboard and tie the ribbons in bows to finish.*

Chintz Headboard

Give your padded headboard a new lease on life with old chintz curtains. The fabric improves with age, as the colors fade and mellow delightfully, and it looks wonderful teamed with crisp white cotton, handmade quilts or plaid wool blankets in a traditional bedroom. Use the very best section of pattern for the bedhead and tuck remaining lengths under the mattress to form a valance. If you prefer a more permanent valance, you could sew pleated lengths of the same chintz fabric around the edges of a fitted sheet.

YOU WILL NEED

pair of floral chintz curtains
scissors
tape measure
headboard
pencil
staple gun and staples

one *Trim the curtains to get rid of any thick seams, curtain tape and bulky hems. Cut a strip of curtain long enough to fold over the front and onto the back of the headboard at the sides, top and bottom. Smooth it over the front of the headboard then move to the back. Draw any curved corners onto the back of the fabric.*

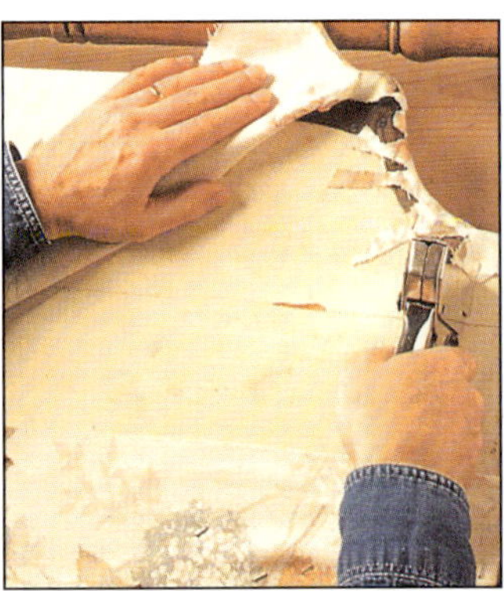

two *Cut notches in the fabric right up to the drawn line, so that the fabric will fit the curve without puckering. Staple each cut strip onto the headboard.*

three *Pull down the top flap tautly and staple it onto the headboard.*

four *Pull up the bottom flap tautly and staple it in place. Staple both side edges in the same way. Cut a panel of fabric to cover all the stapled edges on the back. Turn in the edges and staple the panel flat onto the backing board.*

ENTWINED HEADBOARD

QUITE APART FROM BEING one of the most stylish looks around, rope-wrapping is a real pleasure to do. All you need is a frame, which can be a junk-shop find or a homemade structure made from construction timber. The wood is completely hidden by the coils of rope, so there is no need to prepare the surface in any way. Rope comes in many different twists and thicknesses, some more decorative than others. Some ropes are made from natural fibers and others, like the one used here, are synthetic. An advantage of synthetic rope is that the ends can be sealed by holding them over a flame to melt the fibers together.

YOU WILL NEED

rope
wooden-framed headboard
tape measure
pen
scissors or craft knife
cutting mat or thick cardboard
lighter or matches (optional)
glue gun and glue sticks

one *To calculate the length of rope needed to wrap each wooden post, first divide the height of the post by the thickness of the rope. Multiply this figure by the circumference of the post. Mark the rope at this point.*

two *Cut the lengths of rope required to wrap all the posts. If you are using synthetic rope, seal the ends by holding them briefly over a flame. Use the glue gun to stick the end of the rope to the back of the first post to be wrapped.*

three *Wrap the rope tightly around the post, keeping the coils as close together as possible. To maintain the tension, apply a few dabs of hot glue.*

four *Cut short lengths of rope to cover gaps, loose ends and blobs of glue at the intersection. Glue the ends at the back.*

five *Make sure that all the intersections are finished in the same way so that the symmetry is maintained. Finish with rope decorations.*

SHELL-SHOCKED

AFTER A VACATION, MAKE your shell collection into something really special. We have used them to decorate fine voile curtains, and added interest with eyelets along the top threaded with string loops. Also following this theme, an easy, effective way of trimming a wall is with a length of fine rope attached at chair-rail height. Attach a row of tiny shells above. To complete the look, paint a terra-cotta pot white and attach a small sanddollar to the front.

YOU WILL NEED

iron-on interfacing (optional)
tape measure
dressmaker's scissors
cotton voile, the required drop, plus 4 x the window width
dressmaker's pins
needle and basting thread
sewing machine
matching sewing thread
chrome eyelets
hammer
wooden block
rough natural string
fine beading wire
glue gun and glue sticks
electric drill, with very fine drill bit (optional)
beading needle (optional)
terra-cotta pot
matte white latex paint
paintbrush
sanddollar

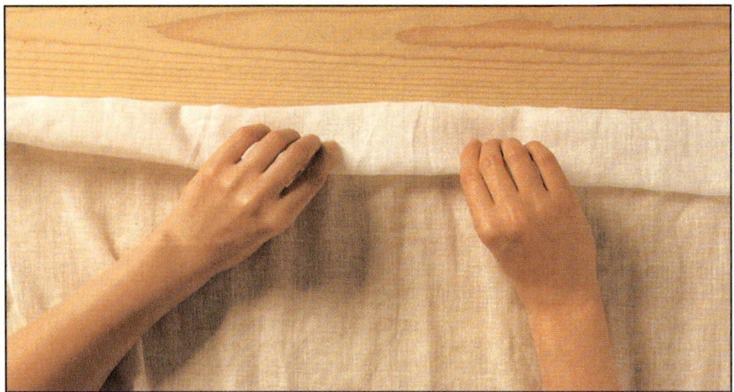

one *To give extra body to the headings of fine fabrics, cut a length of iron-on interfacing 2 inches wide and bond it to the wrong side of the voile. Pin, baste, press and machine-stitch the heading across the top and the hem at the bottom. Then turn under a ½-inch hem down each side. Pin, baste, press and sew. Mark the positions of the eyelets with pins.*

two *Attach the eyelets, following the manufacturer's instructions. Find a secure surface when hammering the eyelets in place.*

three *Cut equal lengths of string, thread the strings through the eyelets and knot the ends. Cut lengths of wire and use a glue gun to stick them onto the shells. Alternatively, drill holes in the shells. A combination of these methods may be helpful, depending on the shape of the shells. Position the shells on the curtains.*

four *Use the beading wire to "sew" the shells on to the curtain by hand, as invisibly as possible.*

five *Paint the terra-cotta pot white. Put a little glue on the side of the pot and attach the sanddollar.*

Sheer Magic

TRIM A PLAIN LINEN or burlap bed cover and pillowcase with the sheerest of voile fabrics to create a look that is simple, tailored and elegant. Large bone buttons and the rougher textures of burlap and linen are the perfect foil to the fineness of the fabric. Cut the voile slightly longer than the drop on the bed so it falls onto the floor all around. The amount of voile given here is for a double bed, but the idea can be adapted to suit any bed size.

YOU WILL NEED

tape measure
about 7½ yards cotton voile
dressmaker's scissors
dressmaker's pins
needle
basting thread
sewing machine
matching sewing thread
16 large bone buttons
fine embroidery scissors
tapestry needle
fine string
burlap or fine linen bed cover
pillow

one *For the top of the cover, you will need a piece of voile the length of the bed plus the drop on one end. The piece should be 6 inches narrower than the width of the bed so the buttons will not be too near the edge. Allow 4 inches all around for double hems. For the sides, you will need two pieces the length of the bed. Measure the drop from the buttons to the floor, allowing 4 inches for hems as before. Pin, baste and sew all the hems.*

two *Mark the position of the buttons and button-holes. They must correspond exactly. Sew the button-holes, then cut the centers carefully. Use a tapestry needle and fine string to sew the buttons in position on the burlap bed cover, and button the voile cover on top.*

three *For the pillowcase, cut a piece of burlap the depth of the pillow and twice the length, plus seam allowances on the long sides. With right sides together, pin, baste and sew the top and bottom edges. Turn right side out and press.*

four *To make a fringed edge, find a thread running across the pillow, just in from the cut edge. Pull gently to fray the edge. Use the same method to make an over-cover for the pillow from voile. Hem all the edges.*

five *Mark the position of the button-holes in each corner. Machine-stitch the button-holes and cut the centers. Sew buttons onto the corners of the burlap pillow cover, and button the voile cover over the top.*

Hammock Quilt

Reclining in a hammock may be the ultimate relaxation, but it is really possible to lie back and enjoy the sway only if you feel completely secure. So make quite sure that your wall fittings are sturdy and properly installed and that the wall itself is strong enough to take the strain. Use strong metal garage hooks with long screws and heavy-duty plastic anchors. Once the issue of safety has been covered, you can then turn your attention to comfort and make this stylish and simple no-sew quilt to dress up your hammock and keep you cozy. The next step is simply to hop in and rock away your cares.

YOU WILL NEED

iron
2¼ yards iron-on batting
5½ yards blue fabric
2¼ yards black cotton fabric
scissors
tape measure
iron-on hemming tape
5½ yards black iron-on mending tape
pins

one *Iron the batting to one half of the wrong side of the blue fabric. Then fold the other half over so that the batting is sandwiched by the blue fabric. This will give the quilt some thickness. Next, cut the black fabric into four 5½-inch-wide strips to fit the quilt edges. Press a ½-inch hem along the long edges. Iron each strip in half to make a long doubled strip 2¼ inches wide. This will be used to border the blue cloth. Place a length of iron-on hemming tape along each edge of the blue fabric and enclose each edge with a doubled black border strip. Iron to bond the fabrics. Fold down the corners of the black edging to achieve a mitered effect. Turn the fabric over and repeat on the other side.*

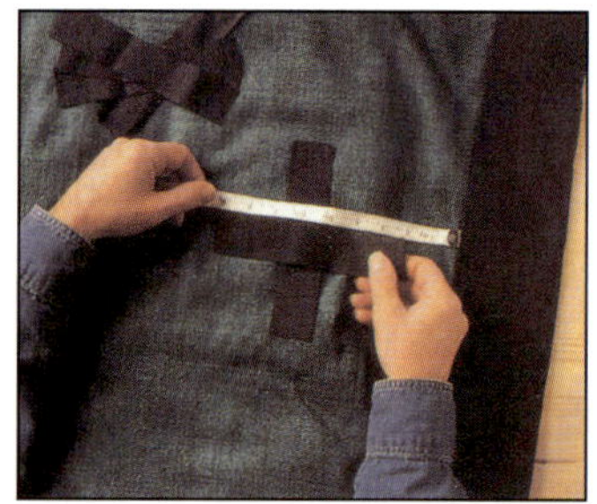

two *Cut twenty-four 8-inch strips of iron-on mending tape and use the tape measure to position them on the quilt in four rows of three crosses.*

three *Pin the crosses in place, if required, then iron them in position.*

CALICO TENT

GET THAT VACATION FEELING every morning when you look out on the day from your tent. This could make a novelty bedhead for a child's bedroom or a stylish feature in a adult's bedroom. The tent is made using a combination of attachments intended for different purposes. The chrome rods are shower rails, finished off in copper with plumber's pipe caps. The thin copper tube is also from the plumbing department—it has an attractive finish and can be bent easily with long-nosed pliers. The stability of the tent is assured by the use of shower rail sockets on the wall and a line of cup hooks on the ceiling. The fabric used here is unbleached calico.

YOU WILL NEED

- 8¾ x 1 yards unbleached calico
- tape measure
- pencil and ruler
- scissors
- 6½ yards iron-on hemming tape
- iron
- hacksaw
- 60-inch length chrome shower rail
- center punch
- hammer
- drill, with bit (the size of the copper tube)
- 1 yard narrow copper tube
- long-nosed pliers
- 3 chrome shower rail sockets
- level
- screwdriver
- 6 chrome cup hooks and plastic anchors
- 4½ yards white cord
- 3 copper pipe caps (to fit shower rail)

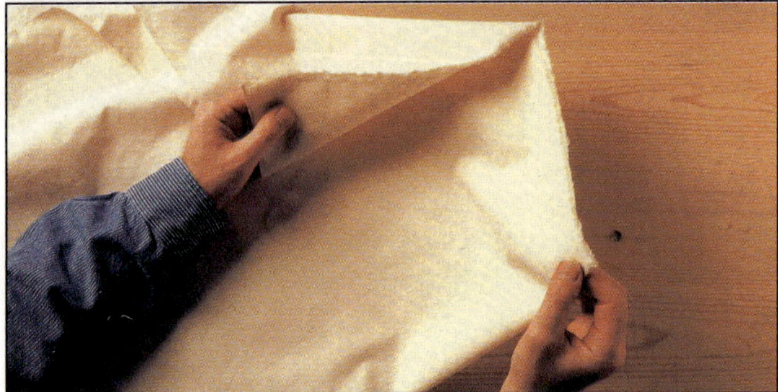

one *Decide on the height of the top of the tent. Measure the fabric and tear it to size. Fold the fabric in four to find the center and mark this point. Measure 14 inches down each short edge and mark the points.*

two *Draw a connecting line between the center point and each of the side points to give the shape for the top.*

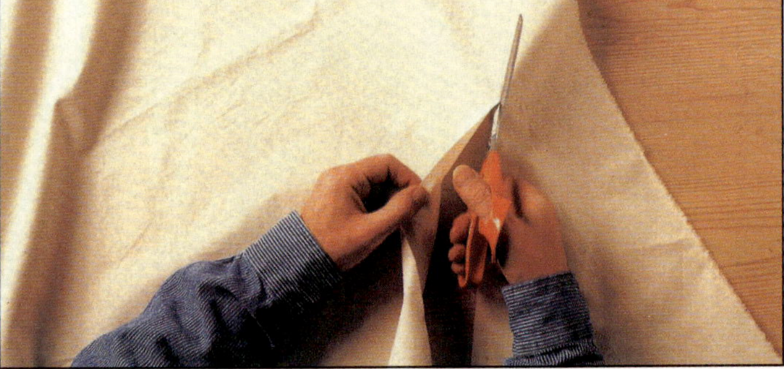

three *Cut along the drawn lines, then cut a 1¼-inch notch at each of the points of the tent shape. Fold the fabric over to make a 1¼-inch seam around the top and sides of the fabric.*

four *Use iron-on hemming tape to hold down the seams neatly. The two pieces should now meet at a right angle to make the tent shape. The sides and top of the tent will fold back to give a double thickness of fabric. Make three holes for the rails at the corner points and reinforce the fabric with an extra square of calico ironed on with hemming tape.*

five *Use a hacksaw to cut the length of chrome shower rail into three 20-inch pieces.*

six *Use a center punch to dent the shower rail where the holes will be drilled, so that the drill does not slip. You will need to drill a hole 2 inches from one end of two of the poles and two holes in the other pole, the first 2 inches from one end and the second ½ inch in from it.*

seven *Drill the holes using a drill bit the same size as the copper tube. Use a hacksaw to cut two lengths of copper tube. Use the long-nosed pliers to bend one end of each copper tube into a hook shape. Use the chrome rail to estimate the curve of the hooks. Each hook should fit snugly around the chrome rail with its end fitting into the drilled hole.*

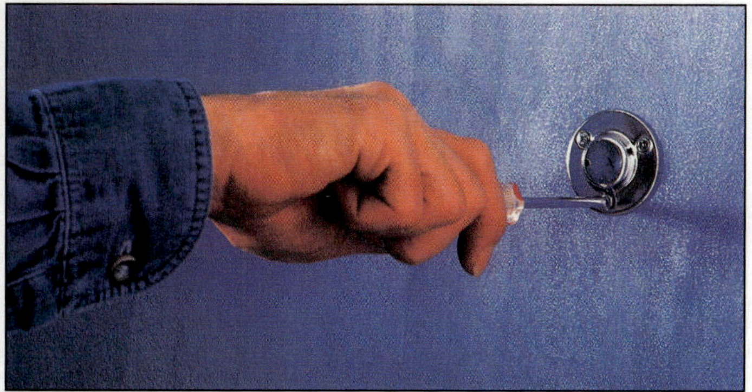

eight *Position the shower rail sockets on the wall so that the rails slot into them. Use a level to check that the outer two are level.*

CONTINUED OVER ➤

Above: The hooked copper tubes fit over and into the chrome rail. The cord is looped around the rail and crossed over to suspend the tent front from the cup hooks. The side rails are finished off with the copper caps and suspended from a crossed cord attached to the cup hooks.

nine *Refer to the diagram below. Push the chrome rails through the holes in the back of the tent, then put the copper tubes in place to hold the front section rigid. Put the straight end of each copper tube into the hole in each side rail. Put the hooked ends over the middle rail and into the two drilled holes. Attach a row of cup hooks to the ceiling directly above the front edge of the tent. Loop white cord around the cup hooks and the chrome rails for added stability. Finally, cap the chrome pipes with the copper caps.*

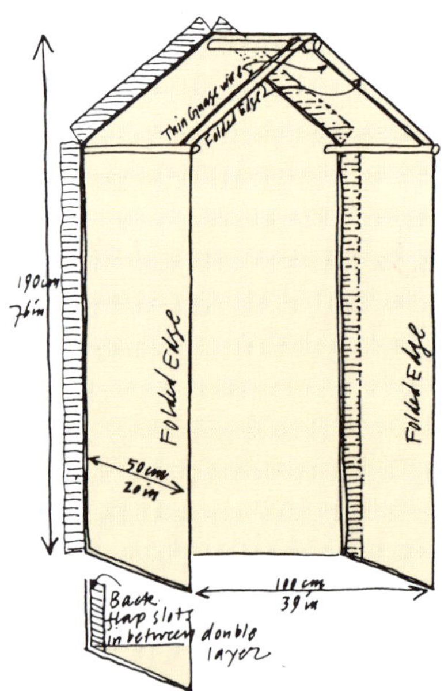

SEASIDE SETTING

SOOTHE THE SOUL AND mind by strolling along the beach and, at the same time, searching the shoreline for all kinds of wonderful things: strands of seaweed, pieces of driftwood, soft gray pebbles, birds' feathers, pearly seashells and chalky white stones with holes ready-made for threading onto pieces of twine. Make the most of your natural treasures by using them to decorate mirrors, picture frames and trinket boxes, or any other unadorned objects—their uses are endless. Seashells also make wonderfully evocative candle holders.

YOU WILL NEED

DRIFTWOOD AND PEBBLE FRAMES

- distressed-wood frames
- white glue (optional)
- medium-grade sandpaper
- wood stain and paintbrush (optional)
- about 20 inches thick rope
- staple gun or hammer and nails
- driftwood
- glue gun and glue sticks
- seaweed
- pebbles and stones
- seashells

PEBBLE AND GLASS NECKLACES

- raffia
- tiny pebbles
- smooth colored glass
- glue gun and glue sticks

SHELL CANDLEHOLDERS

- burnt-down candles
- kitchen knife
- seashells
- safety matches

one *For the driftwood frame, reglue the seams, if necessary. Sand it along the grain and stain it, if desired. To hang the mirror, attach the rope to the top of the frame, with a staple gun or hammer and nails. Arrange the driftwood pieces around the frame. Experiment with different positions until you are happy with the result.*

two *Use a glue gun to attach the driftwood in place, making sure the pieces are perfectly secure.*

three *Work out the position of the seaweed so it drapes gently across the mirror. Add the pebbles, stones and shells, raising them slightly off the edge so they are reflected in the mirror. Glue the pebbles and other materials in place.*

four *For the pebble frame, use a similar frame base to the driftwood frame and sand and stain as before, if required. Select a pleasing variety of stones. Arrange them to your liking and glue them on the frame.*

five *For the pebble and glass necklace, tie a length of raffia around tiny pebbles and pieces of smooth colored glass. Use a glue gun to apply a tiny dot of glue to each knot where the pebble or glass is tied. For the candles in shells, cut the candles right down with a knife and stand them in a shell. Light the candles and let the wax drip down until it fills the shells. Blow out the flame. The wax then solidifies to the shape of the shell.*

Tartan Bedhead

Wool tartan rugs are real comfort blankets, traditionally used on winter car journeys and picnics. The two rugs used in this project are doubled over, with their folded edges meeting in the middle. To complete the Highland hunting lodge atmosphere, the rugs are hung above the bedhead from a rough-hewn "branch."

YOU WILL NEED

2 matching tartan blankets or rugs
kilt pins
tape measure
needle
thick contrasting thread
1-inch wooden dowel (slightly longer than the bed width)
craft knife
fine-grade sandpaper
cloth
shellac
2 iron pipe holders (to fit 1-inch pipe)
drill and plastic anchors
screwdriver

one *Fold each blanket in half lengthwise and pin together along the folded seam. Blanket-stitch the outside edges, then stitch the blankets together along the folded edge. If you don't like sewing, hold the seams closed with three kilt pins.*

two *Start decorating the wooden dowel by roughly carving away both ends of it with a craft knife. Sand the rough edges with sandpaper. Use a cloth to rub shellac into the wood.*

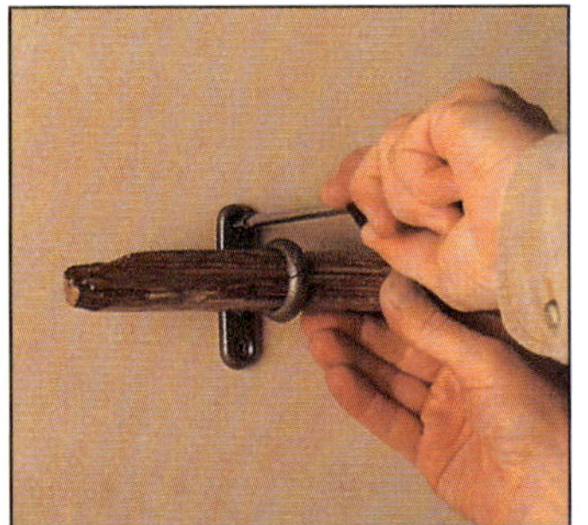

three *Screw the pipe holders to the wall. Attach the dowel in place. Hang the blankets over the dowel, with a 14-inch overlap to make a valance, pinning it in place with kilt pins.*

BUTTERFLY MONTAGE

SURREALISM AND THE WORK of artists such as Ernst, Escher, and Magritte inspire surprising ways of depicting unusual yet familiar objects in designs for montages. This butterfly floor could easily have been made using motifs of flowers, boats or chairs. Strong lines are important, and there are books of wonderful line drawings available. Lay the motifs down in an ordered pattern. Here, the design suggests the flight of butterflies. Protect the montage from wear and tear by applying half a dozen coats of varnish.

YOU WILL NEED

light-colored latex paint
paintbrushes
motifs
craft knife
self-healing cutting mat
wallpaper paste and brush
indelible felt-tipped pen or fine artist's brush and oil-based paints
matte varnish

one *Make sure your floor is completely smooth. If necessary, lay a hardboard or marine-plywood floor. Paint the floor a light color so that the motifs will show up. Photocopy your chosen image(s) in at least seven sizes, ranging from quite small to fairly large.*

two *Using a craft knife and a cutting mat, carefully cut out every image.*

three *Decide on the positions of your images and stick them in place with wallpaper paste.*

four *Add remaining fine details with an indelible felt-tipped pen or a fine artist's brush. Finish by applying at least six coats of varnish to be sure of its durability (some acrylic varnishes dry very quickly) or apply a very strong floor varnish.*

Billowing Muslin

FLOATY BUTTER-COLORED MUSLIN IS one of the cheapest ways to cover a large window without blocking out all the light. The muslin here is in two pieces, each long enough to drape over the rail and down to the floor on both sides. One of the lengths was stamped with a sponge cutout in the shape of a melon half. The two pieces were hung next to each other and knotted about halfway down so the stamped half crosses over to the other side.

YOU WILL NEED

tracing paper

pencil

thin cardboard, for template

block of high-density foam (the type used for camping mattresses)

craft knife

2 lengths butter-colored muslin

2 bamboo poles, window width

sewing machine (optional)

needle

matching sewing thread

fabric paint: coffee-brown and dark brown

plate

paint roller or brush

tape

drill, and masonry bit

plastic anchors and cup hooks

bundle of natural-colored raffia

one *Trace the template, enlarging to the required size. Place it on the foam block, then cut around it. Scoop out the inner area, leaving the printing surface intact. Fold both of the muslin lengths in half. Form a channel along the top of each, about 2 inches down from the fold. It must be the width of the two bamboo poles, as they will slide into it. Sew by machine or hand.*

two *Put some of the coffee-brown fabric paint onto the plate and run the roller through it until it is thoroughly and evenly coated. Use the roller to ink the foam stamp.*

three *Start stamping the pattern, rotating the stamp in your hand each time you print. Leave more or less the same amount of space between prints.*

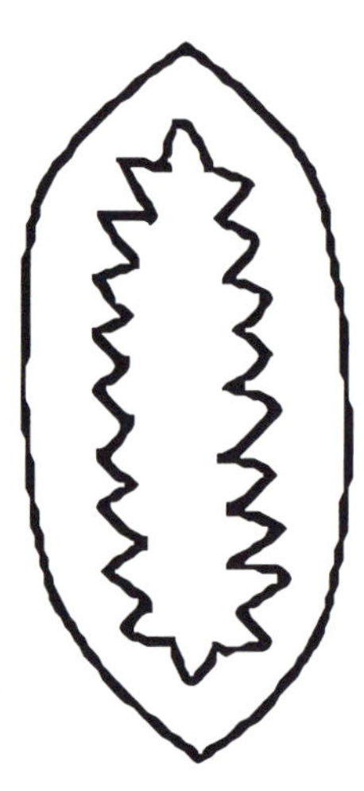

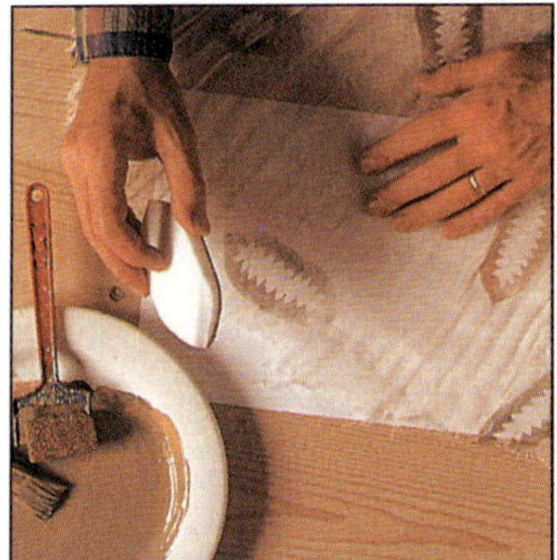

four *Stamp darker prints randomly among lighter ones. Set the fabric paint according to the manufacturer's instructions. Tape over the ends of the bamboo poles so that they do not catch on the muslin, and slide them through the sewn channels in the curtains.*

five *Drill holes and insert the plastic anchors and cup hooks in the top of the window recess, about 4–6 inches in from the sides. Cut ten 18-inch strips of raffia and use five on either side, twisted together into a rope, to bind the bamboo poles together in place of the tape. Use the loose ends to suspend the bamboo rail by tying them to the cup hooks. Tie a knot with the two curtains about halfway down their length. Experiment with different effects, but take your time over the positioning of the knot, its shape and the way the muslin drapes over it.*

RENAISSANCE HEADBOARD

DRAMATIC EFFECTS HAVE BEEN used in this bedroom to create a very distinctive atmosphere, with the large painting dominating the room. It's a good idea to visit a museum store for the best range and quality of art posters—you are certain to find something for all tastes. You can apply a crackle-glaze or antiquing varnish to the poster if you want to create an authentically aged Renaissance look.

YOU WILL NEED

wallpaper paste
poster
medium-density fiberboard (width x height of poster plus mattress-to-floor measurement), plus allowance for frame
pencil
paste brush
ruler
picture rail molding (height of poster x 2, plus width x 1)
mitering block
small saw
viridian green latex paint
paintbrushes
gold spray paint
fine-grade sandpaper
glue gun and glue sticks
crackle-glaze varnish
artist's red oil color
clean cloths
clear varnish
drill and fixtures to attach fiberboard to bed frame (depending on the type of bed)

one *Mix up the wallpaper paste. Mark the position of the poster on the fiberboard and apply paste to that section. Smooth the poster onto the board and let dry. Any air bubbles should disappear as the glue dries.*

two *Measure and mark the lengths of molding for the frame. It goes along the top of the poster and down both sides to mattress height. Saw the corners on a mitering block. Paint a viridian green undercoat. Let dry.*

three *Protect your work surface, then spray a coat of gold spray paint over the green. Let dry. Rub the frame with fine-grade sandpaper, so that the gold is lifted on the highest ridges to reveal the green beneath. Do not overdo the sanding. Use a glue gun to stick the picture frame around the edges of the poster.*

four *Paint the whole surface of the poster with crackle-glaze varnish, following the manufacturer's instructions. Let the varnish crackle. Use a cloth to rub artist's oil color into the surface. Red is used here, but any strong or dark color will also work well. Rub the oil paint right into the cracks and cover the whole surface.*

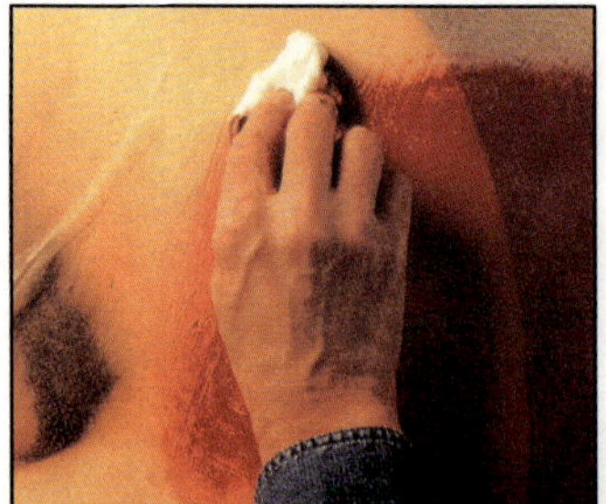

five *Rub the oil paint off the surface with a soft cloth. The color will stay in the cracks. Apply several coats of clear varnish to the poster. When dry, attach the headboard to the bed frame, using the drill and fixtures.*

CORRUGATED HEADBOARD

CORRUGATED CARDBOARD HAS been liberated from its role as a packaging material, as designers realize its potential and versatility. It is strong, rigid, insulating, economical and light as a feather. This project celebrates the natural cardboard color, but colored sheets are also available and are great for adding decorative touches. Corrugated cardboard is perfect for experimentation, especially as it is so inexpensive.

YOU WILL NEED

glue gun and glue sticks

2 x 1 inch lengths wood to fit around the edges of the medium-density fiberboard

rectangle of medium-density fiberboard, to fit behind the bed

roll of corrugated cardboard 1 yard high

triangle

scissors

staple gun and staples

ruler

pencil

scalpel or craft knife

cutting mat or cardboard

small rubber roller

one *Use the glue gun to stick the thin lengths of wood to the back of the fiberboard around the edges. This will be hidden, so any glue drips will not show. Place a large piece of corrugated cardboard over the front of the fiberboard. Use a triangle to press against and crease the cardboard neatly for folding at the corners. Fold the cardboard neatly around the corners in the same way that you would wrap a package.*

two *Trim away any excess cardboard that may cause the corners to look bulky. Staple the flaps down, pressing the gun firmly against the cardboard from above to prevent any kickback that may cause the staples to protrude.*

three *Carefully staple the cardboard along the strips of wood, keeping it taut as you go along. Cut four strips of cardboard 3 inches wide, and approximately 18 inches long. Use the rubber roller to flatten down the ridges. Fold the strips into thirds along their length, so that they are 1 inch wide. Again, use the rubber roller to flatten the strips.*

four *Position the strips to form a diamond shape in the center of the headboard. Allow the ends to overlap each other. Staple the strips in place. Cut through the two overlapping layers with scissors to miter the corners. Staple the strips as closely as possible to the mitered ends.*

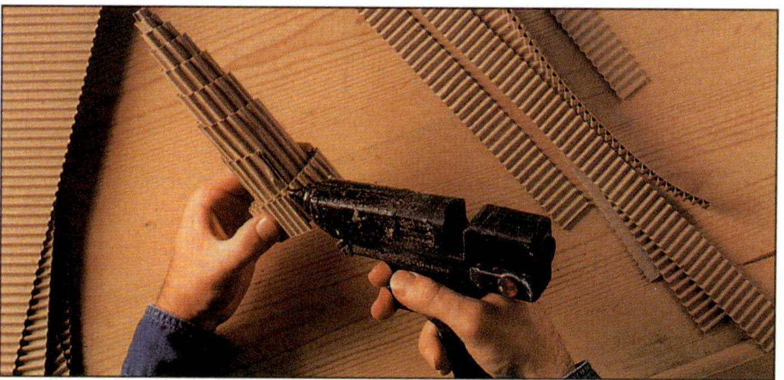

five *For the spiral turrets, cut seven 20-inch strips of cardboard. One long edge of each strip is cut at an angle: Cut the first two strips along a line sloping from one short edge of 4 inches to the other short edge of 2 inches. Cut the second two strips from one edge of $4\frac{3}{4}$ inches to the other of 2 inches. Cut the next two from $5\frac{1}{2}$ inches to 2 inches. Cut the last strip from $6\frac{1}{4}$ inches to 2 inches. Starting at the wider end, roll up the cardboard with the ridges on the outside. Keep the base straight. Use the glue gun to stick down the end of each turret. Arrange the turrets on top of the headboard so that the tallest one is in the middle. Stick them down using the hot-glue gun. Use plenty of glue in the middle and less toward the outside to achieve a good bond without any mess.*

THE NEW WAVE

CORRUGATED CARDBOARD IS A much-maligned material that can look absolutely stunning if used innovatively. It is easy to work with and has myriad uses. Experiment with different shapes to see which looks most pleasing. Triangles would look great bordering a door frame, for example, and perhaps following the lines of the skirting. Bear in mind that corrugated paper crushes very easily, so before starting work, flatten it with a ruler.

YOU WILL NEED

tape measure
roll of natural corrugated cardboard
scissors
ruler
thin cardboard
pencil
craft knife
self-healing cutting mat
spray adhesive
masking tape (optional)
candles
white latex paint
paintbrush
glue gun and glue sticks
natural string
straight-sided vase
fine corrugated paper in different colors
paper glue

one *Measure the width of the sill and cut the corrugated cardboard to this measurement, plus the required drop. Flatten the ridges with a ruler. Draw the design onto cardboard and cut out a template. Draw the shape on the natural corrugated paper, using the template. Cut it out with a craft knife on a cutting mat.*

two *Spray the back of the corrugated cardboard with adhesive and attach in place. If you want to remove the decoration later, stick masking tape under the sill and glue the decoration to the tape.*

three *For the candle-wrappers, cut strips of corrugated paper to the right size and paint them with white latex. Slit the corrugations with scissors. Cut a wider strip and glue it to the back of the white strip. Wrap the decoration around the candles. Cut string long enough to wrap several times around the candles. Use the same technique to make a decoration for a straight-sided vase.*

four *To make the picture frame, measure the image that will be framed and decide on the size and shape required. Draw the frame backing onto corrugated cardboard and cut it out with the craft knife and ruler. Use the backing as a template to draw and cut out the front of the frame from colored corrugated paper. Cut out the central frame area. Stick the image in position with paper glue so the backing color shows through in a thin border all around.*

five *Make a stand for the frame, with a piece of corrugated cardboard cut to the shape shown. Decorate the frame with twisted strips of colored paper.*

Novelty Rooms

Novelty Rooms

This is the perfect place to let your imagination run riot, with customized designs for adults and children. But a word of warning—if you plan to decorate a child's room, first ask the occupant. You may think Pooh Bear makes an excellent wall stencil, but younger decorators may be thinking along the lines of not-so-cuddly extinct creatures...

Whatever you decide on should be regarded as temporary. The first rule of decorating a child's bedroom is not to do anything that can't be changed easily. Tastes change and fads go as quickly as they arrive. Bearing this in mind, make everything as big, bright and bold as possible. You may not agree with the aesthetics of it all, but a room with a sense of humor is a lot of fun—and a stimulating environment for children, especially if they feel able to let themselves go in it. That means don't be too dainty about the room. Everything should be as practical and durable as possible.

Such a decorating challenge opens up endless opportunities. For the floor, choose different colored carpet tiles arranged as for a board game. Kids like writing on walls, so let them—provide a wall-to-wall blackboard with a colorful border.

Comic strips are recognized everywhere, and a montage of well-known characters can be used for a striking decorative focal point in a teenager's bedroom.

Laundry baskets topped with brightly colored domes make great storage containers. Stencil the walls with flags, which are colorful and easy to prepare, or simply turn a wall into a patchwork of color. Our secret for getting the perfect finish is so easy the kids can do it.

Budding astronauts will love the padded headboard covered with space blankets, and you can make individual duvet covers for each child.

Many of our ideas for stenciling and painting can be done by the children, so don't be shy about coming forward to ask for their help. And make sure they have their say about what they want. Their coolness quotient may depend on it.

WALL BLACKBOARD

THIS SIMPLE BLACKBOARD is lots of fun and a highly practical wall treatment for a child's bedroom or playroom. Make sure the wall is flat before you start, and paint it with undercoat and two coats of latex first, if necessary. Bear the height of the child in mind when you are deciding on the size and position of the blackboard. Blackboard paint is available at most good paint suppliers.

YOU WILL NEED

tape measure
pencil
level
straightedge
masking tape
blackboard paint
paintbrushes
latex paint in several colors
tracing paper (optional)
craft knife (optional)
self-healing cutting mat (optional)
stencil brush
hooks
string
chunky chalks

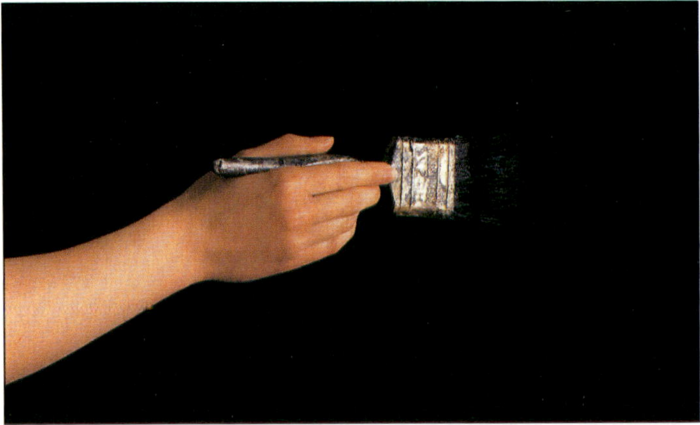

one *Measure and draw the blackboard and the border on the wall, using the level and straightedge. Mask off the blackboard with tape and apply two coats of blackboard paint. Remove the masking tape immediately. Let dry.*

two *Mask off the border and paint with two coats of latex. Remove the masking tape immediately.*

three *Mask off the diamond shape or draw and cut a stencil from tracing paper, using the craft knife and cutting mat. Tape it to the wall. Paint the diamonds with a stencil brush. Paint the hooks. Screw them into the wall and attach the chalks.*

FLAG STENCILS

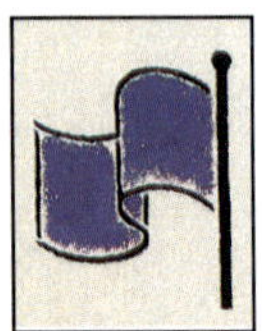

HERE'S A STRONG DESIGN to add lively color and an element of fun to a child's room, while avoiding the conventional and rather predictable motifs and colors available on ready-made children's wallpapers. The easiest way to make a unique stencil is to photocopy a simple motif onto acetate: Here, two complementary flag motifs are combined. Use the stencils as a border at picture- or chair-rail height, randomly around the room or in straight lines to make a feature of, for example, a chimney on one wall or an alcove behind a desk or bookshelves.

YOU WILL NEED

sheet of acetate
craft knife
self-healing cutting mat
tape
black latex paint
stencil brush or small paintbrush
latex paint in several bright colors

one *Photocopy the designs from the back of the book in various sizes to try them out. When you are happy with the size, photocopy them directly onto the acetate.*

two *Cut out the stencils carefully, using a craft knife and cutting mat. Tape the stencil to the wall.*

three *Stencil a bold outline in black.*

four *Use a stencil brush to apply color inside the outline, or paint it free-hand for a looser, more appropriate effect for a child's room.*

WIRED-UP WINDOW

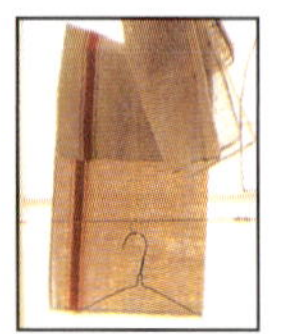

THIS IS A QUIRKY PROJECT for people who see the window as a frame to be filled, but not necessarily frilled. A selection of crisp Irish linen dish towels, linen scrim window cloths, dusters and oven mitts are arranged on a wire framework of tracks and hangers for a practical and stylish window treatment in the kitchen. Yachting supply stores sell good wire with all kinds of interesting odds and ends for fastening and tightening up. Follow the steps here for an explanation of how to use them and ensure that everything connects securely.

Look at this window treatment as a movable feast and re-position the key elements every now and again for a new design at no extra cost.

YOU WILL NEED

- rigging wire, 2 x window width; 1 x ½ window length, plus 12 inches
- both attached and adjustable rigging wire grips and thimbles
- hammer
- pliers
- 2 deck eyes with pulleys
- 2 attached deck eyes
- awl
- rigging screw (tension adjuster)
- connecting rings (key-ring style), various sizes
- wire coat hangers
- selection of dish towels, dusters, and oven mitts

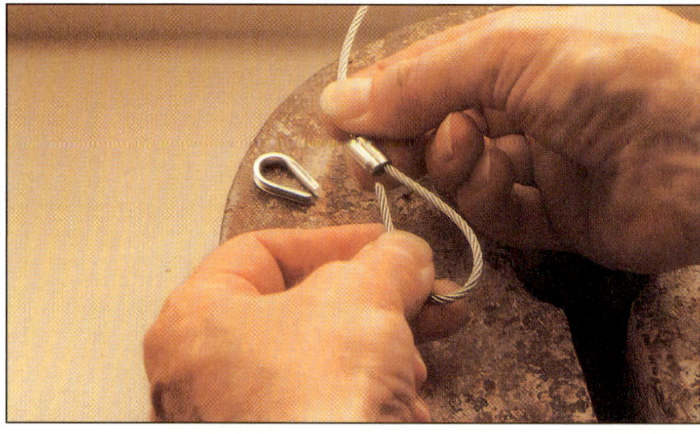

‹ **one** *To make the rigging, thread the rigging wire through the attached wire grip to form a loop with the end.*

two *Place the thimble inside the loop and pull the wire tight, so it fits snugly around the thimble. Place it on a hard surface and hammer the wire grip closed.*

three *Loosen the screw on the adjustable wire grip and thimble and thread the other end of the wire through. Tighten the screw to hold the wire firmly in place.*

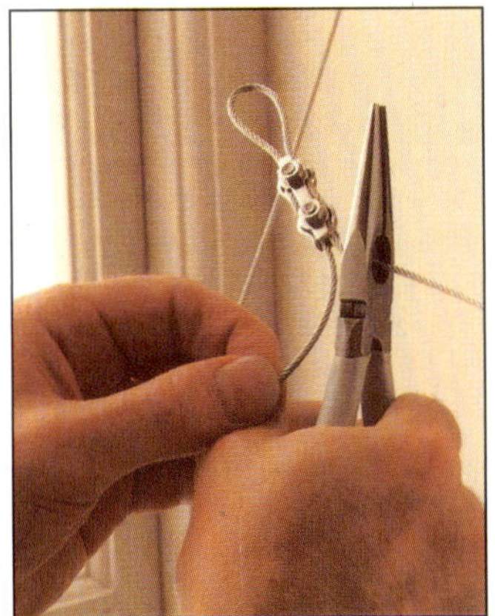

four *Cut off the excess wire at the point where it enters the thimble.*

five *Loop the thimble fitting over a deck eye, then hold it in position to the window frame while you use an awl to make holes for the screws. Screw the deck eye securely into the window frame.*

six *Thread the wire through one of the pulleys and screw this pulley into the window frame opposite the first attachment.*

seven *Thread the wire through the second pulley and screw this pulley into the window frame halfway down the side of the window.*

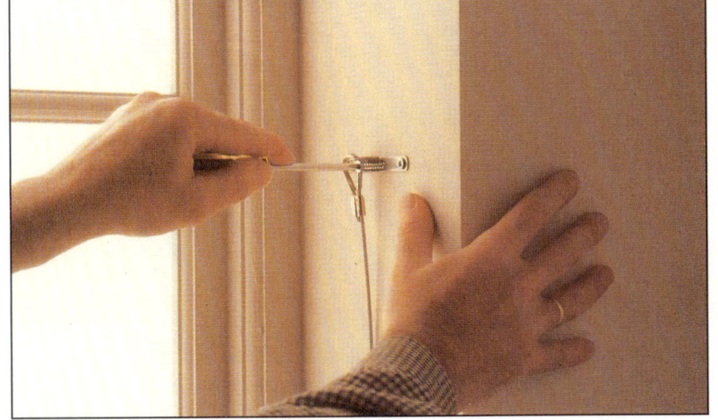

eight *Attach a thimble to the end of the shorter length of wire. Loop this through a deck eye and screw it into the frame halfway down the side of the window—opposite the last pulley.*

CONTINUED OVER ➤

nine *Attach an adjustable wire grip so that it can join onto each end of the rigging screw. Because of the nature of a rigging screw, you will be able to make minor adjustments to centralize it, but aim to cut the wire as accurately as possible to begin with. Twist the rigging screw to increase the tension.*

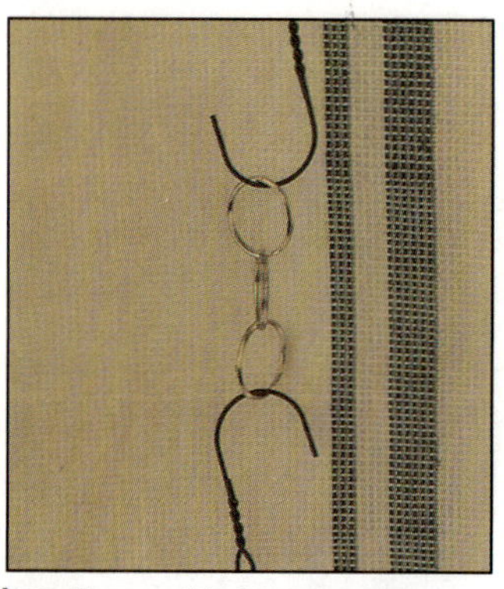

ten *To assemble the arrangement, use connecting rings to link the wire coat hangers together.*

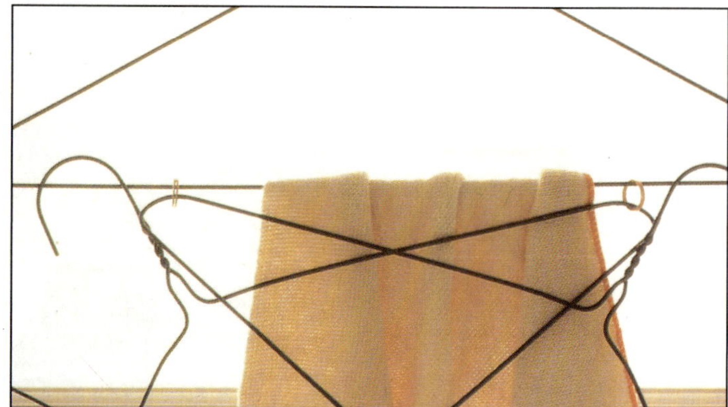

eleven *You could also make up "cat's cradle" shapes by interlinking hangers. Always reinforce the links with rings to make them more secure.*

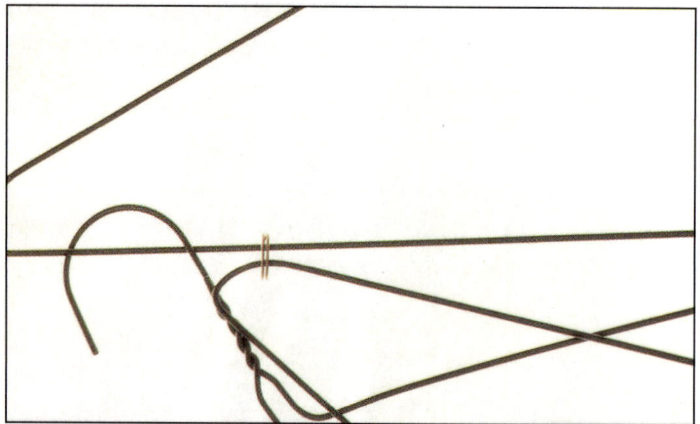

twelve *To make additional variations of the linked coat hangers, experiment with them until you are pleased with the arrangement.*

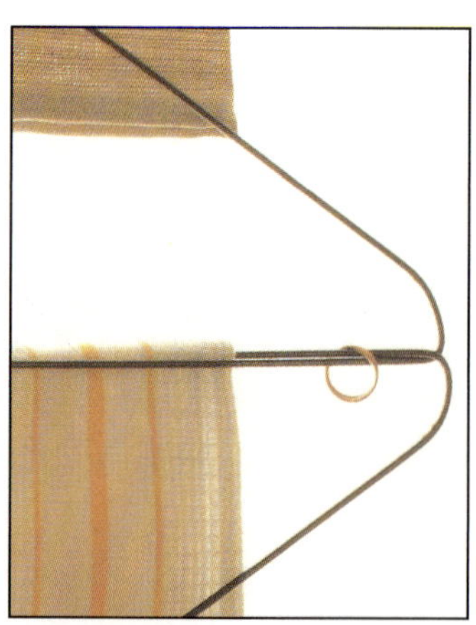

thirteen *Finally, iron the dish towels and fold them over the hangers.*

Purple Playroom

THESE LUSH PURPLE FELT drapes knock the socks off most playroom curtains. They are inspired by the felt shapes that children play with. There is a wide range of topics available —from farms to fairies. When you press out the pre-cut shapes you get a great negative shape as well as your motif. The curtains are attached to a narrow strip of wood, extending 8 inches beyond the frame on both sides above the window.

YOU WILL NEED

- strip of wood 2 x 1 inch thick
- level
- drill, and masonry bit
- plastic anchors and screws
- screwdriver
- pinking shears
- deep purple felt, 2 yards wide x the drop plus 16 inches
- commercial pre-cut felt shapes
- fabric glue
- chalk
- thumb tacks
- staple gun (optional)

one *Attach the strip of wood above the window extending at least 8 inches beyond the frame on both sides. Use pinking shears to cut two strips of curtain felt the width of the curtain fabric and 3/4 inch deeper than the pre-cut felt squares. Stick the felt backgrounds along the strips with fabric glue, allowing space for the gathers.*

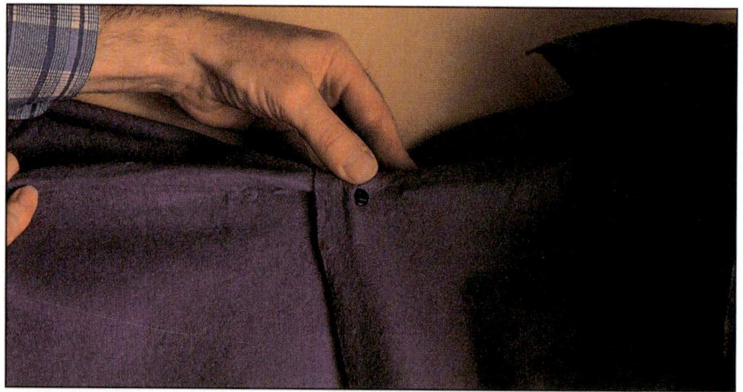

two *Stick the strips on the wrong side of the top edge of the curtains (i.e. the side that will not be decorated). On the right side of the curtain, draw a chalk line 16 inches from the top. Pin the curtain edges to meet in the center of the strip of wood, holding the top 16 inches above it. Pin the outside edges to each end of the strip of wood.*

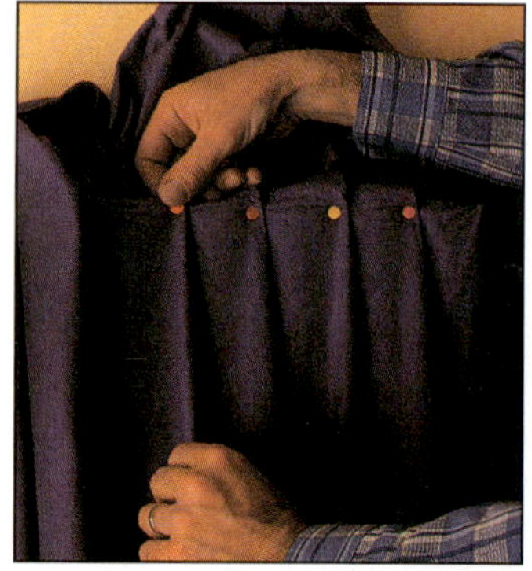

three *Pin or staple the curtains into pleats. If you use pins, you can adjust the pleats as you go. When the pleating is complete, let the valance flop down.*

four *Arrange all the felt shapes randomly on the curtains. They will cling for long enough for you to make a design you like. Stick the shapes in place with fabric glue.*

five *You can make tiebacks in the same style as the valance.*

Mad Hatter

IF YOU HAVE EVER felt like going right over the top with your home decorating, milliner's velvet must be the curtain choice for you. Milliner's velvet comes in gorgeous colors and is great to work with. It is backed with paper and folds into the biggest cabbage roses and most luscious drapes imaginable. A window treatment such as this is definitely not for the shy or retiring.

YOU WILL NEED

wooden strip, window width plus 4 inches on either side
level
drill
plastic anchors and screws
screwdriver
milliner's velvet in dark green and pink
scissors
staple gun
tape measure
2 or more artificial cabbages on wire stems

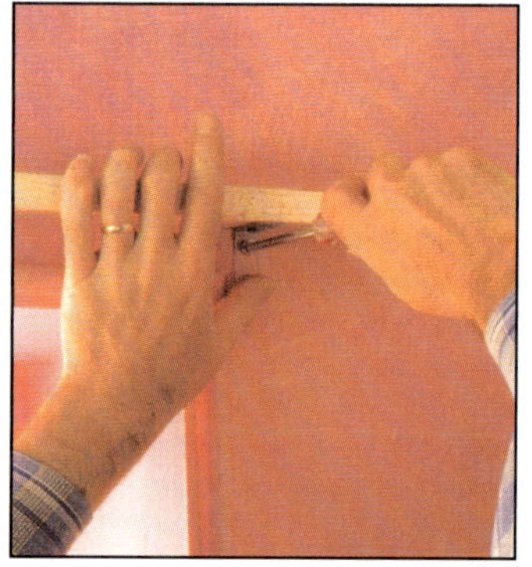

one *Screw the wooden strip above the window. Cut two pieces of green velvet to length and staple them to the strip in pleats, so that they meet in the middle.*

two *Cut two rectangular pieces of green velvet, roughly 1½ times the width of the window. Bunch them up and staple them across the top. Scrunch the pink velvet into three large roses and staple to the top of the valance.*

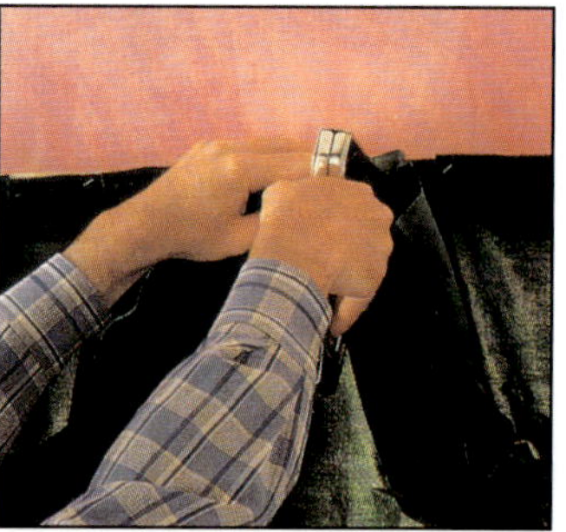

three *Staple the stems of the wire cabbages to the walls on either side of the windows. Then roll the curtains into twists and tuck behind the cabbages. Pull the cabbages in front of the curtains and staple in place.*

BEADED LAUNDRY BASKET

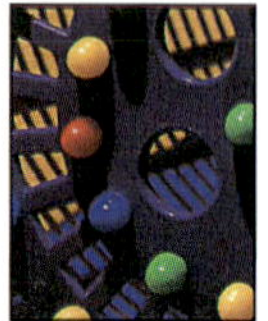

BRIGHTLY COLORED PLASTIC laundry baskets are cheap and practical, but they need help to give them a more individual look. This purple laundry basket was made glamorous with bright Chinese checker pieces taken from an inexpensive children's set. They are ideal, as the domed pieces have spiked backs that can be trimmed to the required depth and glued into holes drilled in the plastic. The attachments are secure, so don't worry about beads scattering all over the bedroom floor. This decorated basket is not suitable for children under three, who might swallow the checker pieces and choke.

YOU WILL NEED

Chinese checker pieces
wire cutters
plastic laundry basket with lid
drill, with fine bit
glue gun with all-purpose glue sticks (or all-purpose glue)
masking tape

one *Sort the Chinese checker pieces into colors. Trim the spikes so that the pieces will fit into the depth of the plastic basket without protruding on the other side.*

two *Drill holes for the spikes—a circle on the lid and lines down the sides.*

three *Sort the pieces into the color sequence you want. Apply glue to one spike at a time and push it into a hole. The glue sets quickly, so work fast.*

four *Run a length of masking tape around the base of the basket as a positioning guide for a straight band of colored pieces. Attach these as you did the other pieces.*

Fake Animal-Skin Rug

GIVING NEW MEANING to the cliché of a baby on a sheepskin rug, this fun idea could be scaled up for a full-size rug. Rather than making a classical bear-, tiger- or lion-skin rug, be more tongue-in-cheek, with shapes such as prehistoric animals or farm animals. Fake furs now come in a range of wonderfully bright colors, so you could take the concept even further from reality and mix up shapes and patterns.

YOU WILL NEED

large sheet of tissue paper
pencil
long ruler
dressmaker's pins
fake fur fabric
scissors
thick felt
pinking shears
iron-on hemming strip and iron, or sewing machine or sewing needle and matching thread

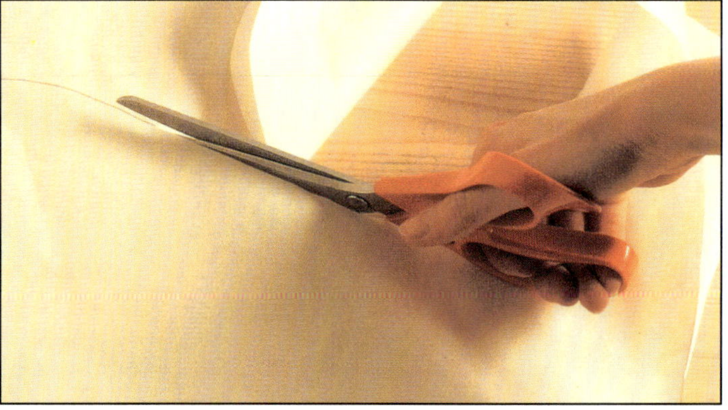

one *Draw a line down the middle of the paper, then draw the outline of half the shape you have chosen—bear, tiger or dinosaur—working out from the line. Fold the paper in half along the line and cut out the shape.*

two *Enlarge the paper pattern to size then pin it to your fur fabric.*

three *Cut your shape out and then cut the shape out again from the felt, using pinking shears. Include a 2½-inch allowance all around.*

four *Stick the wrong side of the fur shape to the right side of the felt shape with the hemming strip, or machine or slip-stitch the two fabrics together.*

PARCHMENT PAPER ART

THERE IS SUCH AN INTERESTING VARIETY of textured and colored papers available at ordinary stationery stores, as well as at specialty art and craft stores, that it is easy to find the right basic ingredients to make some simple but extremely effective pictures without being skilled at painting. Choose your color combination and then make slits in the background paper through which to weave the contrasting colors. These contrasting papers don't need to be clean-cut; in fact, tearing their edges actually enhances the finished look.

YOU WILL NEED

sheets of parchment paper
sheets of colored paper
scrap paper
pencil
self-healing cutting mat
metal ruler
craft knife

one *Decide on the most interesting combination of papers. Use ordinary scrap paper to plan your design first before cutting the parchment.*

two *Draw lines on the scrap paper where you want the slits to be.*

three *Laying the paper on the cutting mat, cut these slits carefully with the craft knife.*

four *Weave paper through the slits. When you are happy with the design, rework using parchment.*

ASTROTURF CHAIR

CLASSIC CONSERVATORY CHAIRS are usually made of expensive hardwood and are often rather boring and conventional in design. To create a truly modern garden room, therefore, why not jazz up a cheap fifties metal chair with strips of astroturf, available at garden centers and do-it-yourself stores. Complete the retro effect with some artificial flowers—although they are, as a rule, considered kitschy, their use is most definitely tongue-in-cheek here. The chair would also be an ideal conversation piece for a garden party.

YOU WILL NEED

metal chair
screwdriver
fine- and coarse-grade astroturf
staple gun
ruler
craft knife
glue gun
artificial flowers

one *Unscrew the seat pad and cut a piece of fine-grade astroturf to cover it. Staple it in place.*

two *Measure and cut strips of a coarser grade of astroturf and attach to the seat with a glue gun.*

three *Cut two matching pieces of coarse astroturf to fit over the central back struts of the chair. Glue the artificial flowers to the front piece.*

four *Fix both pieces over the struts with a glue gun.*

MAGIC CHAIR

COVERED IN NOVA SUEDE, this hard-backed chair has a split personality: It's a kitschy fifties dining chair by day and a theatrical throne in the evening. Throws are often used to cover easy chairs but the limitless possibilities of using them to add drama to a hard chair, totally changing its appearance, are often overlooked. Another advantage is that you can knot throws and tie them onto the uprights of a hard-backed chair, and extras, such as tassels or bindings, can easily be incorporated.

Any fabric that is wide enough is suitable for this treatment, but soft, textured fabrics, such as suede or velvet, are particularly stylish. Practicality is not an issue, because the covers can be whisked off to reveal the practical chair underneath.

YOU WILL NEED

hard-backed chair

large piece of plush fabric; for example, Nova suede

tassels or bindings (optional)

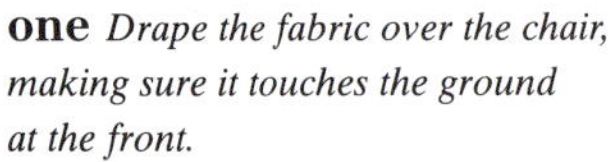

one *Drape the fabric over the chair, making sure it touches the ground at the front.* ›

two *Take up some excess fabric from the back and form a knot over both chair pegs at the back of the chair.*

three *For further embellishment, secure the corners of the fabric with tassels or bindings.*

ROBINSON CRUSOE BLINDS

THIS REALLY MUST BE one of the cheapest, simplest, yet most effective blind solutions ever: It involves two grass beach mats, three cup hooks, a length of rope and some brass paper fasteners. The beach mats are made with colored tape binding, and as they are extremely lightweight, they can be rolled up by hand and tied with rope.

Measure your window carefully—the mats are available in one width only, so they are not suitable for all types and sizes of window.

YOU WILL NEED

awl
3 cup hooks
2 grass beach mats
brass paper fasteners
rope
scissors

one *Make three holes with an awl, one on either side and one in the middle of the window recess. Screw in the cup hooks.*

two *Make a channel for the rope at the top of the blind by folding over the mat 1½ inches and securing with a row of evenly spaced paper fasteners, pushed through and folded back.*

three *Knot the rope onto one of the cup hooks, leaving a tail hanging about a third of the way down the window. Thread the rope through the blind and pull it tight before knotting it onto the middle hook. Cut the rope the same length as before.*

four *Cut a length of rope twice the length of the window drop and knot it in the middle, onto the middle hook. Roll up the blind by hand and tie the two ends of this rope to hold it at the required height. Repeat this process with a second length of rope for the second blind.*

CHILD'S BEDROOM NOOK

CHILDREN LIKE THE security of enclosed sleeping spaces, and older children relish the privacy, especially if the room is shared with a brother or sister. In this project, fiberboard panels are positioned around an existing bed. They can be attached to the bed base or simply rested in a corner so that they enclose the space but cannot be pushed over. The stencils used to decorate the fiberboard panels and the bed linen can also be used on the walls.

YOU WILL NEED

- 2 sheets medium-density fiberboard, 48 inches x width of the bed
- 1 sheet medium-density fiberboard, 48 inches x length of the bed, plus 2 inches
- 2 x 1 inch strip wood, 48 inches long
- drill, with size 10 bit
- screwdriver and suitable screw attachments
- pale gray latex paint
- paintbrush
- paper
- spray adhesive
- stencil cardboard
- scalpel or craft knife
- cutting mat or thick cardboard
- white pillowcase
- iron
- masking tape
- fabric paint: red, blue, yellow
- plate
- stencil brushes
- white sheet or duvet cover
- soft and hard pencils
- jigsaw
- fine-grade sandpaper
- stencil paints (optional)

one *The shorter pieces of fiberboard are used for the head and foot of the bed. To make the bed surroundings, screw the strip of wood to butt up to one 48-inch edge of the head and foot pieces. Butt the long piece of fiberboard at right angles against the strip of wood on the bedhead and screw in place. Repeat with the foot, to make a three-sided surrounding for the bed. The bed surrounding will be stable, but it is advisable to put the long side against a wall. Paint the surrounding with gray latex.*

two *To stencil the bed linen, enlarge the templates overleaf onto paper. Spray the backs lightly with spray adhesive and stick them onto sheets of stencil cardboard. Cut out the stencils carefully, using a scalpel or craft knife on a cutting mat or sheet of thick cardboard to protect your work surface. Peel off the paper patterns.*

three *Wash and iron the pillowcase to be stenciled. Place some cardboard inside the pillowcase. Position the first stencil, holding it in place with masking tape.*

four *Spread each of the fabric paints onto the plate. Using a stencil brush, dab the first color onto the pillowcase. Apply the paint sparingly, as the color is best when built up gradually.*

five *Position the next stencil, being very careful not to smudge the first one, and then stencil the second animal in another color.*

six *Position a third stencil and apply the final color. Continue alternating the stencils and colors to complete the pillowcase. Decorate the sheet or duvet cover in the same way.*

seven *To make the "window," enlarge the crocodile template in sections so that you end up with a good window-sized pattern. Then tape the different sections together. Rub the back of the pattern outline with a soft pencil.*

eight *Place the pattern faceup on the fiberboard and transfer by drawing over the outline with a hard pencil. Drill a hole at any point on the outline as the insertion point for the jigsaw blade.*

CONTINUED OVER ➤

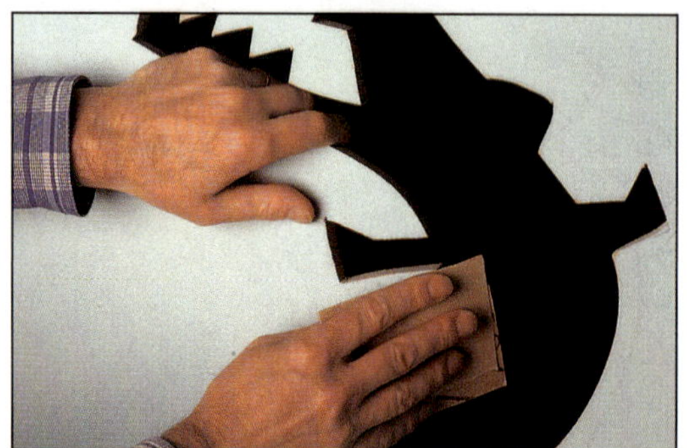

nine *Use the jigsaw to cut out the crocodile shape. Work slowly and hold the blade vertically so that it cuts at its own speed without being pushed or dragged into the fiberboard. Rub down all the edges of the cut-out crocodile shape using fine-grade sandpaper.*

ten *Stencil a frieze of animals around the inside of the bed screen to coordinate with the bed linen. You can use the fabric paints for this, or matching stencil paints.*

Pop Art Floor

Much inspiration for interior decoration is to be gleaned from the pop artists of this century, with their whimsical approach to art. These simple shapes painted on a large surface make use of the pop art conventions of sheer boldness and simplicity, with multiple repetitions of strong images rather than intricate designs. Dramatically discordant colors—orange and shocking pink in this case—are the most appropriate. This idea works best on a concrete floor.

YOU WILL NEED

white matte latex paint
paint roller
tape measure
pencil
masking tape
shocking pink, orange, red and blue matte latex paint
white glue or acrylic varnish

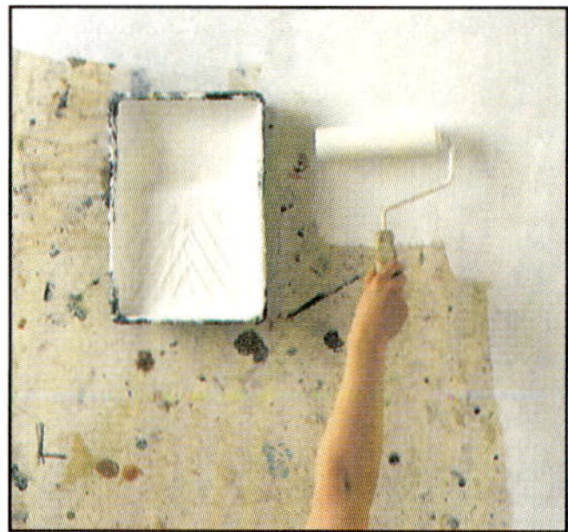

one *Give the floor two coats of white latex, to ensure that the colors of the design ring bright and true.*

two *Measure and draw out your design. Mask off the border, which needs to be crisply painted. Do the same along the outside of the star.*

three *Paint the star, then fill in the area inside the border; taping may not be necessary, as a little white space between the star and border and background makes it look as though silk-screening has been used—a technique common in pop art. Seal the floor with diluted white glue or acrylic varnish.*

SPACE-AGE CHAIRS

FOR AN OVERDOSE of the fantastic, create some space-age simplicity and make a statement that can't be ignored in your bathroom or kitchen. Vacuum-formed chairs appeared in vast numbers in our schools and offices as part of the sixties space-craze. A twenty-first-century update can be given to these forgotten and often discarded chairs by adding yet more space-age technology: Shiny silver space-blankets, used as emergency blankets. These are available at most camping stores and their silver appeal is unsurpassed. Vacuum-formed chairs themselves are the classics of their time and crying out for a facelift. Car spray paint is available in many colors, if you don't want silver.

YOU WILL NEED

2 plastic chairs
silver car spray paint
white glue
paintbrush
1 yard thin batting
1 yard of 54-inch iridescent lycra fabric
needle and strong thread
scissors
4 ping-pong balls
craft knife
space mat
china marker
space blanket

one *Spray the legs of the chairs silver. Apply a coat of white glue to the top and bottom of the first chair and stick on the batting.*

‹ two *Stretch the lycra tautly over the chair. Gather the fabric at the back and stitch it in place. Trim off any excess fabric and turn and baste to neaten the back. Cut holes in the ping-pong balls and insert a leg into each one.*

three *To line the circular hole in the second chair, use the china marker to draw the outline of the hole on the underside of the space mat.*

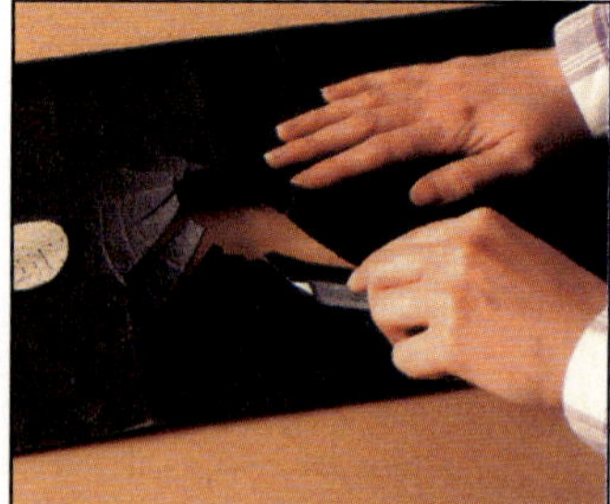

four *With a craft knife, cut a small circle from the center of the outline and then make straight cuts from the inner to the outer circle.*

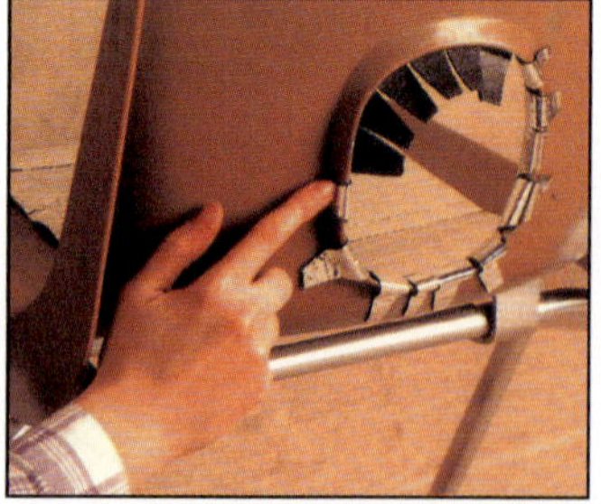

five *Apply white glue to the back of the chair and press the cut sections in place. Once the circle has been centered and the glue is tacky, apply the space blanket as a continuous strip.*

STUDDED FLOOR

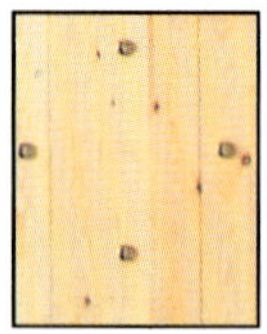

CREATE THE APPEARANCE of the deck of a battleship in your bathroom, with studs positioned at regular intervals across the floor and painted in battleship gray. Alternatively, you could leave the wood natural and studs unpainted. The broad silver studs used here are called "domes of silence," because they are designed to fit under chair legs to help them glide smoothly across the floor without making a noise. However, you can choose any studs, as long as they are sturdy enough to withstand the traffic on the floor and are not sharp or liable to damage shoes or furniture. Sand the floor carefully before beginning.

YOU WILL NEED

pencil
metal ruler or straightedge
studs or "domes of silence"
eraser
acrylic varnish (optional)
paintbrush (optional)
small hammer
cloth, softwood block or carpet scrap
wood glue (optional)

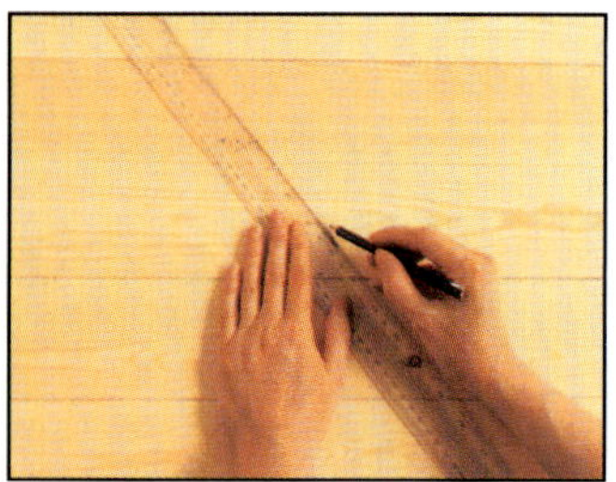

one *Decide on the spacing and pattern of the studs or domes. Draw diagonal grid lines in accordance with your design and mark with a little cross where each stud is to go.*

two *Rub out all markings, except the crosses. If necessary, apply a couple of coats of acrylic varnish to the whole floor, to seal the wood.*

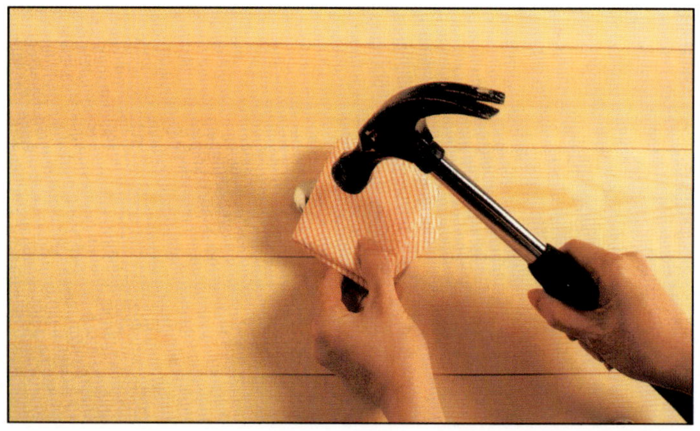

three *Hammer the studs in place over the crosses, using something soft to prevent damage to the studs, such as a folded cloth or softwood block. If you use "domes of silence," which have relatively shallow teeth, hammer them in only halfway to start with. Remove the domes, apply a little wood glue and then replace them and hammer them in all the way. This technique can be used on any decorative wooden floor.*

Fun-Fur Chrome Chair

ANOTHER COMMON flea market find is the chrome-framed chair. Suppliers of second-hand office furniture should have plenty of inexpensive examples. This one was found in very bad condition—the chrome was spotted with rust and the padding torn. The finished picture shows how even a really beat-up chair can be transformed into something chic. The fun-fur covering may seem a touch bizarre but, teamed with the chrome, it turns the chair into a unique furnishing. You need at least twice the length of each pad in fun fur.

YOU WILL NEED

chrome chair
screwdriver
chrome cleaner
soft cloth
craft knife
foam rubber or batting
staple gun
fun-fur fabric

one *Undo and reserve the screws and remove the old seat pads. Clean the chrome frame with chrome cleaner.*

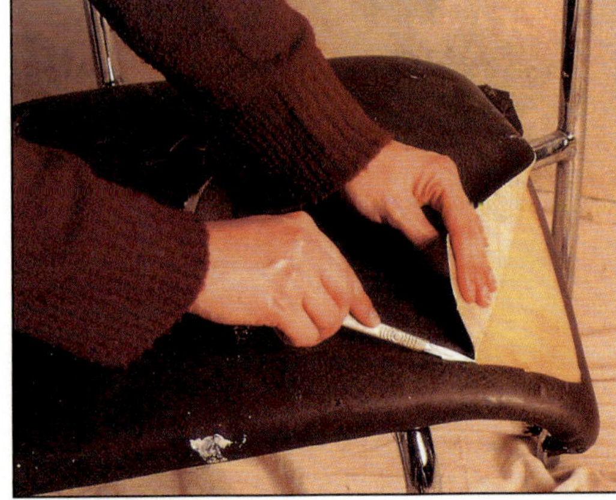

two *Cut away the old covering fabric and padding, to reveal the wooden base of the pads.*

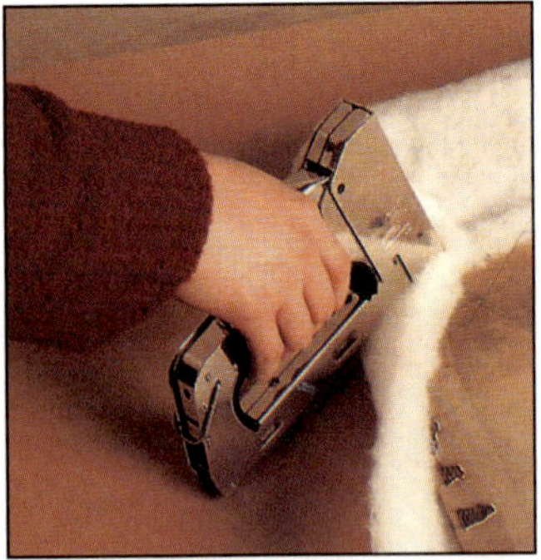

three *Cover the base and seat back with new foam rubber or batting, securing it with a staple gun. Replace the pads.*

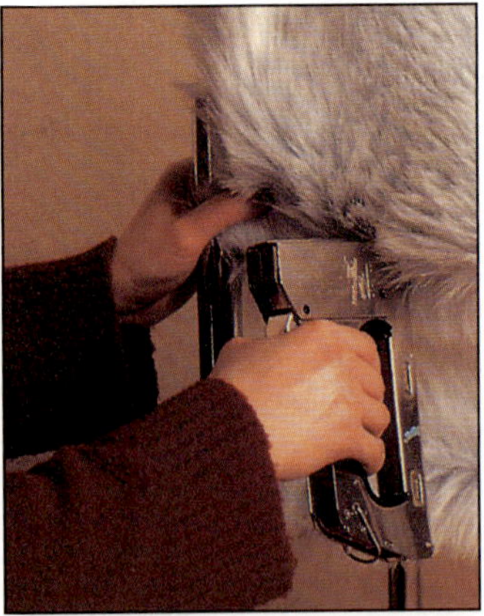

four *Cover the pads with fun-fur fabric, using a staple gun to attach the fabric to the wood. Take into account the nap of the fabric, so it falls nicely over the curved edge. For the longest wear, the pile should run from back to front (i.e. it lies flat when smoothed in that direction). Fold the fabric over the chrome supports. Replace the screws.*

Polynesian Throne

A splendid addition to your conservatory or log-cabin-style summer house, this chair festooned with wheat and rushes is not destined to be a mere garden seat, but a haven for sitting and musing. Gardening has become an extremely popular pastime and garden centers are full of a huge variety of plants and garden paraphernalia. Customized garden furniture is much sought after and pricey, but you can make this stylish throne for very little money, with dried grasses, craft brushes, raffia, bamboo and rushes, which are available at garden centers or florists.

You will need

wooden chair
medium-grade sandpaper
oil-based brown paint
paintbrush
4 large bunches of wheat
large bunch of raffia
double-sided tape
craft rush brushes
saw
staple gun
dried bamboo and rushes

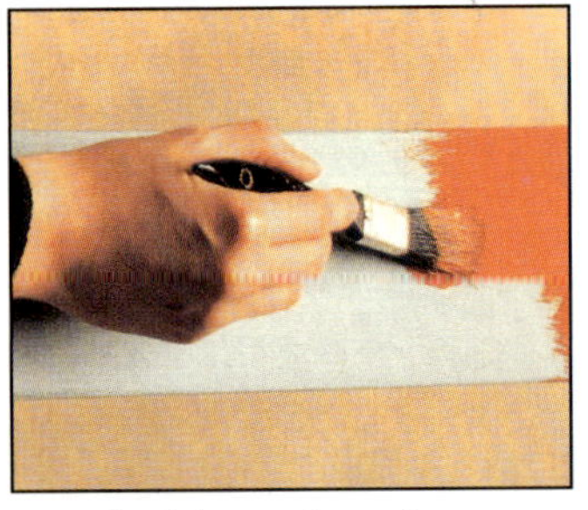

one *Sand the wooden surfaces to provide a key for the paint. Paint the chair with the brown paint to give it a wood-grain effect. You may find it easier to remove the seat.*

‹ **two** *Cover the horizontal strut of the backrest with a few lengths of wheat, tying them in place with raffia. Use the double-sided tape to hold the wheat while you work (the final attaching comes later). Attach two rush brushes diagonally by binding the stalks to the chair frame and at the crossing point with raffia. Shorten the two remaining rush brushes to the length of the vertical chair struts.*

three *To cover the verticals of the backrest, bind them with several strands of raffia. Slip stems of wheat through raffia until wood is covered. Tie two more brushes directly to front horizontals. Tie brushes to verticals.*

four *Bind the two side brushes with many strands of raffia. Discreetly part the brushes and secure them at the top with a few strengthening staples. Add decorative and reinforcing raffia in crisscross fashion to the back of the chair. Knot the raffia to secure it.*

five *Choose thin, flexible bamboo or rushes to bend over the top of the legs, staple in place, then bind with raffia. Staple a rough covering of wheat and rushes over the legs. As a final touch, and also to help it last, knot and crisscross more raffia between your turns.*

HULA-HULA

ORDINARY NYLON SHEETS that are used on the beach can be transformed into instant blinds. They come in a range of lengths with poles in pockets to divide the equal sections, just like a Roman blind, but bolder. All you have to do is saw off the extra piece of pole that would go into the sand and hang the blind on a couple of plumber's pipe fittings. A wide range of bright summer colors is available.

YOU WILL NEED

sheet of nylon, to fit window
scissors
stapler
saw
tape measure
drill
2 plastic anchors
2 plumber's pipe fittings
screwdriver
flower garlands, elastic or rope
string (optional)

one *Hold the sheet of nylon vertically against your window. If the drop is too long, then cut out the nylon mesh and make a new channel for the bottom pole. Fold over a hem, making sure the pole fits, and staple along the edge.*

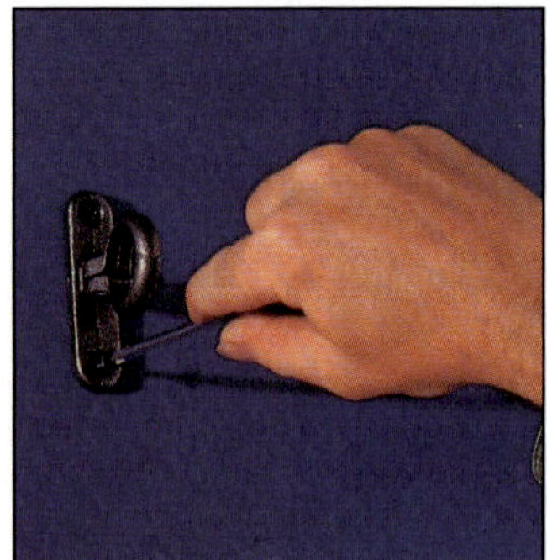

two *Saw off the excess pole, then measure the window and the top of the blind to find the position for the attachments. Drill holes and insert the plastic anchors and plumber's fittings.*

three *Hang the blind, then loop the garlands, elastic or rope between the first and last poles. If the garlands are too long, tie them in divisions with string, to shorten.*

ROBOT CHAIR

A SIMPLE CHAIR MAY not suit a dramatic paint treatment, but you can add to basic chairs to create more height or add drama with a ladder-back effect. The easiest addition to use is already turned dowel, available at lumberyards and do-it-yourself stores, which should be the thickness of your drill bit. If you are prepared for extra work in drilling out larger holes, all kinds of struts could be used, including twisted and carved pieces of the types used for shelving or balustrades. Decorating the chair with computer-age motifs in fluorescent paint adds further impact.

YOU WILL NEED

ladder-back chair
pencil
drill, with wood drill bit
ruler or measuring tape
saw
wooden dowels
medium-grade sandpaper
hammer
royal blue latex paint
medium and fine paintbrushes
acrylic paint: white, fluorescent yellow, green and pink
permanent black marker
clear matte varnish

one *Mark the positions of the holes for the dowels. Drill all the holes. Keep the drill straight, or the dowel won't pass through both holes. Measure the back of the chair. Cut the dowels slightly longer than the chair back and sand the ends.*

two *Pass the dowel through one upright of the chair and line it up with the hole on the second upright.*

three *With a hammer, lightly tap the dowel through the second hole. Leave an equal amount of dowel showing on either side. Paint the whole chair with a blue base coat. Long, slow, even strokes will produce an even finish.*

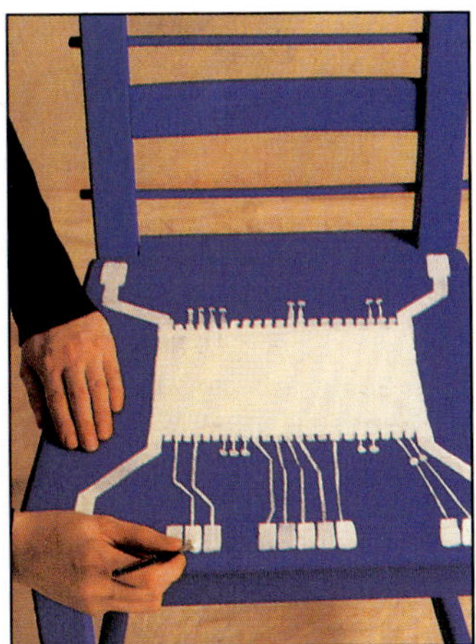

four *With a fine brush and white paint, sketch the outline for the "computer chip" design on the chair seat and on the wide struts of the back. The white provides a good base for the fluorescent paint. Again with a fine brush, paint on the design in yellow, green and pink fluorescent paints.*

five *Outline the design with the marker and add any further detail. Finally, to protect all the paintwork, coat the whole chair with clear varnish.*

CARDBOARD CHAIR

IT'S VERY IMPORTANT that you hunt down the correct cardboard of the heaviest weight direct from a cardboard manufacturer for this chair. An extra thick corrugated cardboard has been used here, resulting in a very sturdy piece of furniture. Remember that, as with wood, the vertical grain is the strongest. Cardboard furniture is particularly suitable for children because of their lighter weight. To hold your cardboard creation securely together, use gum arabic tape, as it is deceptively strong and therefore perfect for this project. The cardboard is left undecorated to create a minimalist look.

YOU WILL NEED

felt-tipped pen
metal ruler
4 sheets of very thick corrugated cardboard, 2 x 1½ yards
scissors
craft knife
self-healing cutting mat
gum arabic tape
4 thin dowels, pencils or chopsticks, 5 inches

one *Draw the design directly onto the cardboard, using the diagrams on the next page as a guide. Make sure that you keep the grain of the cardboard running from the top of the chair to the bottom.*

two *Using the back of a pair of scissors and the metal ruler, score along the fold lines. Cut out all the shapes with a craft knife, then bind the edges with gum arabic tape.*

three *Assemble the chair in the same way as you would make a carton, folding and slotting the cardboard into itself. The backrest of the chair has flaps that fold into the arm rests.*

four *Slot the seat into position, making sure it is securely held in place. To give further support on the struts, insert pieces of dowel, or even pencils or chopsticks, through the cross-struts.*

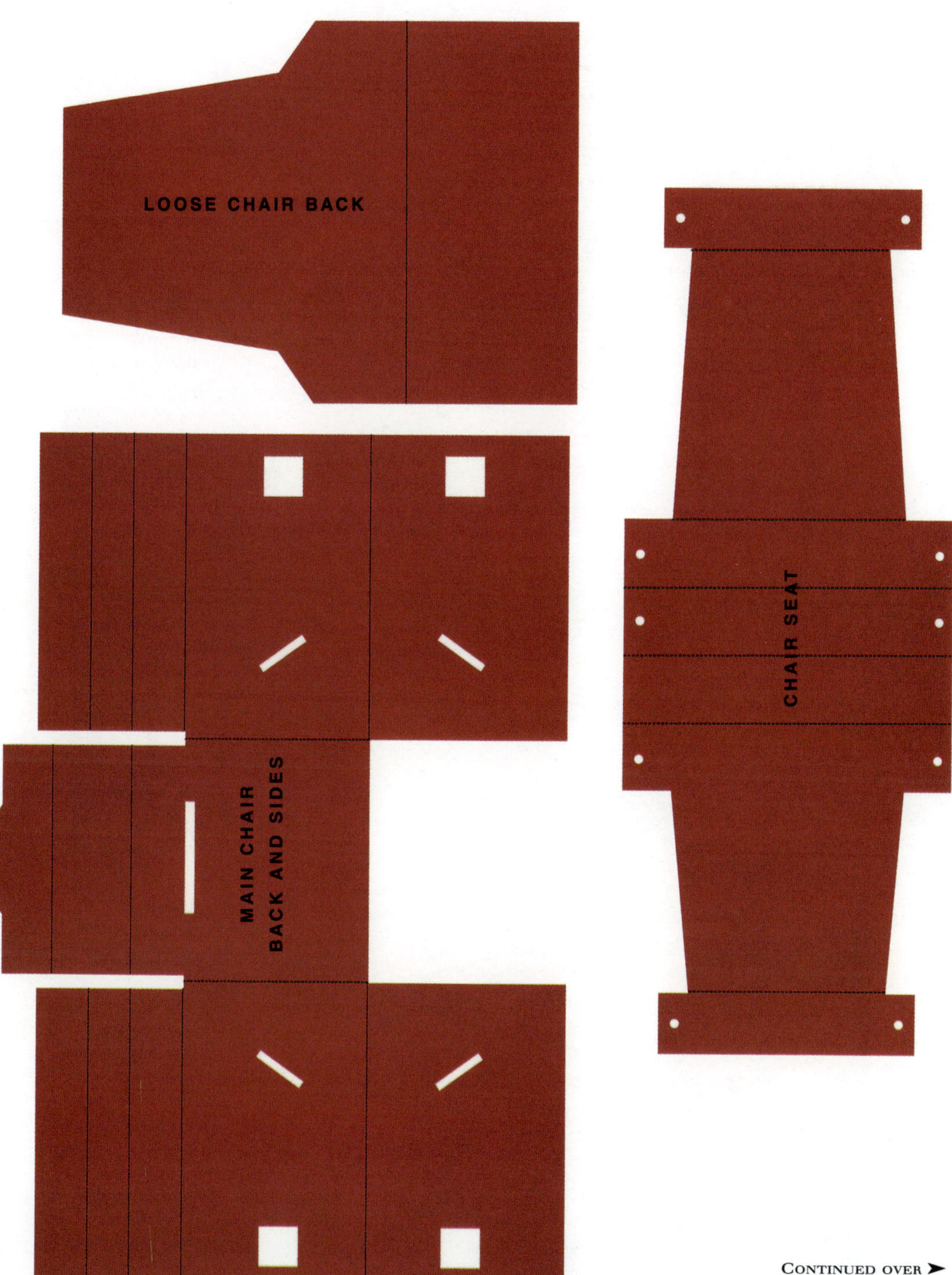

CONTINUED OVER ➤

COLORED STRING

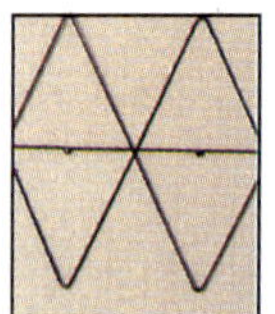

THE IDEA OF DECORATING a wall with colored string wound around tacks might evoke thoughts of nursery-school crafts, but it's surprising what wonderfully graphic patterns and eye-catching designs you can achieve with this simple technique. Set out a grid of tacks on the wall—substitute short nails if the wall won't take tacks—and then you are set to create any design you want. Just wind the string around the tacks tightly and evenly, either running the decoration across a wall from side to side or using it to make interesting borders.

YOU WILL NEED

- level
- straightedge
- pencil
- tacks
- tack hammer
- latex paint to match existing wall color
- paintbrush
- colored string

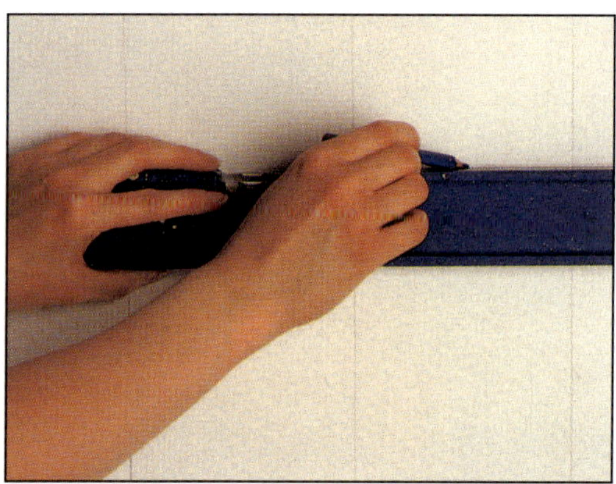

one *Lightly draw a grid on the wall, using the level, straightedge and pencil.*

two *Hammer in the tacks to the same depth at all the cross points of the grid and all around the outside edges.*

three *Paint out the pencil lines with latex paint in the existing wall color.*

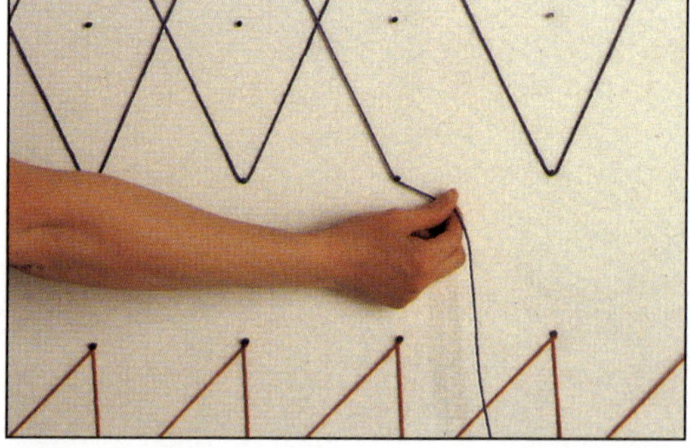

four *Arrange the string. Either buy colored string or dip plain string in colored paint to get exactly the colors you want. Wind the string tightly around the tacks, and start and finish with neat loops.*

SPACE BED

AT LAST, A TERRESTRIAL bed with all the glamour and sparkle of space travel. If the very thought of bedtime has the kids reaching for sci-fi videos, why not let them relax wrapped in their very own shimmering silver "space-blanket" beds? The shape of this headboard is reminiscent of a 1950s tail fin, but you can choose almost any bold shape that can be cut out of fiberboard with a jigsaw. You can buy "space blankets" at outdoor-supply stores.

YOU WILL NEED

1 sheet medium-density fiberboard, width of the bed x height to bed base, plus approximately 1 yard

pen

ruler

string

thumb tack

jigsaw

fine-grade sandpaper

polyester duvet

staple gun and staples

thin silver insulating material

broad, woven adhesive tape

tape measure

thicker-textured silver insulating material (the type used under camping mattresses)

scissors

one *Draw a line across the width of the fiberboard about 16 inches down from the top edge. Tie a 16-inch length of string to a thumb tack and tie a pen to the other end. Push the pin into the line, just in from the left edge of the board. Pull the string taut and adjust its length to reach the top left-hand corner of the board. Using the string as the arm of a compass, draw a curve from the top of the board down to the horizontal line.*

two *Cut out the shape around the curve and along the line with a jigsaw. Sand down the edges.*

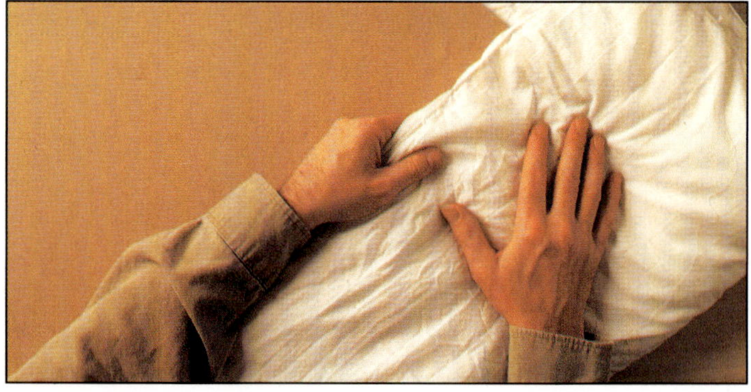

three *Fold the duvet around the fiberboard to create a smooth covering across the front. Fold the edges to the back.*

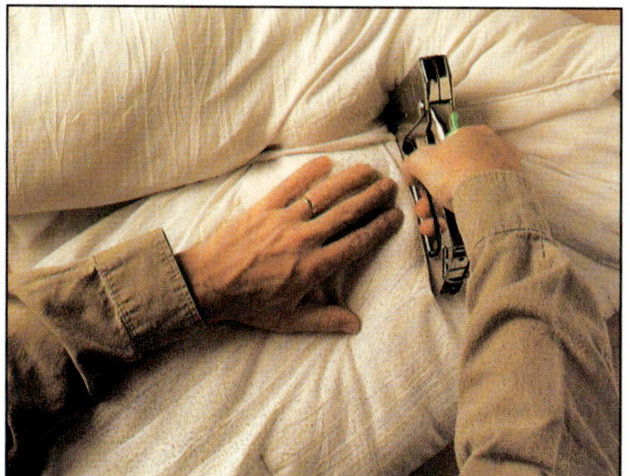

four *Staple the edges to the fiberboard, folding them under and tucking them in to get as even a finish as possible.*

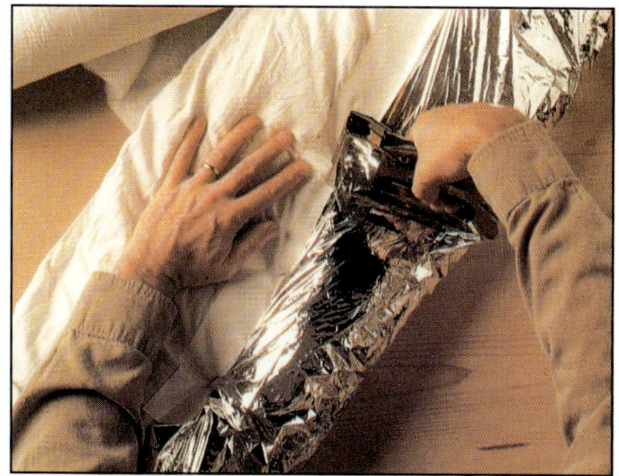

five *Lay the covered shape onto the thin silver insulating material. Fold the edges to the back and staple.*

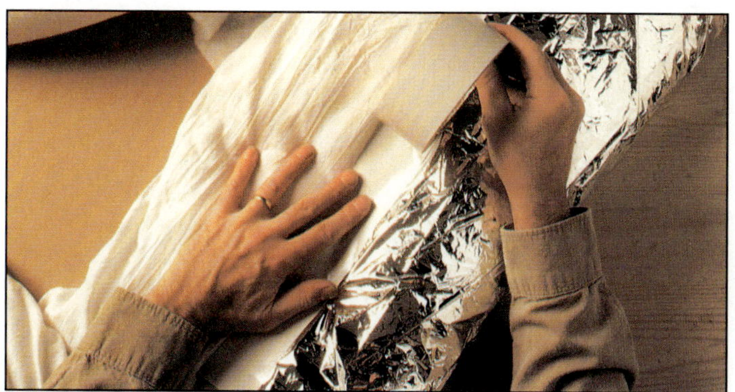

six *Stick a strip of broad woven adhesive tape over the edges of the silver material to cover the staples and give a neat finish.*

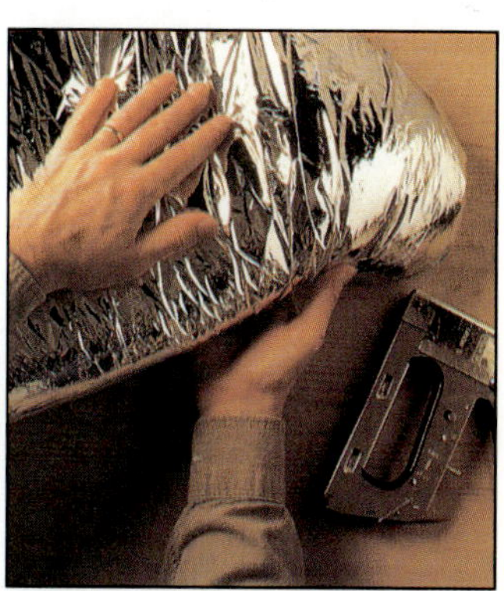

seven *Turn the bedhead over and adjust any wrinkles in the "space blanket."*

eight *Mark points at intervals of 9½ inches along a piece of string.*

nine *Use the piece of string to measure the positions of the quilting buttons on the covered headboard. Mark each point with a small square of woven tape.*

CONTINUED OVER ➤

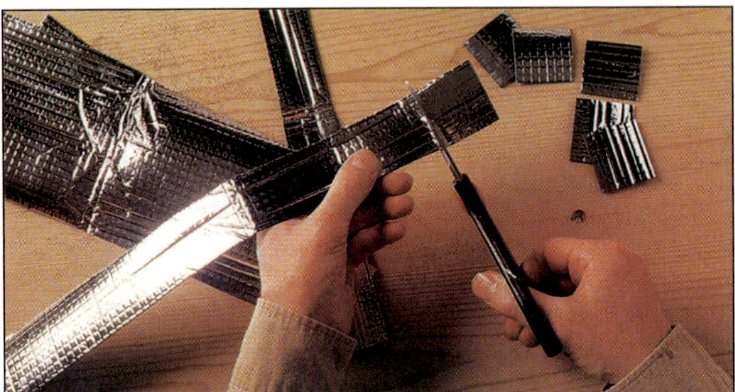

ten *Cut strips of the thicker-textured insulating material into squares to use as "buttons" for the quilting.*

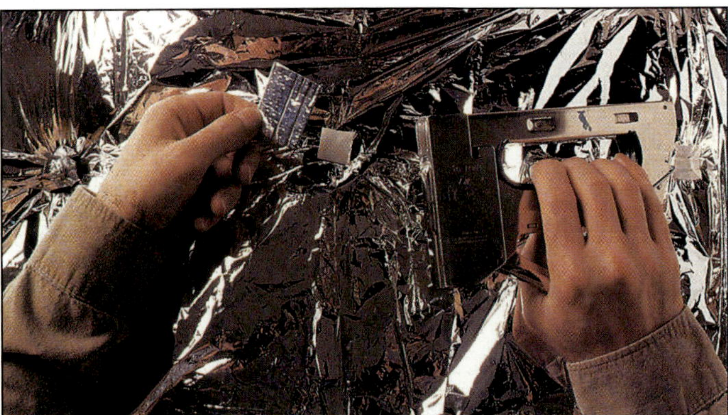

eleven *Staple a silver button on top of each tape square. Make sure that the silver covers up the tape. The tape strengthens the thin silver material and prevents the staples from tearing it.*

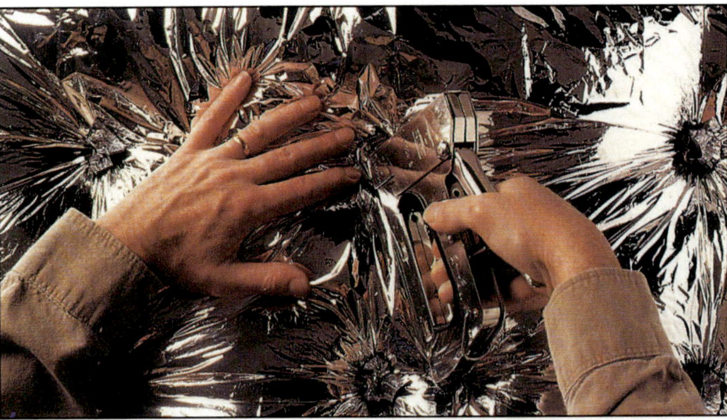

twelve *Push down hard with the staple gun, so that the staple penetrates right through to the fiberboard. Continue stapling the buttons in place until the whole headboard is quilted.*

ANIMAL CUSHIONS

ANIMAL PRINTS HAVE NEVER BEEN more popular, and the quality of fake fur now available is truly fantastic. It is also a delight to animal-lovers and the environmentally conscious. The distinctive boldness of the cowhide print chosen here makes for great cushion covers.

This low bed is draped with lengths of silky smooth velvet tiger- and leopard-skin fabric that spill over onto the floor, adding to the tactile, languorous atmosphere. This project doesn't have to be a permanent fixture, so bring out this special bedding for wild weekends—and it may bring out the animal in you!

YOU WILL NEED

- cardboard
- scissors
- button blanks
- small pieces of black velvet
- hemmed squares of cowhide print, 2 inches smaller than the cushions
- black velvet cushions
- needle and thread
- tiger- and leopard-skin fabrics

one *Cut a circle of cardboard approximately ½ inch larger all around than the button blanks. Use the cardboard pattern to cut circles of black velvet.*

two *Cover the top of each button blank with a velvet circle, tucking in the edges so that they catch onto the spikes underneath.*

three *Press the backing firmly in place to make neatly covered black velvet buttons.*

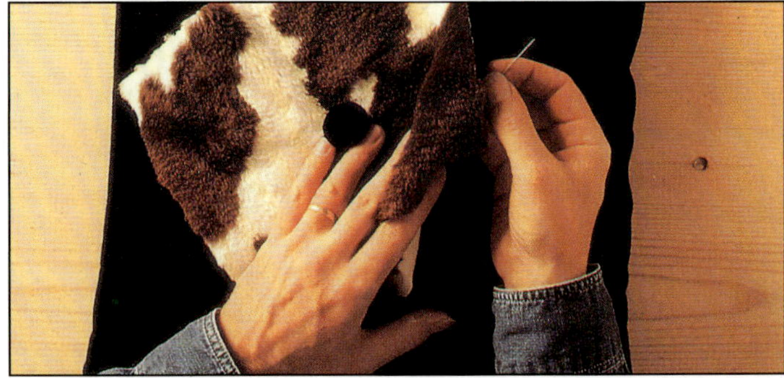

four *Stitch a hemmed cowhide fabric square diagonally on each cushion. Sew a black button onto the center, stitching through both the cowhide print and the black velvet cushion. Arrange the tiger- and leopard-skin fabrics over the bed.*

Comic-Strip Chair

THIS MONTAGE IDEA HAS tons of impact and could be adapted to many different themes. Here, we have chosen comic-strip characters to create a chair that would be welcome in even the coolest teenager's bedroom.The seat cover could use any brightly colored logo or graphic cut from fabric, or make use of a favorite image by taking a picture to a store that transfers pictures onto T-shirts.

YOU WILL NEED

wooden-framed chair
medium-grade sandpaper
scissors
paper motifs
wallpaper paste
paintbrushes
clear gloss varnish or spray gloss varnish
blue stretchy fabric
staple gun
fabric logo (optional)
fabric adhesive (optional)

one *Remove the seat from the chair. Sand the chair lightly all over to provide a key for the paste. Cut out the motifs carefully with sharp-pointed scissors. Apply paste carefully all over the back of the motifs. Let set until tacky.*

two *Brush wallpaper paste over the chair frame, then apply the motifs to the chair, using a brush to prevent tearing them while they are wet. Repeat until you have covered the whole chair. Let dry.*

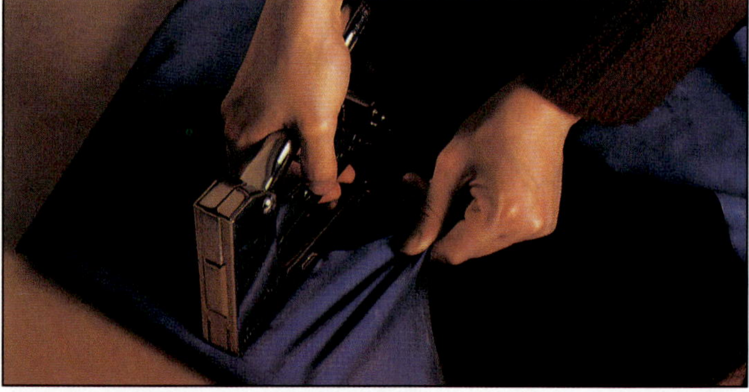

three *Apply a coat of varnish to protect the chair. For the seat cushion, stretch the fabric over the cushion and staple it in place. Pull the fabric taut as you work around the cushion. If you wish to decorate the seat further, find a logo or graphic to go in the center. Apply fabric adhesive to the back and let it become tacky. Position and apply the logo to the seat cushion, pressing it down firmly until the glue has taken hold. Replace the cushion in the chair.*

Board Game Carpet

Along with linoleum tiles, carpet tiles are real winners in the practicality stakes. Almost unbeatable in areas that need to be hardwearing and where children and their accompanying wear and tear are concerned, carpet tiles have the single disadvantage that they never look like wall-to-wall carpet, no matter how well they are laid. Rather than fighting the fact that they come in non-fraying squares, make use of this very quality and create a fun floor-scape, such as this giant board game. Carpet tiles are very forgiving, allowing for slight discrepancies in cutting, and are very easy to replace if an area is damaged. A geometrical design is easiest; it is advisable to leave curves to the experts, but anything else, from a board game to the elegance of a painting by Mondrian, is accessible.

YOU WILL NEED

metal tape measure
pencil
paper
carpet tiles
white crayon or white china pencil
metal ruler
rigid-bladed knife and plenty of spare blades
heavy duty, double-sided carpet tape

one *Measure your room and make sure that the floor is level and all protruding nails have been flattened. Any flat surface will accommodate the carpet tiles, whether it is marine-plywood, hardboard, floorboards or concrete. Plan your design on paper. Most rooms are not perfect rectangles, so leave room for an area of plain tiles to edge the pattern.*

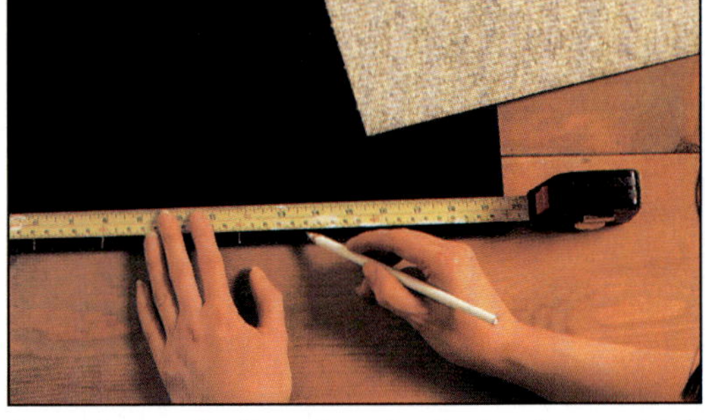

two *Measure the tiles to determine the size of your pointed shapes and to figure out how many tiles will be needed for your pattern. Consider the different weaves and nap of the carpet tiles, and make them work to enhance your chosen plan. Using a white crayon or china pencil, draw the pattern on the reverse of your tiles.*

three *With a metal ruler and a rigid-bladed knife, score along the marked lines. Don't attempt to cut the tile through completely in one action. Starting at the top of the tile, cut down your scored lines. Do this on a solid surface and take extreme care while doing it.*

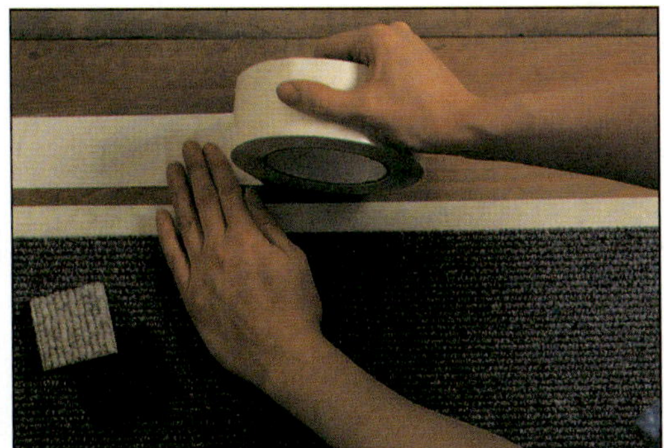

four *Lay down a line of carpet tape and remove the backing. Cut all the tiles for one complete run and place these first, rather than laying little bits at a time.*

five *Stick your cut tiles in place, making sure not to pack them too tightly. Begin by making the entire checkered border. Then fill in, laying strips of carpet tape as you work. Tread the tiles down; uneven cuts will be unnoticeable.*

MINIBUS TOYBOX

EVERY CHILD SHOULD BE ENCOURAGED to put away his or her toys at the end of the day. This eye-catching toybox might just do the trick. The pastel-colored patches behind the bus stamps give the box a 1950s look. These are stenciled onto a light turquoise background. Stamp the buses on randomly so that some extend beyond the background shapes. Keep changing the angle of the stamp—the effect will be almost three-dimensional.

YOU WILL NEED

hinged wooden box

latex paint: turquoise and three pastel colors

paintbrushes

stencil cardboard and scalpel

4 plates

2 rollers

brown stamping ink and minibus stamp

one *Apply two coats of turquoise latex paint to the box. Cut out the background shape stencil. It should be large enough for the whole stamp.*

two *Spread the three pastel-colored paints on plates. Roll the first color through the stencil onto the box. You need a shape for each color. Wash the roller and apply the two remaining colors, painting through the stencil as before. Balance the shapes with an equal amount of background color. Let dry.*

three *Pour some brown ink onto a plate. Coat the rubber stamp with the ink using a rubber roller. Stamp the bus motif onto the pastel background patches.*

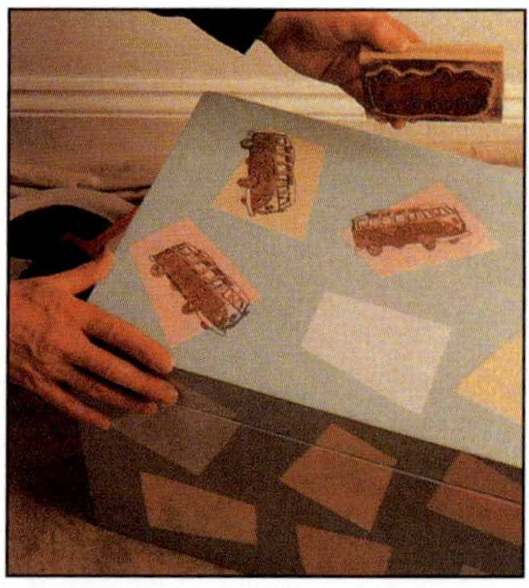

four *Let the stamps overlap the patches and vary the angle.*

BATHROOMS

Bathrooms

Most people's idea of an imaginatively designed bathroom used to be stacking towels according to color and arranging three empty perfume bottles on the windowsill. Not anymore. Bathrooms have come of decorating age, and deservedly so.

Bathrooms are a refuge from the cares of the world, where you can soak and pamper yourself with unashamed self-indulgence. But to get a bathroom that you actually want to spend quality time in, first you must pamper your surroundings.

Cream, white and washed-out pastels are always popular, and for good reason—they make small areas look larger. But there's no need to adhere blindly to white. What about, for example, a beach look?

Brightly colored metal beach buckets hung from a piece of driftwood should do the trick. You could cover a wall with plaster stars or create a mosaic splashback of china. The view from the bath is looking better all the time.

What about views you don't want to see? Cover windows without losing light with blinds made of translucently colored woven scrim, or strips of parched wood from a broken-up orange crate—simple solutions that can be created in a matter of hours. And when night falls, turn off the cold overhead light and switch on a small lamp.

One idea to make your bathroom a bit unusual is to use bright buckets as containers. Buckets from the seaside will remind everyone of summer vacation.

Three chrome flashlights attached to a chrome rod to spotlight special items make a spectacular effect.

Relegate the plastic laundry basket to the kids' room, and in its place put an antique-finished terra-cotta pot. To step over, rather than into, puddles of water on the floor, lay strips of raised wooden duckboards. It's easy and very practical.

The ideas in this chapter provide a bathroom in which you can wash, shower, bathe and unwind. Whether you go for the bright beach look, the classical Roman touch or the crisp, cool serenity of Japanese style, there will be just one problem—once inside, you'll never want to leave!

BATHROOM BUCKETS

ADD AN ELEMENT OF seaside fun to your bathroom—as well as useful extra storage for all those odd-shaped items—by hanging up this row of bright buckets. This trio of enamel-painted buckets was bought at a toy store, but you could take a trip to the seaside where you are bound to find a great selection of buckets in all shapes and sizes. While there, go for a stroll along the shore to find the ideal pieces of driftwood to attach to your wall.

YOU WILL NEED

3 enamel-painted buckets (or plastic seaside ones)
length of driftwood (or an old plank)
pencil
drill, with wood and masonry bits
wire
pliers
wire cutters
masking tape
plastic anchors and screws
screwdriver

one *Line the buckets up at equal distances along the wood. Make two marks, one at each end of the handle where it dips, for the three buckets. Using the wood bit, drill through the six marked positions to make holes through the wood.*

two *Wind wire around each handle end and poke it through the holes. Twist the two ends together at the back to secure. Trim the ends. Then drill a hole near each end of the wood.*

three *Hold the piece of wood in place and mark the positions for the attachments. Place a small piece of masking tape over the tile to prevent it from cracking, then drill the holes and attach the wood to the wall.*

SAVON
BONNE
MERE

SEASHELL BOX

Boxes decorated with seashells can be ugly, and unfortunately the worst ones have given this wonderfully relaxing pastime a bad name. But don't be dismayed—shells are naturally beautiful and there are endless ways of arranging them tastefully. This project combines the contemporary look of corrugated cardboard with a dynamic shell arrangement. For the finishing touch, the box is painted pure white matte.

YOU WILL NEED

selection of seashells

round corrugated cardboard box with lid

glue gun with all-purpose glue sticks (or all-purpose glue)

white acrylic paint (gesso primer is ultra white)

paintbrush

one *Lay out all the shells and sort them into different shapes and sizes. Arrange them on the lid to make the design. Remove the top layer of shells from the middle of the lid and begin sticking them on. Heat the glue gun and glue the outside shells first, gradually moving inward.*

two *Work with the shell shapes, building up the middle section. The glue gun lets you get an instant bond, so the shells will stick to the surface however you want them to.*

three *Paint the box and the lid white. If you are using acrylic gesso primer, two coats will give a good matte covering. If you are using ordinary acrylic or latex, the box will benefit from an extra coat of paint.*

TERRA-COTTA LAUNDRY POT

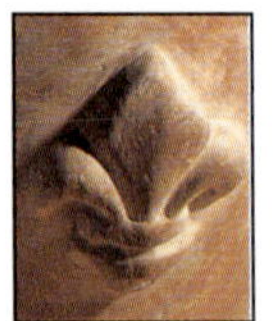

LAUNDRY IN A FLOWERPOT? It certainly sounds unusual, but this idea makes a refreshing change from the ubiquitous wicker basket in the bathroom. Terra-cotta pots are now available in a huge range of shapes and sizes and a visit to your local garden center should provide you with just the right pot. To give a pristine pot an antique feel, follow these simple steps. This project would look good in a bathroom with a Mediterranean decor.

YOU WILL NEED

large terra-cotta flowerpot
rag
shellac button polish
white latex paint
paintbrushes
scouring pad
sandpaper (optional)

one *Soak a rag in button polish and rub all over the surface of the pot with it. The polish will sink in very fast, leaving a yellow sheen.*

two *Mix white latex paint with an equal quantity of water. Stir it thoroughly and apply a coat to the pot. Let the paint wash dry.*

three *Rub the pot with the scouring pad to remove most of the white paint. The paint will cling to the crevices and along the moldings to look like limescale. Either leave the pot like this or rub over it even more with sandpaper to reveal the clay. When you are happy with the effect, apply a coat of button polish with a brush to seal the surface.*

Bucket Stool

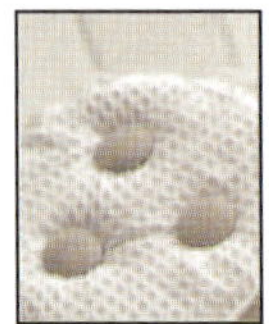

Florist's buckets in galvanized tin are widely available in a variety of heights; obviously, the taller they are, the better. Cover the metal seat pad in any fabric (a waffle-textured towel was used here). For a bathroom you could fill clear plastic fabric with foam chips or fun sponges. Dish cloths also make fun covers, and a layer of dried lavender would make a lovely scented seat.

You Will Need

- 1 yard heavy cord or rope
- 2 florist's buckets
- glue gun
- very large self-cover buttons
- scraps of material for covering buttons
- fabric-cutting tool for buttons
- waffle-textured hand towel
- large sewing needle and matching thread
- circular cushion pad

‹ **one** *Attach the cord to the top rim of one of the buckets with the glue gun.*

two *Place this bucket inside the second bucket, applying glue to its rim, then invert both buckets.*

three *Use the fabric to cover the buttons as per the manufacturer's instructions.*

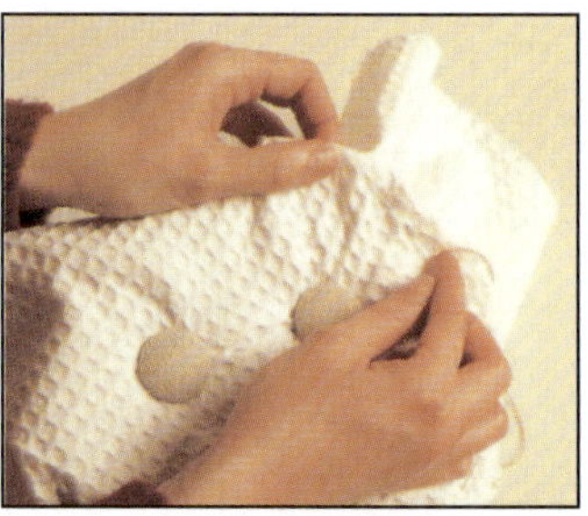

four *Sew the buttons to the center of the waffle-textured hand towel. Then use the towel to cover the cushion pad. Instead of smoothing out the gathering in the fabric, accentuate it, using the buttons as a focus. Glue the pad to the upturned bucket.*

Victorian Stenciling

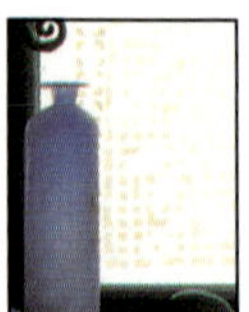

This idea originated from the etched glass windows of the Victorian era. You can easily achieve the frosted, etched look on plain glass by using a stencil cut from stencil cardboard and car enamel paint. The paint needs to be sprayed very lightly, so practice on some picture frame glass first to judge the effect. The stencil design is shown here, but you could easily design your own. Look at examples of lace panels to get some inspiration.

You will need

tape measure
masking tape
tracing paper
stencil cardboard
pencil
craft knife
brown paper
matte white car enamel spray

one *Measure the panes and mark the halfway points with masking tape. Photocopy and enlarge the stencil design and cut it from stencil cardboard. Tape the main stencil pattern in position, then use brown paper to mask off the surrounding area, at least 20 inches deep on all sides. (The spray spreads more than you would think.)*

two *Shake the paint can thoroughly, as this affects the fineness of the spray. Spray from a distance of at least 12 inches, using short puffs of spray.*

three *Depending on the dimensions of the window panes, there may be strips along the sides of the main panel that also need stenciling. This pattern has a border to fit around the edge—you may need to adapt it to fit your pane.*

ORANGE CRATE BLIND

Greengrocers are accustomed to supplying raw materials to their customers, but they might be a little surprised when you ask them for their wooden crates rather than their fruit and vegetables. Get some orange crates if you can, as the thin planks make ideal and original slats for blinds. These wooden blinds work best on a small, permanently obscurable window, such as in the bathroom. Although the blinds look Venetian, they don't actually pull up, but with a bit of perseverance you could probably make them do so. Here the wood was left natural, but it could be stained any color.

YOU WILL NEED

orange crates
pliers
sharp knife
medium- and fine-grade sandpaper
ruler
pencil
drill, and wood bit
string
scissors
2 cup hooks

one *Pull the orange crates apart and select the most interesting parts from the longest sides. Remove any wire staples with pliers. Split some of the planks so that the slats are not all the same size. The final effect is more successful if the pieces are intentionally irregular.*

two *Shave off some of the wood to add character to the finished blind.*

three *Use medium-grade sandpaper first and then fine-grade sandpaper to smooth the wood and round off the edges.*

four *Place the slats side by side so that the edges line up. Mark a point 2 inches from each end and 1¼ inches from the bottom long edge. Although the slats are different widths, the holes should be drilled through points that line up on the front of the blind.*

five *Drill through the positions you have marked. The holes should be big enough to take the string through twice, but no bigger.*

six *Begin threading the string through the blind. Go through the blind from the back and pull a long length, about twice the drop of the window. It must be threaded all the way down the blind, to include all the looping around the slats.*

seven *Loop the string back over the slat and thread it through the hole a second time.*

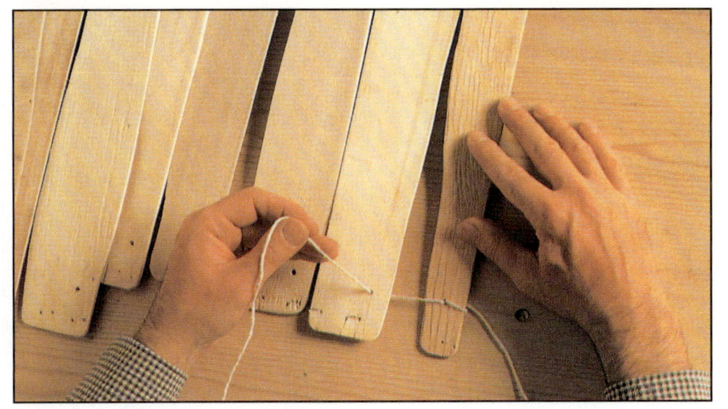

◄
eight *Take the string up through the second slat. Continue as you did with the first, looping it around and through each slat twice, working all the way up the slats.*

CONTINUED OVER ►

nine *When you get to the last slat, tie the string in a double knot and cut it off. Repeat this process on the other side. This is what the blind will look like from the "working side."*

ten *Turn the blind around as shown to hang it up so that you only see the string entering and leaving each slat. Screw two hooks up into the window frame and hang up the blind.*

Mosaic Splashback

Mosaics look complicated and elaborate but are actually very simple to do; you just need time and patience to complete the job. Use broken tiles or look for chipped flea market finds to make a unique splashback for behind a sink. You can have as simple or as complicated a color scheme as you wish. You need a good selection of differently sized pieces. Break up the tiles, plates and so on by putting them between two pieces of cardboard and hammering them gently, but firmly. The cardboard will prevent tiny chips from flying around. Work on a piece of fiberboard so that you can sit down with the mosaic on a table, which is less back-breaking than applying the mosaic directly onto a wall.

YOU WILL NEED

- tape measure
- sheet of medium-density fiberboard
- pencil
- triangle or ruler
- jigsaw
- drill, with wood and masonry bits
- beading
- miter block and saw or miter saw
- wood glue
- white latex paint
- paintbrush
- selection of broken tiles and ceramic fragments
- glue gun and glue sticks
- screws
- grout
- plastic anchors
- screwdriver

one *Measure the fiberboard to fit the width of your sink. Draw your chosen splashback shape onto the fiberboard using a pencil and a triangle or ruler.*

two *Carefully cut out the shape using a jigsaw.*

three *Mark the position of the holes that will be used to attach the splashback to the wall. Drill the holes.*

four *Measure the beading that will frame the fiberboard. Miter the beading using a miter block or miter saw.*

five *Glue the beading in place with wood glue, following the manufacturer's instructions.*

six *When the glue is dry, paint the whole splashback white. Let dry.*

seven *Arrange the ceramic pieces on the splashback. Experiment until you have created a pleasing pattern.*

eight *Glue the ceramic pieces in place using the glue gun.*

nine *Put screws into the screw holes, to prevent grout from getting into the holes. Grout over the mosaic, being careful near any raised, pointed bits.*

CONTINUED OVER ➤

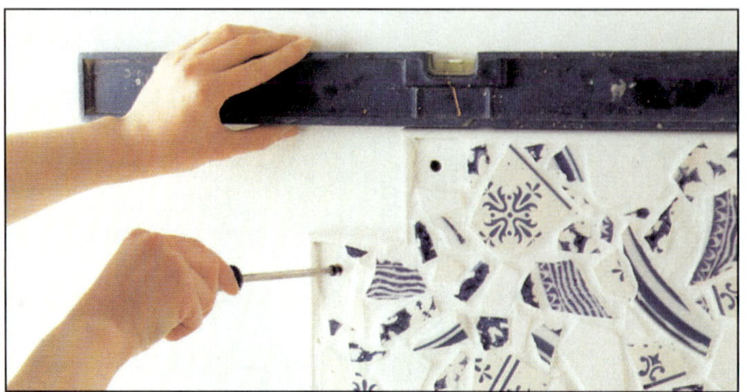

ten *Drill holes into the wall and insert the plastic anchors. Then screw the splashback into position onto the wall.*

eleven *Glue on more ceramic pieces, to hide the screws.*

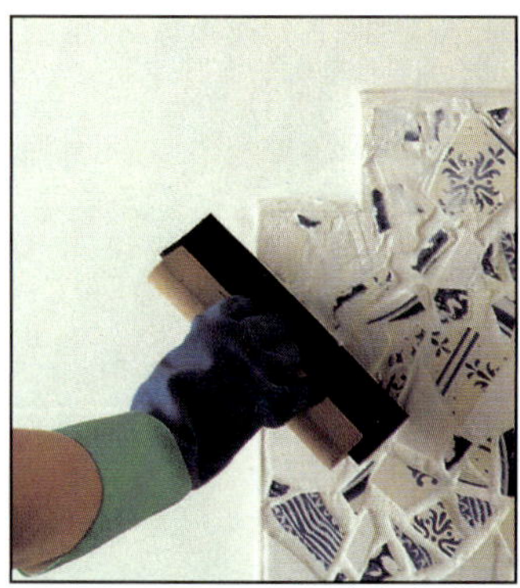

twelve *Re-grout over these pieces.*

Rubber Mats

Available at rubber manufacturers, this safety matting is valued for its non-slip and protective qualities, and since it is waterproof, it is particularly useful in, say, a bathroom. Rubber matting doesn't fray when cut and will happily absorb any lumps or strange seams in a floor. Attach it in place using a rubber contact adhesive then clean and seal the matting with silicone spray. Make sure your floor is sanded or put in a layer of fiberboard underneath before starting.

YOU WILL NEED

2 types of rubber safety mat
tape measure
metal ruler or straightedge
craft knife
rubber floor tiles in different patterns
rubber contact adhesive
WD-40 or silicone spray

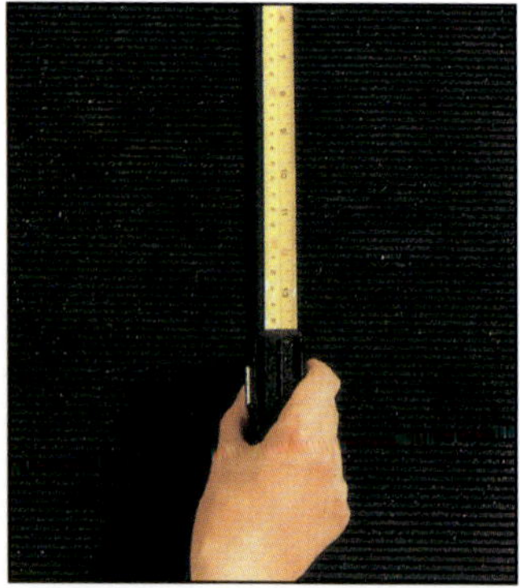

one *Measure the floor and the rubber matting and carefully trim the matting to size.*

two *For the corners, cut four squares. Divide these diagonally and make four squares by placing two triangles together, with the grooves running across and top to bottom. Position these and the runners around the edge of the room.*

three *Cut pieces from the other matting to fit the central section. Cut the tiles into squares, then cut holes in the mat at regular intervals to take the squares.*

four *Secure all the pieces with rubber adhesive, applied to both surfaces. Spray with WD-40 or silicone spray.*

DECKING

THE JAPANESE BATHHOUSE is the inspiration for this floor treatment, preventing pools of water from turning your bathroom into a skating rink and, at the same time, imparting the serenity of a Zen garden. In this project the decking forms a pontoon or walkway across the bathroom, but you could also use sections and cut them around the bathroom furniture. Ready-made decking is also available in strips or squares.

YOU WILL NEED

- tape measure
- saw
- quadrant beading
- decking or duckboards
- drill, with wood bit and pilot bit
- soft cloth
- paintbrush
- wood stain
- wood screws

one *Make sure you have a clean, level floor: cork tiles, wood and linoleum are all suitable. The existing floor will show through, so if you want to change the color, do so now. Measure and cut the two lengths of beading to the same length as the runners on the decking or duckboards. Drill holes through these new runners. Stain the two new long runners to the same color as the decking or duckboards.*

two *Measure the distance between the runners on the decking or duckboards.*

three *Space the new runners at a distance that will let the decking or duckboard runners slide between them, holding the board steady but letting it be lifted up for cleaning. Screw in place by drilling through the subfloor, using the correct type of bit for the type of floor you have. Slide the boards into place.*

CHECKED FLOOR MATS

FLOOR MATS ARE EASILY available, extremely inexpensive and particularly useful, as you can usually cut them without their edges fraying. They are manufactured in many finishes, some even incorporating words, symbols or pictures, and all are produced in manageable rectangles. When these heavily textured gray polypropylene mats are arranged with the pile alternately running in different directions, an interesting checker-board effect is achieved. For a different style of room, you could create a less subtle or even thoroughly funky effect by combining two or more colors. Make sure your floor surface is smooth before starting.

YOU WILL NEED

string
white crayon or chalk
tape measure
gray polypropylene floor mats
long metal ruler or straightedge
craft knife
notched spreader
floor adhesive

one *Stretch strings across the floor to find its center and mark the spot with a cross. If possible, link the opposite pairs of walls. Measure the floor and figure out how many floor mats you will need. Mark the cuts with a white crayon or chalk on the reverse of the floor mats.*

two *If the mats are of carpet quality, first score along the lines before cutting them with the craft knife. Then cut the mats to size.*

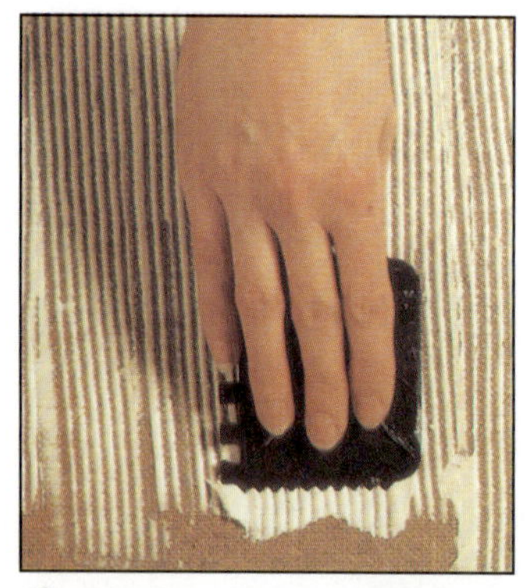

three *Using a notched spreader, apply floor adhesive to the floor.*

four *Starting at the center, carefully lay the mats in position, remembering that, for the checkerboard effect shown here, you need to alternate the weaves.*

PATCHWORK EFFECT TILES

Bathrooms and shower rooms are often thought of simply as basic utility rooms because they tend to get heavily splashed and also, with today's busy lifestyle, most people spend little time there. Consequently, their floorings are frequently correspondingly spartan. However, the wide range of ceramic tiles now available enables you to achieve stunning good looks without sacrificing practicality. Here we opted for stylish blue tiles in the same color range, accented by deep indigo.

YOU WILL NEED

pencil
ruler
tile adhesive (waterproof for bathrooms; flexible if on a suspended floor)
ceramic tiles
notched spreader
tile spacers
straightedge (optional)
squeegee
grout
damp sponge
lint-free dry cloth
dowel scrap

one *Draw a grid on the floor for the tiles. Using the spreader, spread some adhesive on an area of the floor small enough to be reached easily. Start laying the tiles. As you do so, use spacers to ensure that the gaps between them are even. Use a straightedge to check that all the tiles are horizontal and level. When all the tiles have been laid, use a squeegee to spread grout over them and fill all the seams—this is for both appearance and waterproofing.*

two *Wipe off the surplus grout with a damp sponge before it dries.*

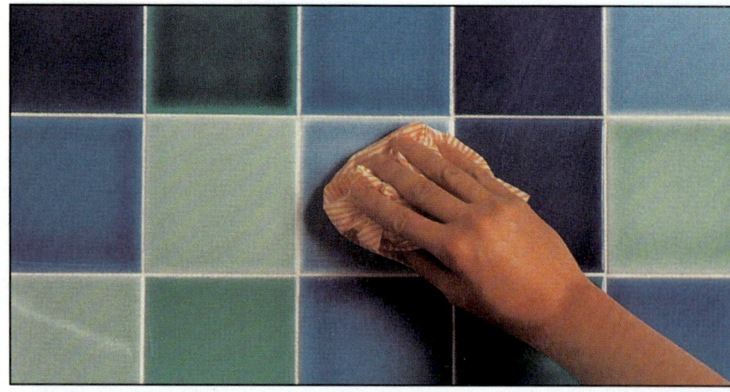

three *Buff with a dry cloth when the grout has hardened, then smooth the grout with the scrap piece of dowel.*

FISH FOOTSTOOL

THIS LOW STOOL decorated with the leaping fish motif looks good in a bathroom but can be used anywhere in the house where you need to put your feet up. Any small and useful stool that looks as if it is handmade can be a suitable candidate for this treatment. The fish and border blocks are cut from high-density foam, and the primitive designs, printed in off-white and light and dark blue, make patterns reminiscent of Balinese batik prints.

YOU WILL NEED

small stool
latex paint: dark blue, light blue and off-white
paintbrushes
tracing paper and pencil
scalpel
spray adhesive
high-density foam
scrap paper and plate

one *Give the stool two coats of dark blue paint and let dry. Trace, transfer and cut out the pattern shapes from the template section. Spray the shapes with adhesive and glue to the foam. Cut around the outlines and scoop out the details.*

two *Print five fish shapes onto paper and cut them out. Use them to plan the position of the fish on the stool.*

three *Apply off-white paint to the top of the fish and light blue to the bottom.*

four *Make a test print then stamp the fish lightly on the stool, printing both colors at the same time*

five *Paint the border stamp using the off-white paint. Stamp the design in a slightly haphazard fashion.*

Woven Blind

THIS COLORED MESH RIBBON is one of the new natural materials now available. It is stiff enough to hold its shape and be folded into sharp creases to make a blind. Use this treatment for a window that must be obscured from prying eyes while still allowing maximum light to penetrate the room—a bathroom, shower room or toilet. To make the most of their interesting texture and soft colors, the ribbons have been interwoven.

YOU WILL NEED

strips of woven mesh ribbon in 3 colors, 2½ inches wide

scissors

tape measure

2 broom handles

staple gun

awl

2 plumbers' pipe attachments

screwdriver

one *Cut lengths of woven mesh ribbon to the length of the drop, plus 8 inches. Wrap a 4-inch length around a broom handle and secure it with a staple gun. Leaving 1¼-inch gaps between each ribbon, continue attaching the ribbons along the broom handle with the staple gun. Finish with 3½ inches of bare wood at the end. Repeat this process to attach the ends of the strips to the second broom handle.*

two *Cut the remaining two colors into strips to fit the width of the blind, plus a 1¼-inch allowance on each side. Weave these through the first ribbons.*

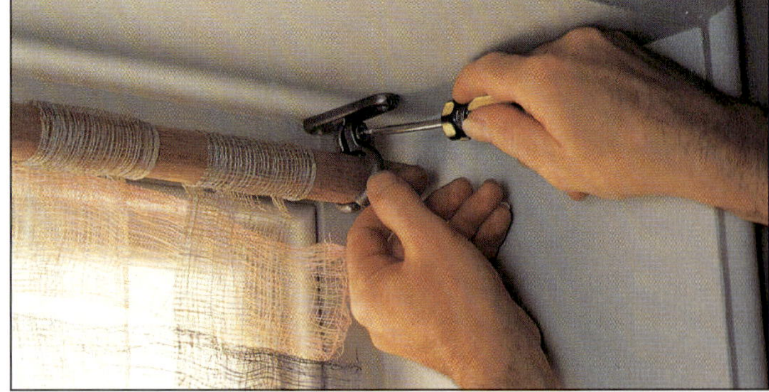

three *At each side, turn the seam over and crease it with your thumbnail, then staple the two ribbons together. Use an awl to make two small holes on either side of the underside of the top recess, then screw in the plumbers' fittings. Put the broom handle in position, then screw the front section of the fittings into position.*

HAND-PRINTED "TILES"

THESE IMITATION TILES ARE, in fact, hand-printed onto the wall using a homemade foam stamp. This is a quicker and less expensive alternative to ceramic tiles, and there are endless color combinations. If you opt for shades of one color, it is inexpensive because you can buy one pot of paint and lighten it with white to achieve different shades. Making a sponge stamp to apply the color is a quick and foolproof way of getting squares of color onto the wall. If you start with a white wall, the lines left between the fake tiles will look like the grouting between real tiles.

YOU WILL NEED

ruler
pencil
scrap paper
high-density foam
glue
craft knife
self-healing cutting mat
latex paint in 2 colors, plus white
paintbrushes
scissors
straightedge
level
old plates
small roller
small brush
clear varnish
varnish brush

one *Decide on the size of the tiles. Draw your design for the stamp on paper. Glue it to the foam and cut out unwanted areas. Angle the cut outward slightly from top to bottom. Make a stamp for each color. For this design you need six stamps.*

two *Use smaller pieces of foam to make a handle on the back of each stamp.*

three *Choose your colors—aquatic greens and blues work well in bathrooms. Here, a scheme of six shades, made from two basic colors, was used. One-third of each color was mixed together to make a third color, and then these three colors were halved again and lightened with white.*

four *Decide on the pattern; small-scale paper squares, painted in the different colors and/or shades, will help you plan the design.*

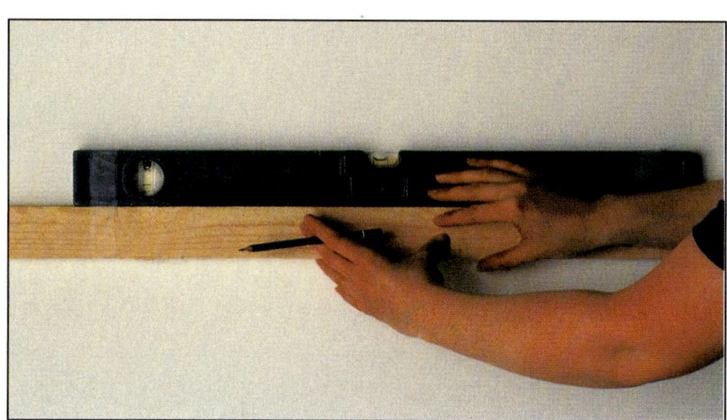

five *Mark horizontal guidelines on the wall with faint pencil lines, using a straightedge and a level.*

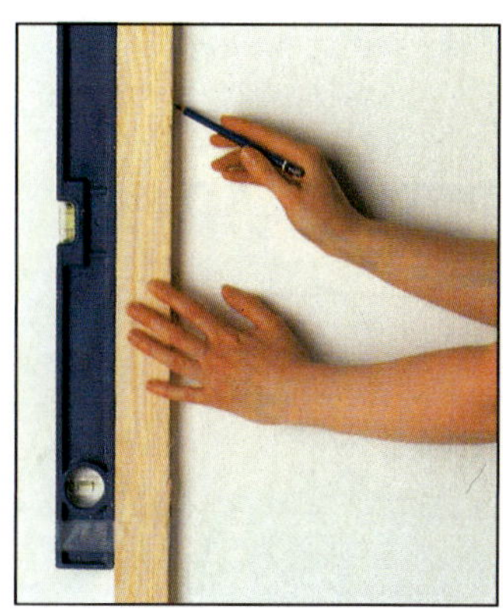

six *Mark vertical guidelines in the same way.*

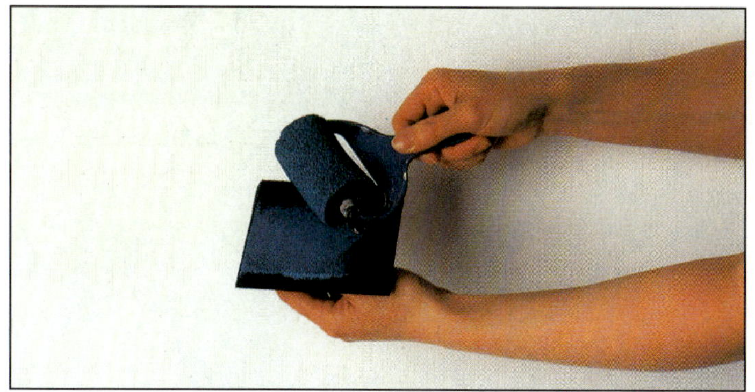

seven *Put some paint onto a plate and run the roller through it until it is evenly coated, then roll the paint onto the first stamp.*

CONTINUED OVER ➤

eight *Stamp the "tile" pattern onto the wall, pressing down firmly with your fingers. Go around the "grout" area and touch up any smudges with white paint and a small brush. Make sure no pencil guidelines are visible.*

nine *When dry, apply two coats of varnish to protect the surface and give it a wipeable finish.*

H
C

PLASTER STARS

Plaster has a powdery quality and a pure white color, which make it an especially interesting wall embellishment. Also, of course, it can be painted in any color of your choice. Most decorative plaster firms have lots of simple shapes—both modern and traditional—to choose from and will make a mold of virtually anything you like, so the possible variations of this effect are endless. This idea works well as a border above a skirting board or around a door, as well as in a defined area, such as behind a sink, as shown here.

YOU WILL NEED

plaster stars
scissors
masking tape
white glue or clear varnish
paintbrush
wall adhesive
wood scrap

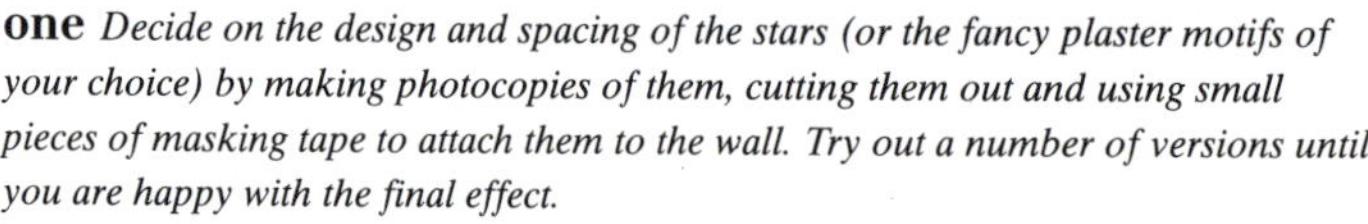

one *Decide on the design and spacing of the stars (or the fancy plaster motifs of your choice) by making photocopies of them, cutting them out and using small pieces of masking tape to attach them to the wall. Try out a number of versions until you are happy with the final effect.*

two *Seal the stars with clear varnish or white glue mixed with water.*

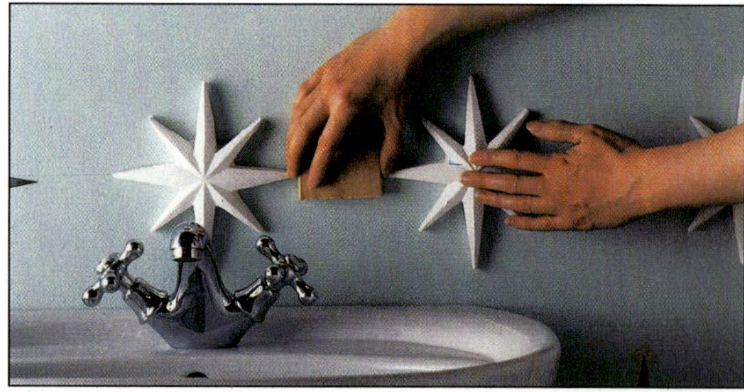

three *When the stars are dry, use wall adhesive to attach them to the walls. Use a wood scrap as a spacer for positioning the stars on the wall.*

GREEK KEY BATHROOM

This bathroom looks far too stylish to have been decorated by an amateur. The border design is a classic Greek key interspaced with a bold square and a cross. The black and gold look stunning on a pure white tiled wall. Every bathroom has different features, so use the border to make the most of the best ones, while drawing attention away from the duller areas. If you want a coordinated scheme, you could print a border on a set of towels, using fabric inks.

YOU WILL NEED

- tracing paper
- pencil
- spray adhesive
- high-density foam, such as upholstery foam
- scalpel
- acrylic enamel paint: black and gold
- 2 plates
- length of wood, 3/4-1 1/4 inches wide, depending on the bathroom
- masking tape

one *Trace and transfer the pattern shapes from the template. Lightly spray the shapes with adhesive and place them on the foam. To cut out the shapes, cut the outline first, then undercut and remove any excess, leaving the pattern shape standing free from the foam.*

two *Apply an even coating of black paint onto a plate. Place the length of wood up next to the door frame to keep the border an even distance from it. Make a test print on scrap paper, then begin by stamping one black outline square in the bottom corner, at chair-rail height. Print a key shape above it, being careful not to smudge the adjoining edge of the previous print.* ➤

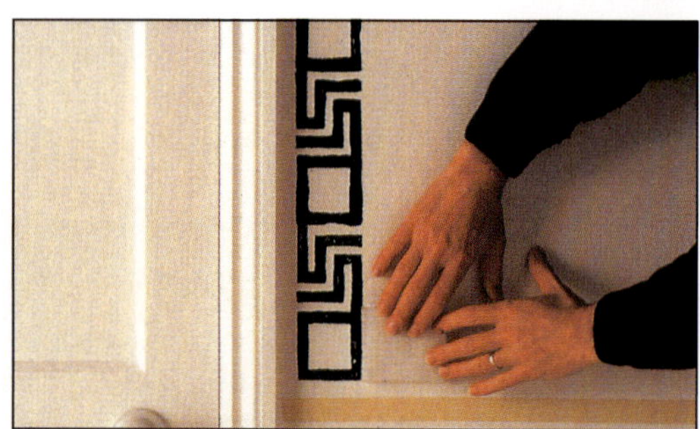

three *Continue alternating the stamps around the door. Mark the base line at chair-rail height with masking tape and alternate the designs along this line.*

four *Place a coating of gold paint onto a plate and dip the cross shape into it. Make a test print on scrap paper, then print the shape in the square frames.*

LAMPS AND LIGHTING

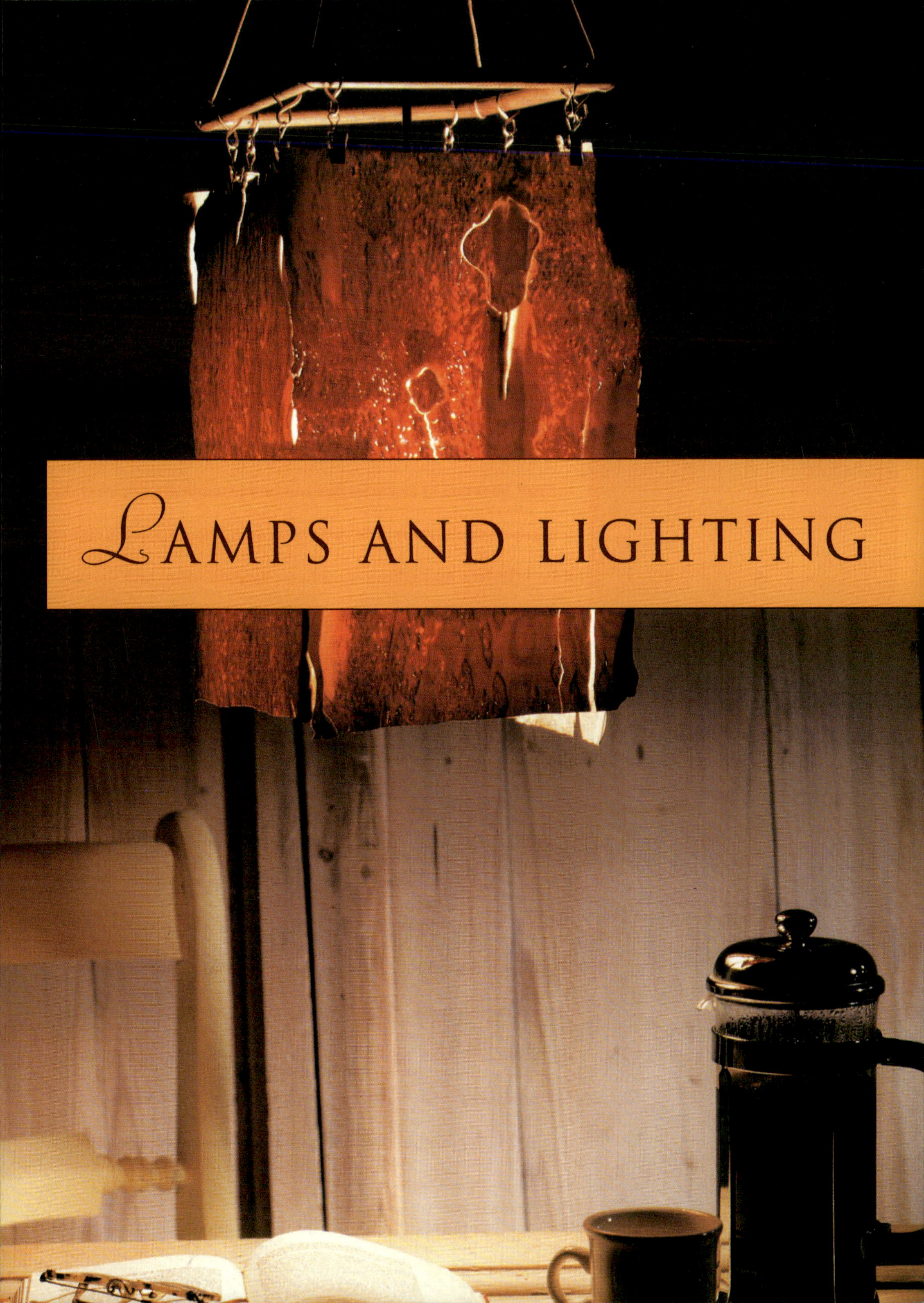

LAMPS AND LIGHTING

THE LIGHTING IN ANY ROOM IS CRUCIAL—it has a huge impact on the overall atmosphere. You can use it to highlight the contours of a room, to draw attention to desirable features and to tempt the eye away from less impressive corners. The options for interesting lights are endless, from high-tech spotlights to traditional standard lamps and classical sconces, and in this chapter we have tried to explore plenty of alternatives. Simple, step-by-step photographs show how to transform everyday lampshades and bases by using interesting paint techniques, by embellishing them with raffia or by covering them with beads. You can take a basic frame and cover it with tissue paper, or wrap it with muslin, or create a table lamp from bamboo—all the projects we have chosen are clearly photographed and provide a stunning array of different treatments for painting, adapting and decorating light fittings of all kinds. A good starting point is to look at the lights that are already in your home. Some of the quick projects could be just what is needed to give them an injection of style. Bases and shades can both be transformed with simple paint techniques or bead fringing, or stamped with paper designs. Patterns can be cut out of paper shades,

Left: The bird shapes stamped onto this paper lampshade are inspired by traditional Inca patterns.

to allow shards of light to escape, and tin shades can be drilled or pierced for a similar effect. Old-fashioned wall lights that you want to get rid of can be replaced with small spotlights and creatively shaded with unusual objects such as baskets, colanders or roof slates ... or perhaps you will come up with an unusual idea of your own. Lighting is more than a practical necessity, it is one of the interior designer's most powerful tools, so use it creatively and really enjoy transforming the look of your rooms.

STRING-BOUND LAMP BASE

STRING-BINDING IS AN INNOVATIVE way to disguise an unappealing lamp base or to dress up a cheap flea market find. Look for a lamp base with good proportions and a pleasing shape. There are many kinds of string to choose from, ranging from smooth, fine, waxy and white to fat, loose-weave brown twine, and all give different effects. You can paint the string afterward if you want it to fit in with a room's color scheme.

YOU WILL NEED

glue gun with all-purpose glue sticks

china, glass or wooden lamp base

ball of string

scalpel or scissors

one *Heat the glue gun and apply a dot of hot glue below the flex on the bottom edge of the lamp base. Press the string in place. Apply a thin line of glue to the string and wind it around the lamp base, keeping the string taut as you wind.*

two *Wind the string up around the base, dotting it with glue in key positions to hold the rows tightly together. When you reach the flex, cut the string. Apply a dot of glue on the other side of the hole and start the winding again with a new piece of string.*

three *Apply the glue at intervals as you wind and glue. Use plenty of glue when winding around concave shapes, as this is where the string may sag if it is not held firmly enough.*

four *At the top of the lamp base, apply an extra dot of glue and cut the string at an angle so that it lies flat.*

BIRD CAGE

ALREADY DECORATIVE AND DESIGNED to hang at eye level, birdcages need little adaptation to turn them into unusual Asian-style shades. This charming little wooden cage was made in the Far East. However, judging by the spacing of the bars, it cannot have been intended for keeping a real bird. Look for wooden or bamboo cages like this in gift stores, florist's or import stores and even at flea markets and yard sales (just make sure that they are in good condition). If necessary, adapt the steps to suit the shape of the cage. Hang the lampshade from a chain so that it can twist in passing air currents and use a low-watt bulb for safety.

YOU WILL NEED

small wooden or bamboo birdcage
saw
wire cutters
tissue paper
pencil
scissors
ready-mixed wallpaper paste
paintbrush
pendant lamp fitting

one *Using a saw and a strong pair of wire cutters, cut off the struts that make up the base of the cage.*

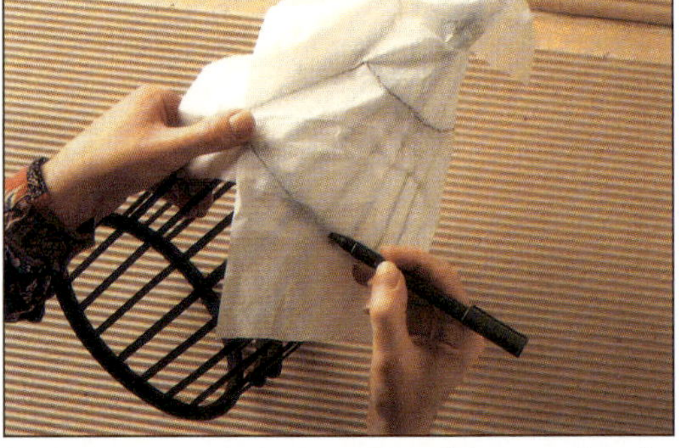

two *Roll a sheet of tissue paper around the top section of the cage—here it is conical. Mark the shape in pencil.*

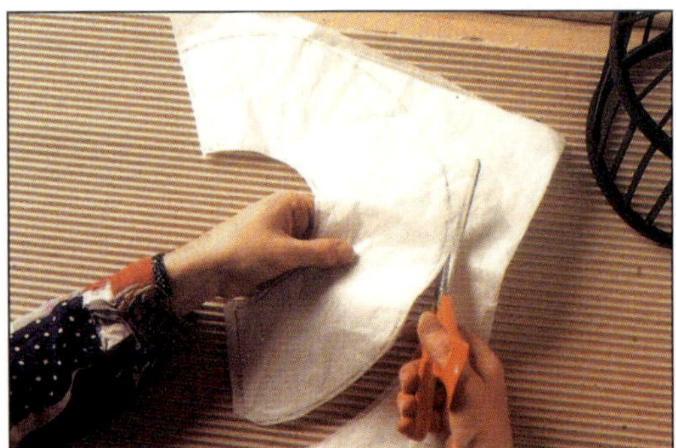

three *Cut out the shape. Apply wallpaper paste to the inside of the struts of the top section. Roll up the tissue paper, then unfold it inside the cage, pressing it against the pasted struts to form a lining. Trim away any excess.*

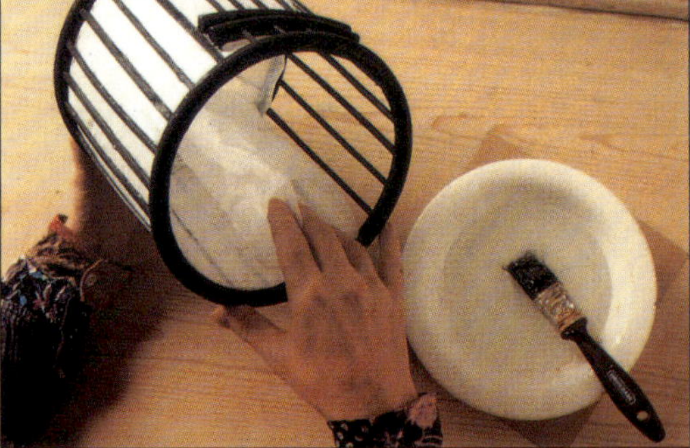

four *Cut out a rectangle of tissue paper to line the rest of the cage. Paste the inside of the struts, then place the tissue paper inside the cage, as before. Let dry. Ask an electrician to attach the pendant lamp fitting and to wire it to an electric switch.*

PINK TISSUE SHADE

THIS BRILLIANT PINK PAPER lampshade will make a stunning centerpiece for a room and will cast a flattering pink light over everything—and everyone—at the same time. Make the size of the lampshade appropriate for your room. As it is very lightweight, it can be made quite big, which is useful if your house has high ceilings. Attach equal lengths of chain to the curled hooks and hang the light fitting in the center, so that the hot air rises out of the top of the shade.

YOU WILL NEED

bonsai-training wire
wire cutters
thinner wire
long-nosed pliers
chains to hang the shade
glue gun with all-purpose glue sticks
bright pink, good-quality tissue paper
water-based varnish
paintbrush

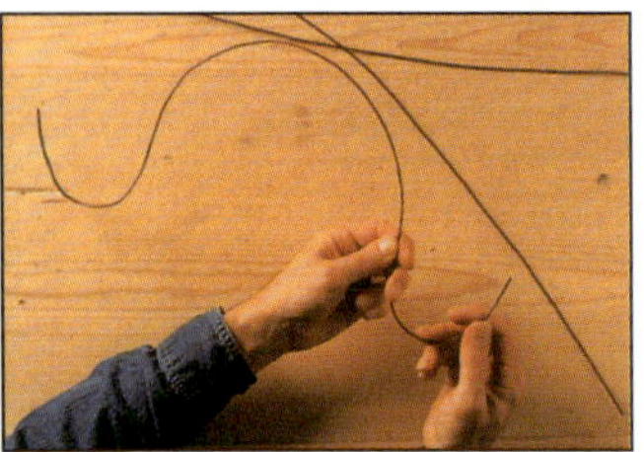

one *Cut three equal lengths of bonsai wire for the struts. Bend them into wavy shapes. You can exaggerate the shape, as the wire will spring back a little. Bind the ends together with thinner wire, using long-nosed pliers.*

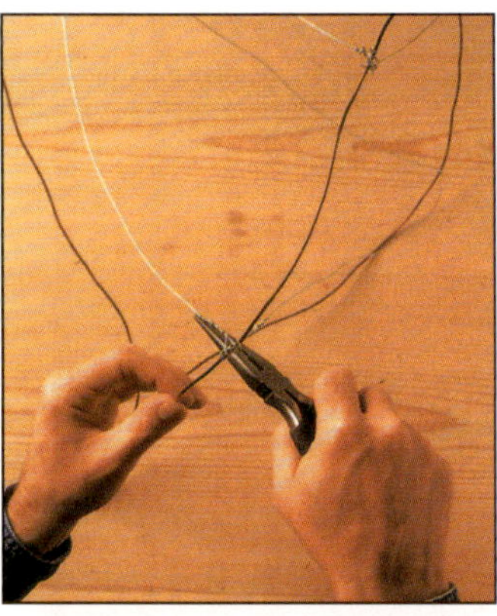

‹ two *Attach a length of the thinner wire about 4¾ inches from the end of one strut, winding it around to secure it. Then take it around the other two struts in the same way. This will form the top of the framework. Wind around two more lengths of the thinner wire in the same way.*

three *Using the pliers, curl the ends of the struts where the chains will be attached. Apply glue to one of the struts and fold the edge of a piece of tissue paper over it. Stretch the tissue across and glue it to the next strut.*

four *Continue in this way, overlapping where necessary, until the framework is covered. Wind and glue a strip around the point where the three struts are joined. Brush on a coat of varnish to tighten up the paper and bond the layers.*

LIME-WASHED LAMP BASE

ONE OF THE MOST effective ways of updating a dull lamp is to give the base a fashionable paint finish and add a fresh new shade. Look for second-hand bargains at flea markets or antique stores, then give them new life with a special paint treatment. This turned-wood lamp base has been given a limed look by applying and rubbing back two colors. The first, blue-gray coat of paint is rubbed off but remains in the grain and the grooves. The second coat of white paint is also rubbed back, leaving a transparent, lime-washed look.

YOU WILL NEED

plain turned-wood lamp base

fine-grade sandpaper

latex paint: blue-gray and white

paintbrushes

2 cloths

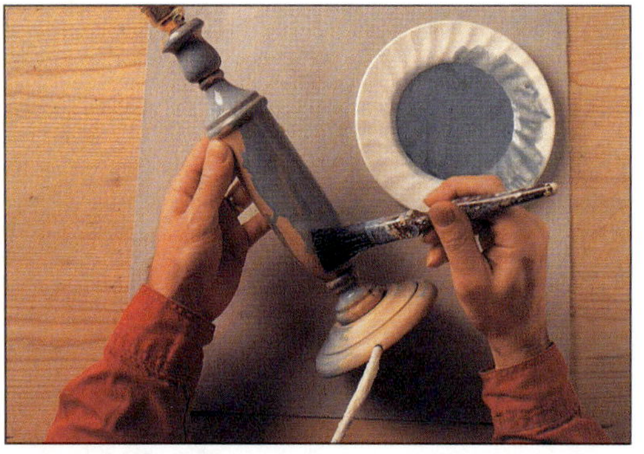

one *Remove any surface finish on the base and sand it to a smooth finish. Then paint the bare wood with a coat of blue-gray paint.*

two *Before the paint has dried, rub it off with a cloth, leaving some color in the grooves and grain. Let dry.*

three *Gently rub the decorative, raised parts of the lamp base with fine-grade sandpaper.*

four *Paint the whole lamp base with white latex. Rub off the paint before it has dried, using another cloth, and then let dry. Gently sand the decorative raised parts to create the lime-washed look.*

GILDED PAPER PATCHWORK

GIVE TWO PLAIN LAMPSHADES a glittering new look by covering them in paper patchwork in two different styles. Although the techniques for each shade differ slightly, they have enough in common to be used as a stunning pair. The paper can be any type that is not too thick: newsprint, tissue paper, brown wrapping paper, photocopied typescript, sheet music or fine woven paper. Make a feature of ragged edges and avoid a regular, neat finish. The very special finishing touch is added with flashes of brilliant gold. The leaf used here is called Dutch metal. It is applied in the same way as gold leaf but costs much less. If you have never done any gilding before, these shades are a good starting point.

YOU WILL NEED

CUT-PAPER PATCHWORK

selection of interesting paper materials: corrugated cardboard, colored scrim ribbon, brown wrapping paper, handmade papers, paper mesh

scissors

plain cream fabric or paper lampshade

ready-made wallpaper paste or white glue

household paintbrushes for applying glue, an artist's paintbrush and a firm-bristled brush

gold size

Dutch metal leaf

soft cloth

TORN-PAPER PATCHWORK

selection of interesting paper materials: photocopied typescript, paper mesh, brown wrapping paper, handmade fiber paper, handmade paper, tracing paper

shellac

household paintbrushes for applying stains and glue, and an artist's paintbrush

turpentine

water-based stain: a natural wood shade

plain cream paper lampshade

ready-made wallpaper paste or white glue

gold size

Dutch metal leaf

soft cloth

CUT-PAPER PATCHWORK

one *Cut out "squares" from the different materials. Make them roughly equally sized, but trim them at an angle on both sides to taper slightly to fit the shade's conical shape.*

two *Try various combinations of texture and color until you are happy with the arrangement. Apply a coat of wallpaper paste or white glue to the backs of the shapes and stick them in place on the shade. Make sure the edges meet in order to form a solid patchwork.*

three *Paint "stitches" of gold size to link the squares together. Think of patchwork stitching, and make the lines vertical on the top and bottom and horizontal on the sides.*

four *Cut the Dutch metal leaf into strips, still on the backing sheet. Gently press the leaf onto the tacky gold size.*

five *Use a firm-bristled brush to clean away all the excess leaf, leaving just the stitches. Burnish with a soft cloth.*

TORN-PAPER PATCHWORK

one *Tear the different papers into similarly sized shapes, leaving the edges ragged and uneven.*

two *Tint one-third of the shapes with shellac. It is fast-drying and will make the papers stiffer and also slightly transparent. The brush will need cleaning with turpentine.*

three *Tint another third of the paper shapes using water-based stain and let them dry.*

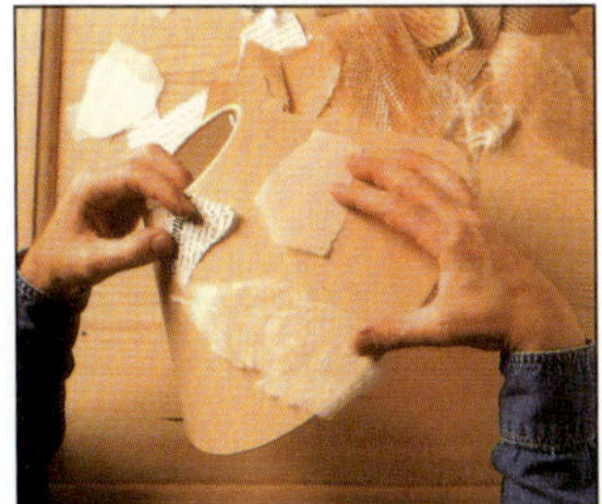

four *Arrange the shapes on the shade, overlapping them in places and making a feature of the ragged edges. Practice with different arrangements until you are happy with the result.*

five *Apply wallpaper paste or white glue to the backs of the shapes and stick them onto the shade, using the stained shapes first. Space them wide apart to start and build up gradually.*

six *Fill in the gaps with the untinted torn papers.*

CONTINUED OVER ➤

seven *Paint a neat ½-inch borderline all around the top and bottom of the lampshade with gold size.*

eight *Cut the sheets of Dutch metal leaf into strips, leaving the backing sheet still in place.*

nine *Press the strips against the tacky gold size along both edges. Overlap them when you need to; the leaf will only stick to the sized sections.*

ten *Finally, rub off any excess metal leaf and burnish the entire design to a shine with a soft cloth.*

SKEWBALD SHADE

A SKEWBALD PATTERN—brown patches on a white pony—is perhaps the boldest of animal-skin prints and always makes a strong style statement. It is very adaptable and can be used in a contemporary, minimalist room, a child's bedroom, a study or as a classic Tex-Mex decorating style. Brown packing paper is strong and makes satisfactory stencils; the shapes of the patches need to be irregular to imitate the unique character of a skewbald pattern.

YOU WILL NEED

felt-tipped pen
brown packing paper
scalpel
cutting mat
spray adhesive
plain fabric lampshade
brown acrylic paint
paintbrush
glue gun with all-purpose glue sticks
brown fringing

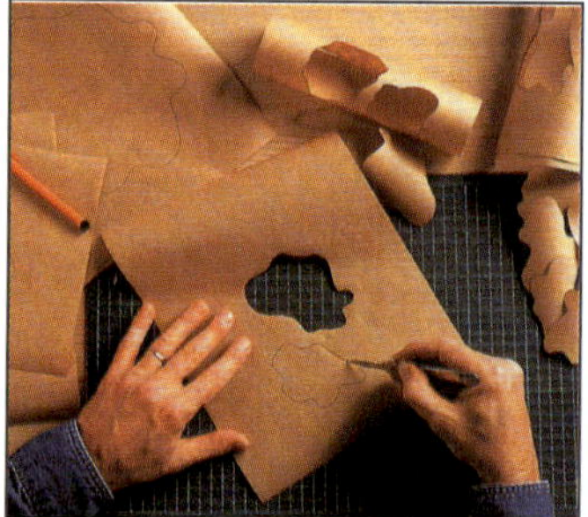

one *Draw irregular cloud-like shapes on brown packing paper. You need several small ones and a bigger one. Keep the shapes curved, with no sharp angles. Use a scalpel to cut out the stencils.*

two *Spray the backs of the stencils very lightly with adhesive and arrange them on the shade. Position the large shape to overlap the rim. Stencil the brown shapes onto the shade, working inward from the edges and making sure the paint gets into the weave of the fabric.*

three *Stencil the larger shape right up against any edging strip, or over the rim of the shade. The pattern will appear more natural if you do it this way. Use the glue gun to stick the fringing around the bottom rim.*

ECCENTRIC CREPE

CREPE BANDAGE IS GREAT material to work with and makes a fun lampshade. It has just enough stretch to give a good tight fit, and the textured surface clings to itself as you layer the bandage. Keep an even tension as you wind it around a wire frame and use hot glue at key points, if necessary, to prevent any slipping or sagging. Make sure you leave an opening at the top to let the hot air escape.

YOU WILL NEED

copper bonsai-training wire
wire cutters
long-nosed pliers
thinner wire
glue gun with all-purpose glue sticks
rolls of bandage

one *Cut three equal lengths of bonsai-training wire and bend each into three curves, using the pliers. The wire will straighten up when you release it, so exaggerate the shapes as you bend them.*

two *Bind the three ends of the bonsai wire firmly together with the thinner wire. Be generous with the amount of wire because you need to make a solid fixture. Use the long-nosed pliers to help you to bind tightly.*

three *Run another length of wire between the three struts winding it tightly around each strut to form the lowest of three enclosing wires that will later provide the framework for the bandage binding.*

four *Wind around two more lengths of wire to complete the frame. Twist the ends of the struts into curved "feet."*

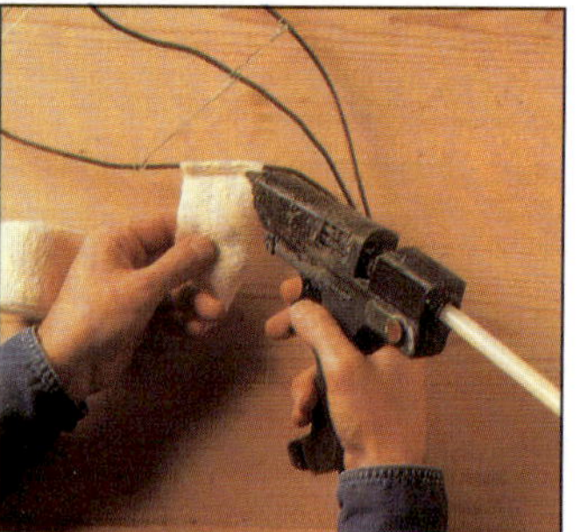

five *Glue the bandage to a strut about 2 inches from the binding at the top. Wrap tightly to secure. Wrap the bandage around the framework, pulling it to get the tension right. Apply glue whenever it crosses a strut.*

six *Wrap and glue a small length of bandage to cover the wire binding right at the top of the framework. Use the glue gun to seal the edge and be sure to leave a 2-inch gap around the top in order for the heat to escape.*

CORRUGATED LAMP BASE

CORRUGATED CARDBOARD HAS SCULPTURAL qualities that elevate it from a boring packaging material. Its construction, with one smooth and one rigid side, means that it can be rolled into even, tubular shapes to make a lamp base. This is one project in which the fact that corrugated cardboard is very lightweight might be a disadvantage, so take care to site the lamp where it is unlikely to be knocked over.

YOU WILL NEED

roll of corrugated cardboard
ruler
pencil
scalpel and cutting mat
glue gun with all-purpose glue sticks
bottle adapter lamp fitting

one *Cut a 20½ x 13¾-inch rectangle of corrugated cardboard and roll it lengthwise, leaving the center hollow for the lamp fitting. Glue the loose edge.*

two *Cut a 53 x 1½-inch rectangle from the corrugated cardboard. Measure in 7¼ inches from the top-left corner, draw a line between this point and the bottom-right corner and cut along this line. Apply glue to the square end and line it up with the column base. Wrap it around, gluing to hold the layers together. Keep the base flat.*

three *Cut a 20½ x 1½-inch rectangle of corrugated cardboard, then glue and wrap it around the base to add extra stability.*

four *Cut another 53 x 1½-inch rectangle of corrugated cardboard, then glue and wrap this around the top of the column. Keep the top flat. Ask an electrician to install the bottle adapter lamp fitting and to wire it to a cord.*

Starry Night

Capture a small piece of the midnight sky by making this cut-out lampshade. Choose the deepest of blue shades, as the effect will be best if the light is completely blocked except by the star-shaped holes. The stars should be ½–¾ inch wide; any smaller or larger and the effect will be lost. Use a very sharp scalpel to cut the points of the stars, and always cut from the top of a point toward the middle. The lampshade looks spectacular at night, but you will get a similar effect by day with the decoration of raised metal stars. Available at notions stores, these have spikes at the back that are pressed through the shade and folded flat on the inside.

You will need

- white paper
- pencil
- scissors
- spray adhesive
- navy blue paper lampshade
- cutting mat
- scalpel
- metal-star studs
- high-density foam rubber

one *Using the template, draw 50 stars on white paper. Cut the paper into small squares with one star in the center of each. Spray the backs of the squares with adhesive and stick them inside the shade. Arrange them randomly rather than spacing them in a pattern.*

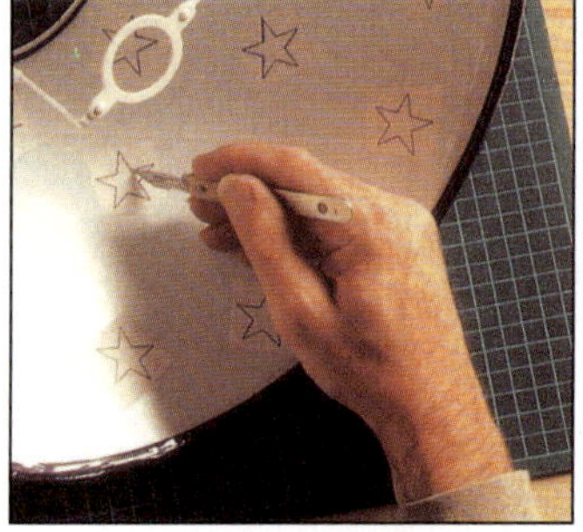

two *Rest the shade on the cutting mat, and cut out the stars using a scalpel. Working from the right side of the shade, cut through any threads that remain and gently push the stars inward to remove them.*

three *Make sure that the spikes on the backs of the metal stars are all straight, otherwise they will not penetrate the shade. Hold a piece of dense foam rubber inside the shade to give you something to push against, then press the stars through and fold the spikes over at the back.*

CHINESE LANTERN

THIS STICK-AND-CARDBOARD lampshade has a natural look by day, but lights up like a skyscraper at night. Sheets of corrugated cardboard can be bought in a range of colors, from natural to fluorescent, and the wooden skewers can also be painted. You can use the lantern over any small table lamp or even a candle. If using a candle, place it in a secure holder.

YOU WILL NEED

metal ruler, approximately 1¼ inches wide

pen or pencil

13¾ x 10¼ inch sheet corrugated cardboard

scalpel

cutting mat

scrap paper

gold spray paint

package of wooden skewers

one *Use the width of the ruler as a spacer and draw vertical lines and slits across the cardboard. Cut slits across alternate columns, starting one in from the edge. Move the ruler down a width at a time; continue cutting to the bottom of the cardboard.*

two *Cut through the uncut rows in the same way, but starting with the ruler a half-drop down, so that the slits fall halfway between the first ones. Continue until the sheet is covered with a "brickwork" pattern of slits.*

three *Protect your work surface with scrap paper, then spray the smooth side of the cardboard with gold paint. Turn the cardboard over and weave the skewers in and out of the slits. Allow about 1 inch to protrude on one edge to give the shade legs to stand on. Trim the last column to within ½ inch of the slits so that the seam will not be too bulky. Overlapping the two edges (with the gold side inside), weave the last skewer through the double thickness to attach the lampshade edges together.*

TRIMMED SHADE

TURN A RATHER BORING, plain-colored lampshade into a completely wacky extrovert by adding a dangling fringe of unusual trimmings. Almost anything non-perishable that will thread can be used—the brighter, the better. The choice is yours. Check out the toy store, particularly the inexpensive selection, where bright beads, miniature dolls and animals and fluorescent plastic balls are all waiting to be snapped up. Another good source is a stationery store; multicolored plastic paper clips can be put to a decorative use their inventors would never have imagined.

YOU WILL NEED

plain conical lampshade
square of paper or cardboard
pencil
triangle
hole punch
strong thread
needle
selection of beads, toys, baubles, etc.
glue (optional)

one *Place the lampshade on a square of paper or cardboard and draw around the bottom edge in pencil.*

two *Use a triangle to divide the circle into eight equal segments.*

three *Replace the shade on the paper or cardboard and mark the divisions around the edge in pencil.*

four *Use the hole punch to make eight small holes about ½ inch up from the edge of the shade, in line with the pencil marks.*

five *Attach a bead securely at the end of the length of thread, as an anchor, then thread on a selection of your chosen baubles and beads.*

six *Attach the thread to the shade by sewing it through one of the punched holes several times, then finishing with a secure knot. An extra bead can be glued to the edge of the shade to cover the thread. Decorate the rest of the shade in the same way.*

HANDMADE-PAPER GLOBE

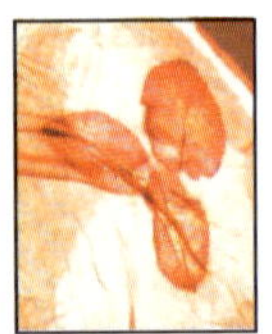

COVERING AN INFLATED BALLOON with papier-mâché may not be the most original creative technique, but old ideas are often the best ones. You could use a variety of different papers; here, light tissue paper has been mixed with fibrous handmade-paper scraps containing dried flower petals and leaves. Keep the same thickness across the top of the balloon, but let it taper off toward the tied end.

YOU WILL NEED

handmade-paper scraps containing leaves and flower petals
ready-mixed wallpaper paste
paintbrush
inflated balloon
cream or white tissue paper
gauze or mesh
pin
scissors
pendant lamp fitting
cardboard ring
all-purpose glue

one *Apply paste to small pieces of paper and stick them onto the balloon in a random overlapping arrangement, beginning at the top.*

two *Cover the top two-thirds of the balloon with three layers of paper, tissue paper and gauze or mesh. Set aside until bone-dry; this may take several days. Use a pin to burst the balloon and remove it from the shade.*

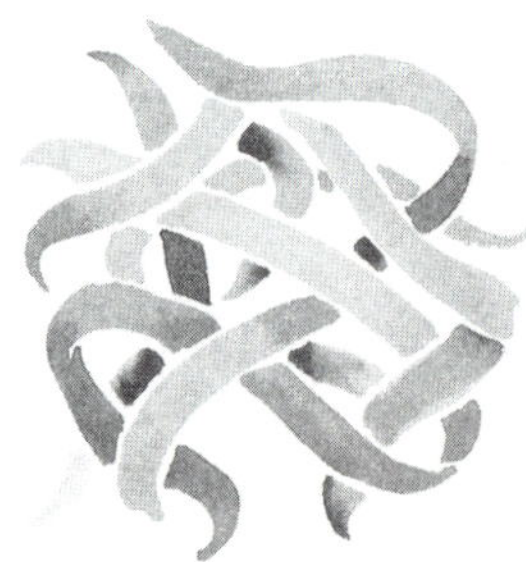

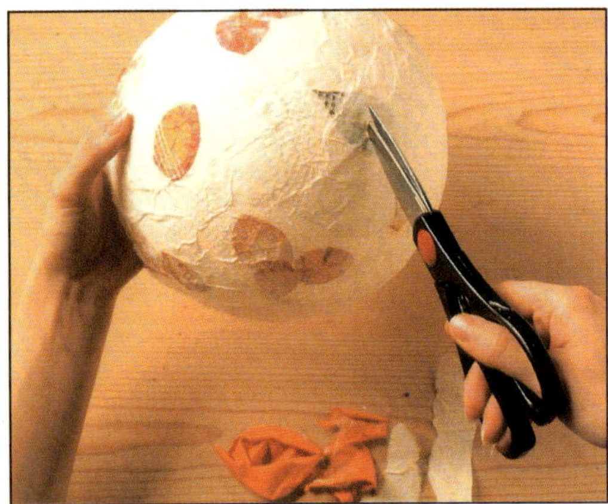

three *Cut a small hole in the top of the shade, using the lamp fitting as a guide to the right size.*

four *Reinforce the hole by gluing a cardboard ring inside the shade. Screw the two halves of the pendant lamp fitting together, one on either side of the shade, and ask an electrician to wire the fitting to an electrical cord.*

TRIPOD LIGHT

THIS CONTEMPORARY-LOOKING standard lamp appears quite delicate, but the tripod legs are very stable. The simple design makes it ideal for a Japanese-style room, particularly if a plain shade is used. The base consists of three pieces of wooden dowel fitted into angled holes drilled in a circle of wood. The frame of the shade is covered with butter-colored muslin. The lamp is assembled by screwing a lamp attachment to the wooden disc, over a central hole through which the cord passes.

YOU WILL NEED

- dark oak wood stain
- 1-yard lengths wooden dowel
- soft cloth
- pencil
- compass (optional)
- square piece of wood
- clamp
- 2 scraps wood
- coping saw
- drill, with twist bit
- craft knife or scalpel
- wood glue
- tape measure
- large cylindrical shade frame
- dressmaker's scissors
- 3 yards unbleached butter-colored muslin
- dressmaker's pins
- rust-colored 4-ply yarn
- darning needle
- shade holder

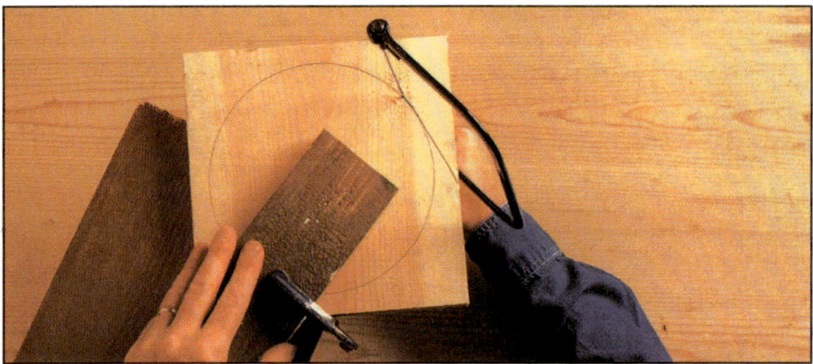

one *Rub the wood stain into the dowel with the cloth. Draw a circle with a 7-inch diameter on the square of wood, then clamp it ready for sawing. Protect it from the clamp with scraps of wood. Saw in from the edge at an angle and follow the curve with the blade. Move the wood around so that you can saw comfortably.*

two *Using a drill bit that is marginally narrower than the dowel, drill three angled holes through the wood circle. To do this, hold the drill directly above the center, then tilt it slightly toward the edge; the angle will then be correct.*

three *Shave the ends of the lengths of dowel slightly with a craft knife or scalpel, apply wood glue and then push them into the drilled holes. Apply glue to the lengths of dowel where they intersect. Let dry. To cover the frame, measure around the circumference and height. Cut a double thickness of muslin 4 inches wider than the height of the shade and long enough to fit around it, with an extra 1½ inches as a seam allowance. Pin one end of the muslin along a strut, leaving ¾ inch at each end for a seam, and gathering the fabric slightly as you go.*

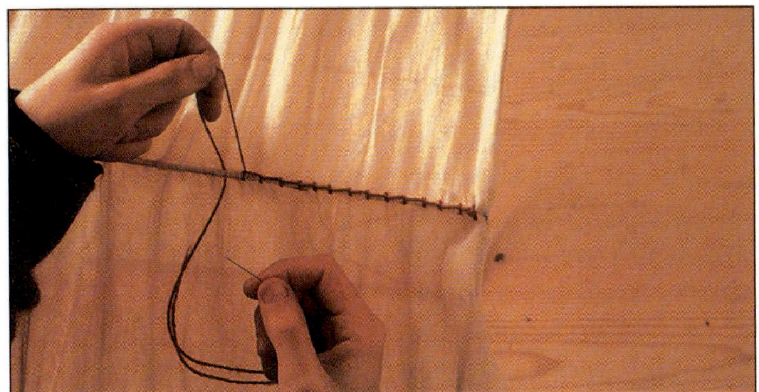

four *Pin the muslin along the next strut and sew in place using a blanket stitch. To sew a blanket stitch, insert the needle behind the strut and pull it out in front. Do not pull the yarn through. Take the needle through the loop of yarn, then pull the yarn tight. Continue stitching the muslin to each strut in the same way until you reach the first pinned seam. When you reach the final strut, join the two edges and stitch them together, still using blanket stitch.*

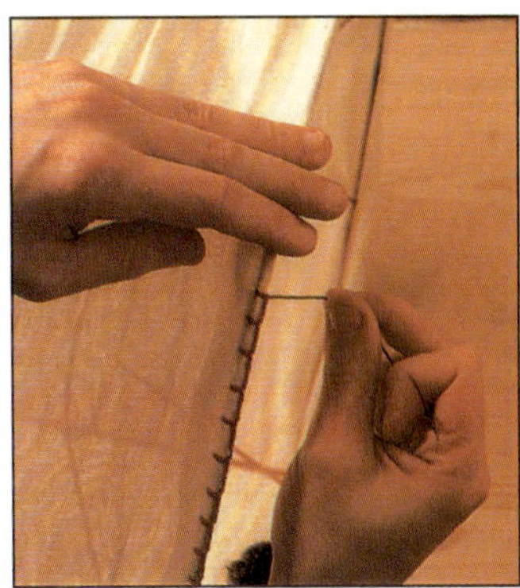

five *Finish off the top and bottom of the shade by rolling the edges around the wire frame, then pin and stitch them in place. Ask an electrician to attach the light attachments to the tripod, then place the shade on the holder.*

RAFFIA STANDARD

Standard lamps provide the perfect overhead light to read by without killing the atmosphere of a room as bright central ceiling lights often do. Placing one in the corner means that an individual can see what he or she is doing, while the rest of the room can be dimmed for watching television or general relaxation. Here, a turned-wood standard lamp has been enclosed in a sheath of raffia which is finished off by a "thatched" base that resembles a very clean chimney-sweep's brush.

YOU WILL NEED

turned-wood standard lamp
rubber bands
several bunches of natural-colored raffia
scissors
colored raffia

one *Place a rubber band at the base of the lamp pole, near the floor. Unravel the raffia and cut a handful of 15-inch lengths. Fold the lengths in half and tuck them under the band, so that it holds them in place just below the fold. Continue inserting folded lengths until the base is completely covered.*

two *Wind a strand of raffia around the rubber band several times and tie it tightly to hold the raffia base in place.*

three *Place a rubber band around the top of the lamp. Tuck bunches of raffia under it until the pole is covered. About 10 inches down from the band, wind a strand of raffia around the pole. Continue at intervals.*

four *At the base, tuck the raffia into the top of the base raffia, then bind to cover the seam. Trim any loose ends. Cover the plain raffia bindings with colored raffia.*

INCA BIRD PRINT

MAKE AN IMPRESSION on a tall conical lampshade by stamping it all over with a strong printed pattern. The shade used here is made of thin, mottled cardboard that resembles vellum in appearance and casts a warm glow when the lamp is lit. The stamp is based on an Inca bird design that is bold enough for a beginner to cut and is even enhanced by a slightly rough cutting style.

YOU WILL NEED

- white paper
- spray adhesive
- high-density foam rubber
- scalpel
- white glue
- flat plate
- ready-made wallpaper paste
- golden brown and darker brown ready-mixed watercolor paint in droppered bottle
- small paint roller
- conical paper lampshade

one *Photocopy the motif from this page. Spray the back of the copy lightly with adhesive and stick it onto the foam block. Cut around the shape with the scalpel and scoop away the background so that the motif stands out.*

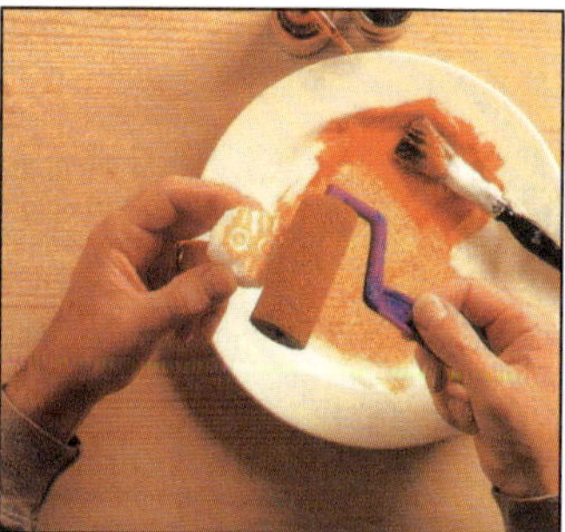

two *Put a spoonful of white glue on the plate. Add a similar amount of wallpaper paste and a few drops of golden brown paint and mix well. Run the roller through the mixture to coat it evenly and use it to coat the stamp.*

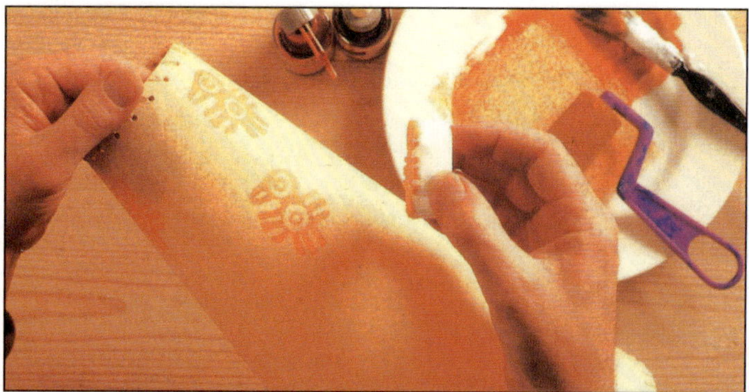

three *Print the bird motif on the lampshade by pressing the stamp onto the surface and then removing it directly. The wallpaper paste makes the paint gelatinous, leaving an interesting texture when you lift the stamp.*

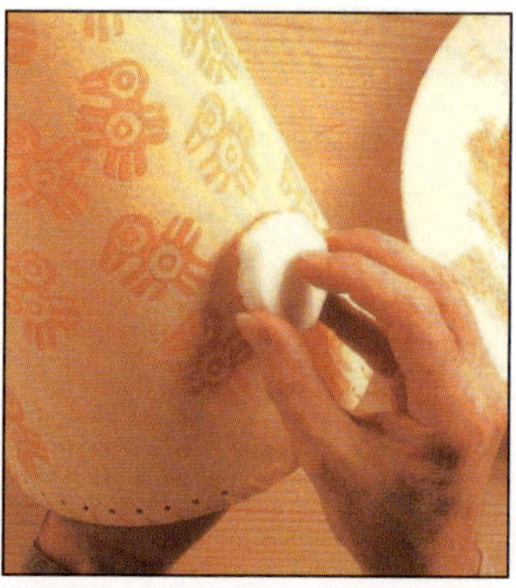

four *Add a few drops of the darker paint to the mixture and stamp more motifs on the shade.*

新潮
日本文学
小辞典
新潮社

STAINED-GLASS BULB

LIGHT BULBS CAN BE PAINTED in jewel-like colors to look like little illuminated stained-glass balls and create an unusual and impressive conversation piece. Ordinary light bulbs can be used, but the one shown here is a large 60-watt decorative globe bulb. Painted bulbs deserve to be shown off, so hang them low over a table, with a shallow shade that will not distract attention from the pretty patterns cast by the colored shapes. Special glass paints are available at art and craft stores. You don't need to buy much, as a little paint will go a long way.

YOU WILL NEED

- waterproof marker
- 3 pieces of cardboard
- light bulb
- scalpel and cutting mat
- strip of corrugated cardboard
- sticky tape
- glass paints: pink, green, yellow, blue and black
- paintbrushes

one *Draw a circle on each piece of cardboard: one the size of the widest part of the bulb, one the size of the center of the star design and the third in between the two. Cut out the circles. Slip each piece of cardboard in turn over the bulb and draw a guideline on the glass where each sits. Carefully draw the guidelines for the rest of the design.* ›

two *Roll up the corrugated cardboard strip to make a base for supporting the bulb. Secure the roll with sticky tape.*

three *Begin painting the top of the bulb. Start with the central dot and radiating arms of the star. Support your painting hand with your free hand to steady it.*

four *Working carefully, fill in all the different parts of the design, applying more than one coat where necessary to build up the color. Let the paint dry, then paint a thick black line around each color section to give a stained-glass effect.*

CLOTH SHADE

LOOSELY WOVEN COTTON, such as that used to make dishcloths, is the ideal fabric for this rustic lampshade. In this project, the fabric is used to cover an ordinary lampshade frame. The tube is opened out and pulled down over the bare lampshade frame. A second layer of fabric then covers the first and is attached so that the edges roll over to create an interesting pattern. Finally a third layer of fabric is pulled over to strengthen and protect the design.

YOU WILL NEED

lampshade frame
tape measure
scissors
$1\frac{1}{2}$ yards loosely woven cotton
dressmaker's pins
needle
matching cotton thread
embroidery needle
yellow embroidery floss

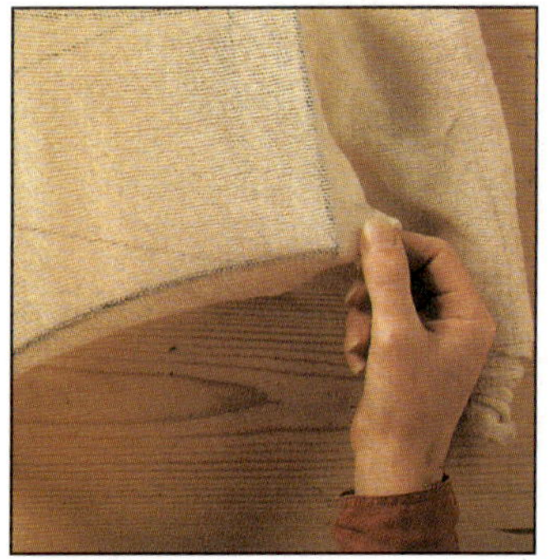

one *Cut a length of cloth three times the height of the frame. Pull the cloth down over the frame so that you have just enough to roll under the bottom.*

two *Divide the remaining cloth in two, then pull a second length down over the frame. Catch the middle of each side along the top and bottom of the frame and pin. The unpinned edges will roll up. Sew the first layer and the pinned section of the second layer securely to the frame.*

three *Pull the third length of cloth down over the frame and pin all around the top and bottom edges. Then stitch to secure the cloth in place.*

four *Cross-stitch around the top and bottom of the shade with a length of yellow embroidery floss to add a subtle finishing touch of color to the shade.*

PRIMARY PLASTIC

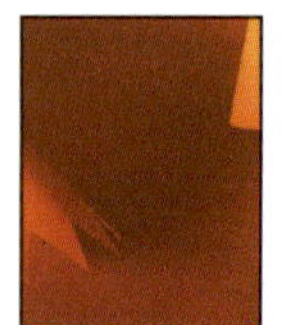

THIN SHEETS OF OPAQUE, colored plastic, which are available at art supply stores, make excellent lampshade materials. They are available in a range of colors, and the edges can be cut decoratively, with no need for seaming, and fastened in place with nuts and bolts. As plastic is a fairly rigid material, it does not require a supporting frame, although you can use one for a template if you wish.

YOU WILL NEED

brown paper
spray adhesive
sheet of red or yellow plastic
craft knife
cutting mat
pen
ruler
broad cloth tape
masking tape
scrap of wood
drill, with twist bit
nuts and bolts
shade carrier (optional)

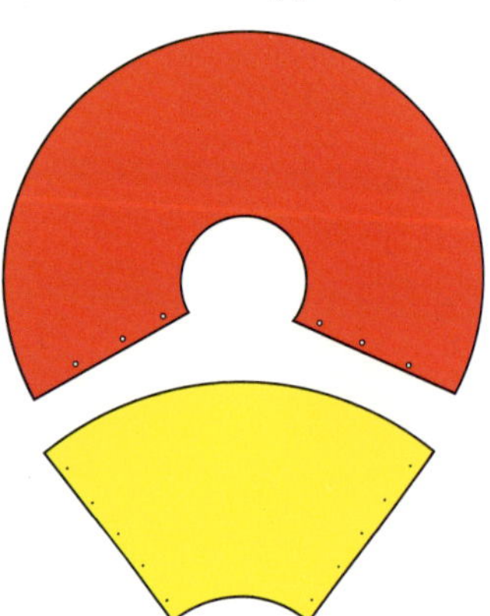

RED SHADE

one *Enlarge the template and transfer it onto brown paper. Spray the back with adhesive and stick it onto a sheet of red plastic. Cut out the shade with a craft knife. Make a cardboard template for the sawtooth pattern. Place it on the edge of the brown-paper pattern, on the plastic sheet, and draw around it to create a zigzag.*

two *Cut out the sawtooth border. Cut toward the outside edge every time. Remove the paper and attach the long edges of the shade together with cloth tape. Place a strip of masking tape along this seam. Place the wood block behind the seam, then drill three holes through the plastic. Remove the tape and screw in the nuts and bolts.*

YELLOW SHADE

one *Enlarge the template and transfer it to brown paper. Spray the back with adhesive and stick it onto a sheet of yellow plastic. Place on the cutting mat and cut out the shade using a craft knife.*

two *Overlap the two long edges of the shade and secure with a strip of cloth tape. Then place a strip of masking tape along this seam.*

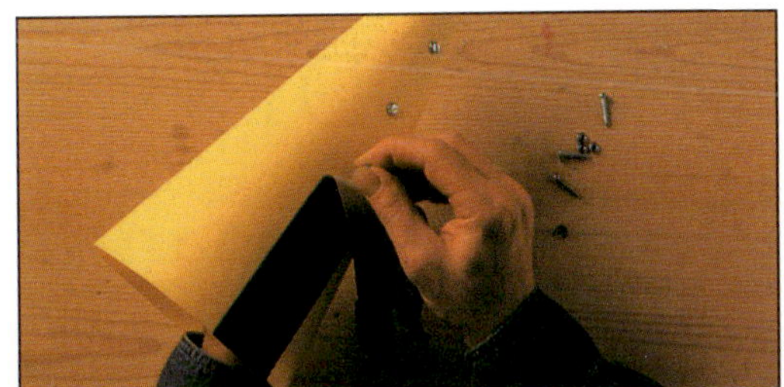

three *Using a ruler, mark five equal divisions along the seam. Place a wooden block behind the seam and carefully drill a hole through the plastic at each mark. Start peeling off the tape at the top of the shade and screw in a nut and bolt each time a drilled hole is exposed.*

TRIO OF LAMPSHADES

NOTHING COULD BE QUICKER, easier or cheaper than painting squiggles, spots or flecks of color on a few plain lampshades to add a touch of individuality to any room. The three shades shown here have each been made using a different decorative technique. All are fun to do, and only the black-and-white stripes require a steady hand. Use plain fabric shades and experiment with color, using it to reinforce an existing decorating theme or to add a spark of brilliance and give a quick face lift to a monotonous color scheme.

YOU WILL NEED

BLOTTING-PAPER EFFECT

plain fabric lampshade

paintbrushes

bright blue ready-mixed watercolor paint

droppered bottle

PAINTED-LINE EFFECT

cardboard

scalpel

cutting mat

metal ruler

plain fabric lampshade

black acrylic paint

paintbrushes: large square-tipped and small

FLECKED EFFECT

plain fabric lampshade

cardboard

pencil

scalpel

cutting mat

toothbrush

water-based acrylic, poster, watercolor or gouache paints: yellow ocher, brick-red and cream

paintbrush

BLOTTING-PAPER EFFECT

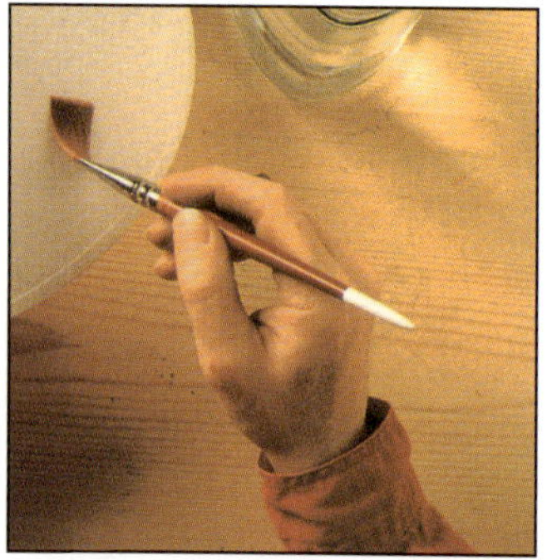

one *Dampen the whole outer surface of the fabric lampshade with water, using a paintbrush.*

two *Fill the droppered bottle with blue paint and squeeze it gently to leave one small drop on the shade. Watch the blot spread so that you can judge where to position the next drop.*

three *Turn the lampshade with your free hand and, as you do so, drop equal amounts of paint, spaced fairly evenly all around the shade.*

four *Fill the spaces between the blots with a more random pattern of differently sized dots, but be careful not to cover the original lampshade color completely.*

five *Holding the lampshade from the inside with your free hand and resting your painting hand on the work surface, paint the top and bottom rims solid blue.*

PAINTED-LINE EFFECT

one *Cut a right-angled piece of cardboard with one edge the same length as the height of the shade. Angle the other side to make it easy to hold.*

two *Hold the square-edged cardboard up against the shade and paint a wide squiggle to the right of it, using the large brush. After each squiggle, move the cardboard along; this will ensure that you paint vertically and don't slide off in one direction, which is very easily done when painting a shape like this.*

three *Paint fine squiggly lines between the fatter ones, using the small paintbrush. Support the wrist of your painting hand with your free hand to keep it steady.*

four *Finish off the lampshade by painting the top and bottom rims with a solid black line.*

CONTINUED OVER ➤

FLECKED EFFECT

one *Place the shade upside down on the piece of cardboard and draw around the inside of the top rim. Cut this circle out, just slightly larger than the drawn pencil line, and place it on top of the shade to prevent any paint from dripping onto the inside.*

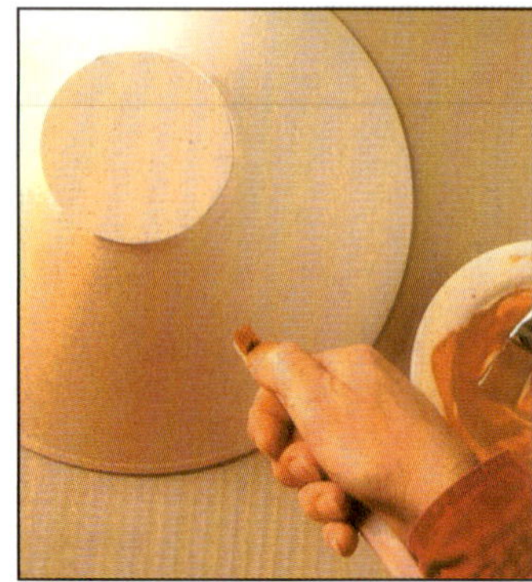

two *Place the shade on a protected work surface. Fill the toothbrush with the yellow ocher paint, then draw your thumb backward over the bristles to fleck the lampshade with color. Try to get a fine, even covering, but let the background show through.*

three *Clean the toothbrush, then dip it into the brick-red paint. Using the brush at an angle, make randomly placed wedge-shaped marks at different angles over the flecked pattern. Don't try for a regular pattern: Look at the example shown here to judge the effect you are after.*

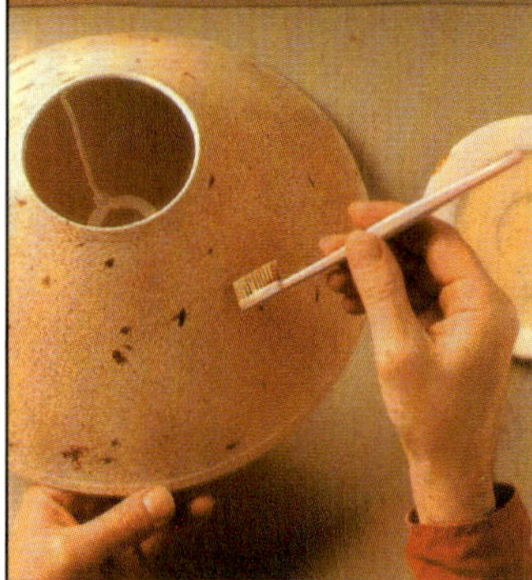

four *To finish the decoration, clean the toothbrush, then apply the cream paint in the same way as the red. It may not show up much, but when the lamp is lit at night, all will be revealed.*

ASIAN SHADE

THE GLOBAL SUPERMARKET is now well and truly a part of our lives, and strings of brightly colored fabric birds from Asia have become as familiar to us as imports from closer to home. The lampshade made here is a combination of Chinese bamboo weaving and Indian textile work, put together in a way that is reminiscent of an Australian bush hat. The lampshade looks best when hung low over a kitchen table or anywhere that needs light combined with vibrant color.

YOU WILL NEED

string of Indian hanging textile birds
scissors
needle
embroidery floss
assorted beads
bamboo lampshade
scrap-paper measuring strip

one *Cut the retaining bead off the string of hanging birds, and remove the cord to separate the birds and beads.*

two *Thread the needle with about 12 inches of embroidery floss and tie a bead at the end of the floss. Push the needle up through the existing hole in one of the birds, and then thread on three more beads.*

three *Attach the bird to the shade, letting it hang down three finger-widths from the rim. Divide the rim into ten equal sections and attach a bird at each division.*

four *Attach an inner row of birds one-third of the way up the shade. Position them so that they hang between the birds on the outer row and at a slightly higher level. Use a paper measuring strip to calculate the floss lengths required.*

WOODY NIGHTSHADE

WOOD VENEER IS A THIN SHEET shaved from a seasoned tree trunk and is sold at lumberyards that supply furniture makers. Each sheet is unique, so choose the veneer with the best grain; it will look even better with light shining through it. The lampshade shown here is made from flamed-ash veneer. The veneer hangs from a simple wooden frame but you could use a square picture frame (without the glass). Carefully remove one edge of the frame, thread on the curtain rings and glue the piece back. Suspend the veneer from the frame using clipped curtain rings. Hang the lampshade on leather thongs or cord from a ceiling hook, with a pendant lamp fitting and bulb dangling inside it.

YOU WILL NEED

- 4 equal lengths of wooden dowel, mitered
- glue gun with all-purpose glue sticks
- curtain rings with clip attachments
- metal ruler
- scalpel
- sheet of wood veneer
- 4 equal lengths of cord or leather thongs

one *Attach three pieces of dowel using the glue gun. Thread the rings onto the frame before gluing the last piece of dowel in place.*

two *Measure the width of one side of the frame and, using the scalpel, cut four strips of veneer, one for each side. Make the length roughly twice the width; for a natural look the pieces should not be precisely the same size.*

three *To finish, attach two clips to each sheet of veneer, then tie a cord or thong to each corner for hanging.*

LEADING LIGHTS

CHANGE YOUR SHADE and lamp base to something unique and quite sensational within the space of just an hour. Here, a basic shade was decorated with rough string threaded through punched holes. It is very easy to punch holes around the top and base of any shade, using a hole punch, and then thread through string, raffia, ribbon or yarn. To continue this idea, put small string bows at intervals around the shade and intersperse them with dried leaves.

YOU WILL NEED

lamp base and shade
hole punch
rough string
scissors
glue gun and glue sticks
dried leaves

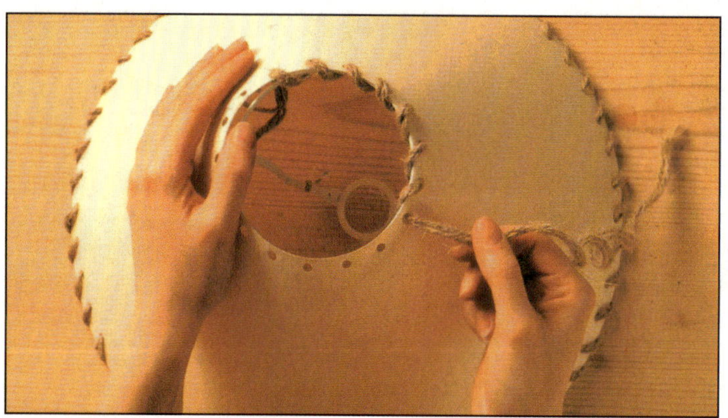

one *Punch evenly spaced holes around the top and bottom of the shade. Thread lengths of string through the holes, top and bottom.*

two *Use the glue gun to stick the leaves around the shade.*

three *Tie small string bows and glue them between the leaves.*

four *Put a line of glue down the back of the metal base. Starting from the top, bind a long length of string tightly around the stem. Use glue and a second length of string to cover the base. Press to make sure the string binding is absolutely firm. Make sure that the ends are glued securely in place.*

BENT-WIRE CHANDELIER

MAGICALLY CRAFTED FROM A roll of wire, this delicate little chandelier was twisted and curled into shape with long-nosed pliers. Making it is so much fun that you will probably want to make a pair. Bonsai-training wire, sold at garden centers and by bonsai-tree specialists, was used here. Hang the chandelier from a chain and hook so that it can twist and turn in passing air currents.

YOU WILL NEED

roll of silver bonsai-training wire

wire cutters

long-nosed pliers

roll of gardening wire

4 reinforced screws and screwdriver

glue gun with all-purpose glue sticks

4 thumb-tacks

4 nightlights

large sequins

one *Cut a 13¾-inch length of bonsai wire for the first kidney-shaped curl. Hold the wire with one hand, grip the end with the pliers and shape a curl. Holding the first curl in your hand, curl the other end. Make a single curl from a smaller piece of wire.*

two *Make two more single curls. Each branch is made of these four pieces. Cut a 4¾-inch length of gardening wire and bind the kidney-shaped curl and two of the single curls together, as shown. Wind the wire around neatly like a spring.*

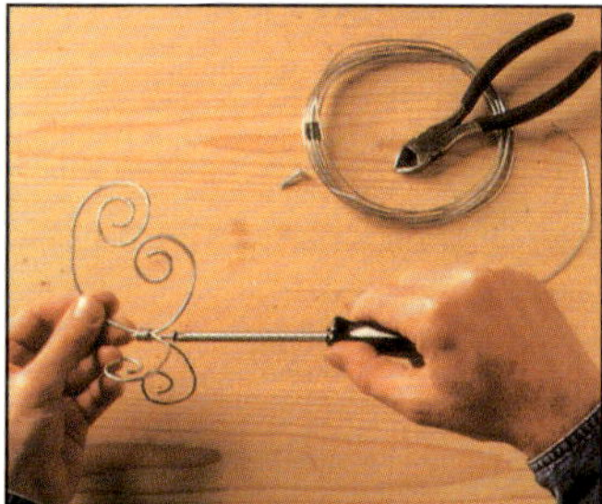

three *Screw a self-tapping screw into the center of the binding, leaving at least ½ inch protruding at the top.*

four *Bind the third single curl onto the back of the kidney shape, winding a length of gardening wire into a neat binding as before. Snip off the end of the gardening wire at an angle, close to the binding. Repeat the above steps to make the four branches.*

five *Cut a 20-inch length of bonsai wire for the central column. Twist one end into a spiral and the other into a small hook. Make two small, tight curls and bind them into the top end of the column, facing inward. Bind the four branches onto the column.*

six *Apply a dot of glue to one of the screw heads and immediately sit a drawing pin on it, pointing upward. Repeat with the three remaining screw heads. Press a nightlight down onto each of the drawing pins. Thread the large sequins onto the curls.*

CHICKEN-WIRE TORCH

THIS DRAMATIC SHADE WOULD look fabulous in an entrance hall or at the top of a staircase, especially if it is teamed with an interesting paint finish. The basic shape is a cone, but the shade's character relies on the layers of chicken wire interwoven with silver solder and copper wire. Spirals of wire, creating an unusual textural patchwork, hold the ragged, torn paper in place. The shade is hooked over a small halogen wall spotlight by means of a slit cut into the wire mesh. The light picks up the colors of the silver solder and the copper wire, adding another layer of brilliance on top of the grayish wire mesh, and shines through the different paper textures. The shade is very lightweight, but a coat of black latex applied to the base of the cone will add visual weight and create a feeling of substance and balance.

YOU WILL NEED

36 x 24 inches chicken wire
long-nosed pliers
hammer
wire cutters
small halogen wall-light fixture
silver solder
copper wire
3 different, highly textured natural-weave papers
black latex paint
paintbrush
screw and screwdriver

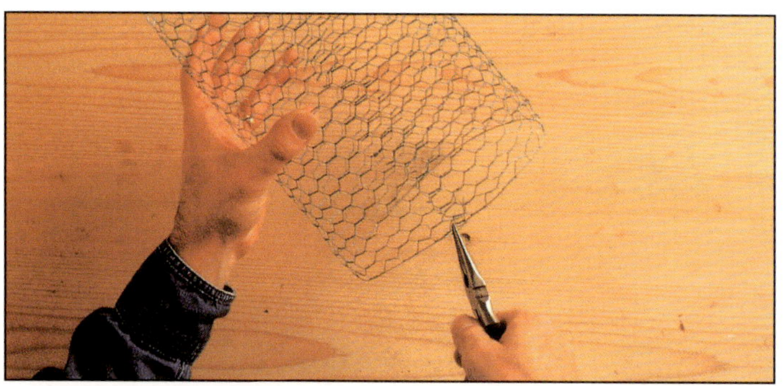

‹ **one** *Roll the chicken wire into a tube with a 6½-inch diameter. Using the pliers, pinch and twist the cut edges to make one end neat.*

two *Roll the tube into a cone shape, so that the unneatened end tapers down to a point. Pinch and twist the cut wire to hold the shape firm.*

three *Compress the narrow end of the chicken-wire shape by hammering it on a hard surface. The wire mesh will scrunch up into a fairly solid mass.*

four *Use the wire cutters to make a slit in the back of the cone. This should be large enough to fit over the base of the wall-light fixture and let the cone lie flat against the wall.*

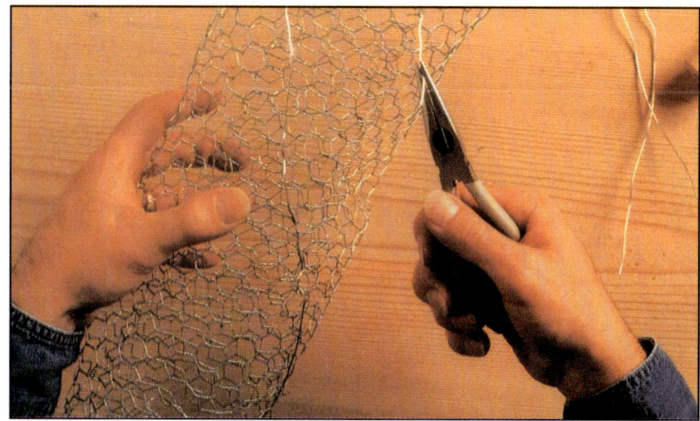

five *Cut two 20-inch lengths of solder and weave them in and out of the mesh. Follow the shape of the cone, spiraling the wire upward.*

six *Cut similar lengths of copper wire and weave them through the mesh. Here, a zigzag pattern is used.*

seven *Wind copper wire around the outside of the cone, "sewing" it through the mesh in places.*

eight *Add a patchwork of chicken-wire pieces. The different depths of wire will be picked out and enhanced by the light when it is switched on.*

nine *Tear up the three sheets of paper. The edges should be rough and ragged. Tear some pieces into strips and others into random shapes.*

CONTINUED OVER ➤

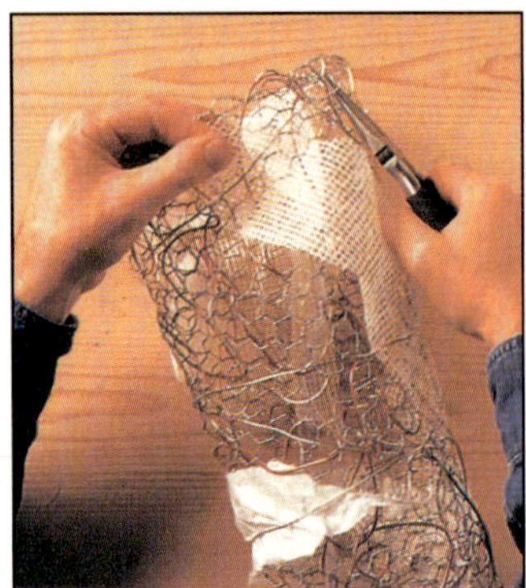

ten *Place the paper pieces randomly on the outside of the cone, and use spiraling strands of wire to bind them into place.*

eleven *Use the long-nosed pliers to tweak and pinch the paper in places, so that it becomes a part of the structure instead of just sitting on the outside.*

twelve *Carefully dry-brush black latex paint onto the narrow base of the torch to give a matte-black charcoal finish.*

thirteen *Fit the torch over the wall-light fixture. Bend the mesh so that it fits snugly around the base and put a screw in the wall near the top of the torch to hold it in place.*

Above: Chicken wire is cheap and surprisingly easy to work with. You can form the wire into elegant candleholders, candlesticks and shimmering bead domes.

ANGULAR WALL LIGHT

THIS UNUSUAL WALL LIGHT IS a two-colored plastic shade slotted over a standard mini-spotlight. The two halves of the shade are simply clamped together with two shiny metal clips on each side. Before fitting the two pieces together, cut a hole in the back piece to slot over the base of the spotlight. Make the hole the same size as the spotlight base so that it fits snugly and will not slip. Place the back of the shade in position first, making sure that the bulb remains far enough from the plastic to avoid both accidents and damage to the shade.

YOU WILL NEED

brown wrapping paper
pencil
ruler and triangle
scissors
spray adhesive
sheet of yellow plastic
sheet of red plastic
craft knife and cutting mat
small halogen wall-light fixture
4 small metal clips

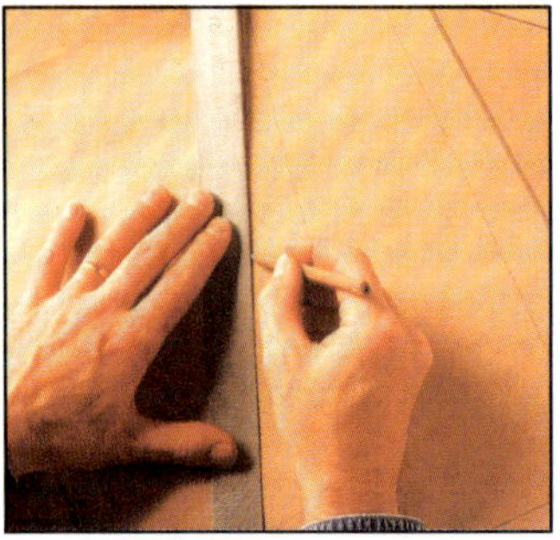

one *Enlarge the template on a photocopier. Transfer it twice to brown wrapping paper. Cut out the two patterns, leaving a ¾-inch seam allowance all around the edges.*

two *Spray the paper patterns with adhesive and stick one on each plastic sheet. Cut out the shapes and nick the ends of the fold lines, so that they will be obvious from both sides.*

three *Remove the paper, then score the fold lines, but be careful not to cut more than the surface. Practice on the scraps first to get the pressure right.*

four *Turn the sheets over and score the fold lines again, working between the nicks at each end. Fold up the shades. Cut a hole in the back shade to fit the spotlight base, place it over the spotlight, then attach the front piece with metal clips.*

FLASHLIGHTS

A ROW OF ANGLED chrome spotlights adds a designer touch to any shelf display, but wiring and attaching them can be a time-consuming and expensive undertaking, especially with the extra safety factors essential in a bathroom. Here is a way to obtain an even better effect without spending a lot of money or even plugging anything into the electrical circuit. All you need is three cheap chrome flashlights, a length of towel rail with sockets, a few fixtures and an hour to spare.

YOU WILL NEED

3 small or medium chrome flashlights
3 small leather straps
pencil
hole punch
3 small jubilee clips
chrome shower rail with 2 sockets
screwdriver
drill, with masonry bit
plastic anchors and screws
level

one *Wrap a strap around a flashlight and mark the point where the buckle spike should enter. This will guarantee a good tight fit. Mark all the other straps in the same way.*

two *Punch a hole in each strap where marked. Slide the jubilee clips over the rail, loop a strap through each, then use a screwdriver to tighten the clips.*

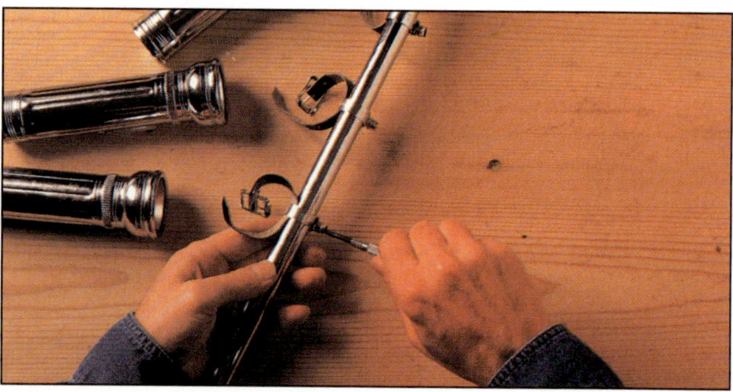

three *Ensure that they are spaced evenly. Put the rail into the sockets and attach these to the wall. Use a level to ensure that the rail is level before attaching. Buckle the flashlights to the rail.*

CONTAINERS

CONTAINERS

CONTAINER DECORATING PROVIDES highly imaginative and innovative projects for transforming old containers or creating new ones in quick, simple, stylish and beautiful ways. Put an end to cluttered shelves and overcrowded closets, protect your belongings from dust, spills and breakage and find exciting ways to jazz up your home. If you've always thought of containers as mere practical objects in which to store anything from flowers to cookies, then you will be amazed by how cheap, everyday items can be easily transformed into chic containers, bringing a personal dash of style into every room in your house. Take old paint cans, jam jars, bottles, bags, baskets or shoe boxes and give them a new lease on life by converting them into plant pots, shoe racks or funky bureaus—cover them with fabric, perhaps, or glue on buttons, beads or shells. There are no limits to what you can do. The projects in this chapter will serve as a rich source of ideas to help you add a variety of colors, textures, patterns and shapes to whatever style of organization you opt for. Whichever project you choose to make, you can simply use our suggestions as a springboard for your own

Choose containers with interesting shapes, such as the bottles pictured below, then all you need to do is to emphasize their basic forms by adding texture to surfaces.

creativity, so don't be afraid to amend or embellish any of the projects you discover here once your confidence has grown. Adapt ideas and techniques to suit your own style and existing decor. An afternoon spent taping and gluing is totally absorbing and satisfying, and at the end of the day you will have a wonderful sense of achievement, too.

All the techniques used here are clearly photographed for each project and are designed to be easy to follow.

STRING BOTTLES

LIQUEUR BOTTLES HAVE SUCH attractive shapes that it seems a shame to put them into the recycling bin. This method of recycling enables you to continue enjoying them even after you have enjoyed their contents. The bottles used here are sherry, crème de menthe and Armagnac. This project is very easy to do and it can almost seem like therapy once you've gathered together a ball of string, some glue, a pair of scissors and three interestingly shaped bottles. Make yourself comfortable, put on some relaxing music and start winding the string around the bottles.

YOU WILL NEED

ball of thick string

glue gun with all-purpose glue sticks (or all-purpose glue)

3 interestingly shaped bottles

scissors

one *Coil one end of the string around like a coaster to make a base. Place a dot of glue in the center of the bottle base. Heat the glue gun and apply glue in spokes over the base. Press the string onto them. Draw a ring of glue around the edge to make the base secure.*

two *Circle the bottle with the string, working your way up and applying sufficient glue as you go. Make sure you get a good bonding on the bends and curves.*

three *When you reach the top of the bottle, cut the end of the string and apply plenty of glue to it so the finish is neat with no fraying. Repeat these steps with the other bottles.*

FANCIFUL SHOE BOX

IF YOU ARE ONE of those people who always takes the shoe box home with new shoes, only to throw it away reluctantly a while later, then this is the project for you. Your instincts to take the box in the first place are right, as shoe boxes are the perfect shape and size to make useful containers. This box is covered with brown wrapping paper—yet more good recycling—that was rolled and twisted, then unraveled and stuck onto the box to provide an interesting textured surface. The "bark" is made from torn strips of white paper, coated with wood stain to give a streaky finish. The end result is a unique, natural-looking container suitable for anything from potpourri to an index card system.

YOU WILL NEED

shoe box
cream latex paint
paintbrushes
brown wrapping paper
pre-mixed wallpaper paste and cheap brush
scissors
white glue
thick white paper
wood stain (such as antique pine)
thick, coarse string
square of calico, 4 x 4 inches
clips or pegs
glue gun with all-purpose glue sticks (or all-purpose glue)

one *Paint the shoe box with cream paint until all of the lettering is completely covered. Let dry.*

two *Roll up some brown paper, crumpling it. Fold up, then twist it as small as possible. Untwist and open it out.*

three *Apply a coat of wallpaper paste to the box. Place the box centrally on the brown paper.*

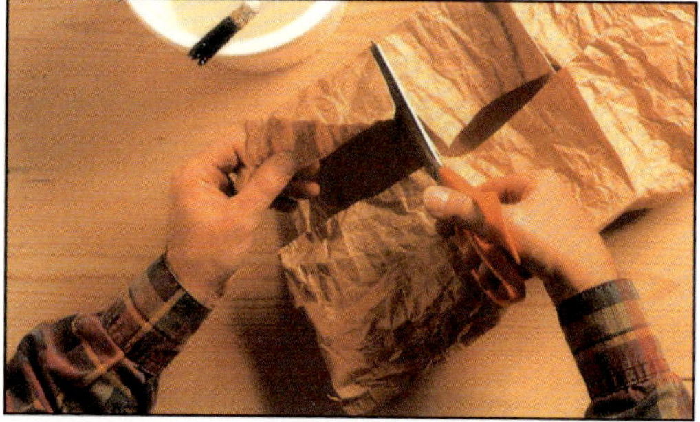

four *Fold the brown paper around the box, pressing it into the pasted surface, but not smoothing it too much. Pinch the paper along the edges of the box and cut along these. Fold the end flaps inside, sticking them in place with wallpaper paste.*

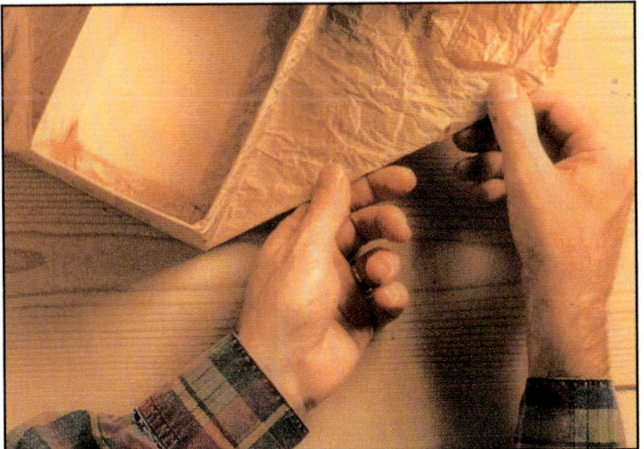

five *Fold the brown paper around the sides of the box, one end at a time, pasting one on top of the other to create two large triangular shapes.*

six *Fold the triangular shapes up over the sides and paste them against the inside of the box.*

seven *Neaten the inside by cutting a piece of brown paper to fit the base exactly. Paste it over the paper edges.*

eight *Using a dry brush, paint a streaky coat of undiluted white glue on the white paper. Leave some areas of the paper unpainted to let the wood stain show through. Let dry completely.*

nine *Brush wood stain onto the white paper. It will be resisted by the white glue where it is at its thickest and part-resisted in other places. This creates the bark effect.*

ten *Tear the paper into rough triangular shapes. If you tear at a slight angle, the paper will rip through its thickness and make the edges white and thin. Paint these white edges with wood stain so that they blend in.*

CONTINUED OVER ➤

eleven *Roll up the paper triangles, beginning with the widest part and rolling toward the point. Bundle the strips together with string and tie a reef knot. Separate the strands of string so that they bush out from the knot.*

twelve *Fray the edges of the calico piece, then scrunch it up in the middle, using clips or pegs to hold the shape. Heat the glue gun and apply glue to the scrunched folds. Press the calico onto the center of the box lid.*

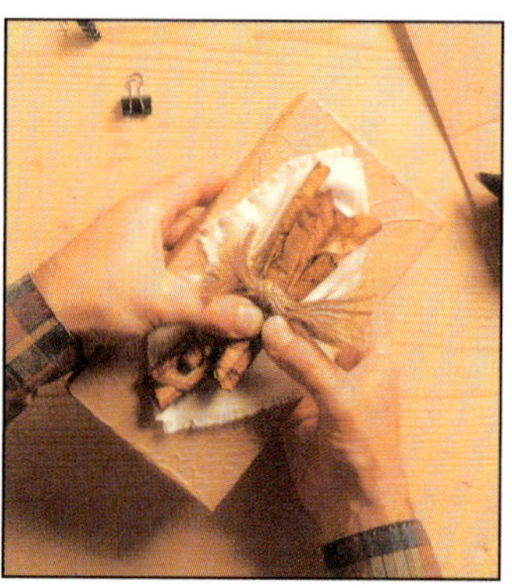

thirteen *Remove the clips or pegs from the calico and apply more hot glue. Press the bark bundle on top of the calico.*

fourteen *If you are using the box to store index cards, write labeling on some spare "bark" paper and glue it to one end of the box.*

Gilded Boxes

There is no paint or spray that gives a finish to compare with gold leaf, or its cheaper counterpart, Dutch metal leaf. It glows and glitters and can be burnished with a soft cloth to leave a gleaming surface. The art of gilding is surrounded by mystique because it requires a great deal of skill to lay the fragile sheets of gold leaf onto gold size or glue. This design was created using a kit suitable for beginners, which can be bought at art and craft suppliers. The flat surface of the box makes it easy to apply, but it is important to follow the manufacturer's instructions, as the drying time is crucial to the success of the project.

YOU WILL NEED

design tracing or photocopy
spray adhesive
high-density foam rubber
craft knife
round painted wooden box with lid
fine-grade sandpaper
pencil
gold leaf kit
paintbrush
plate
small foam roller
cotton balls
fine steel wool (optional)

one *Select a suitable design or motif from a source book, and photocopy or trace to size. Spray the back of the design with adhesive and stick it onto a block of foam rubber.*

two *Carefully cut out the design, starting in the middle. Then cut around the outside.*

three *Once the cutting is complete, carefully peel off the paper pattern.*

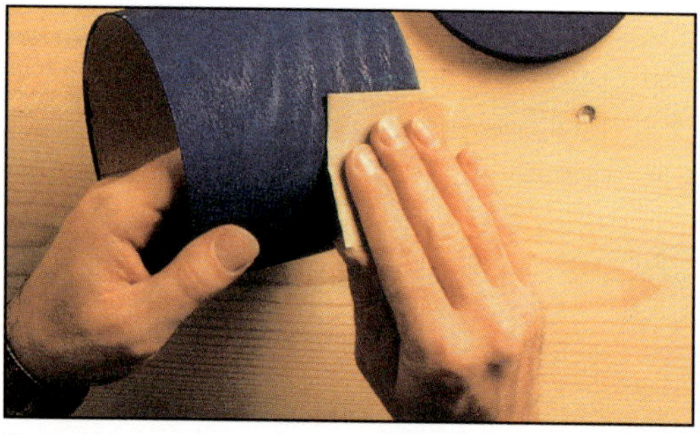

four *Rub the entire surface of the painted box lightly with fine-grade sandpaper to make a rough surface for applying the gold size.*

five *Draw a pencil line around the top edge of the lid. Use your fingers to keep the line an even distance from the edge.*

six *Carefully paint a strip of gold size between the edge of the box lid and the pencil line and also around the top and bottom edges of the lid sides.*

seven *Put some size on a plate and run the roller through it until it is evenly coated. Using the roller, coat the foam stamp thoroughly and evenly.*

eight *Stamp an even pattern around the side of the box, re-coating the stamp after each print. Stamp four shapes inside the lid border line and one in the center.*

nine *Leave the size until it has the right degree of "tack" (according to the manufacturer's instructions), then invert the lid onto a sheet of gold leaf. Smooth the gold leaf over the edges so that it is in contact with all of the size.*

ten *Holding the lid at an angle, apply the sheets of gold leaf around the sides in the same way.*

CONTINUED OVER ➤

eleven *Rub the surface with cotton balls. All the "un-sized" gold will flake off, leaving the design behind.*

twelve *If the brand new gleaming design overwhelms you, rub the box lightly with steel wool to create an antiqued look.*

ALL THE TRIMMINGS

CHOOSE THE CHEERFUL PRIMARY colors of blue and red and team them with white for a crisp, clean look with a slightly nautical feel. You can also trim black with white for classic appeal or use several shades of one color to add a subtle lift. Felt is an easy, lovely and inexpensive way to trim plain fabrics, whether on shoe bags, linen bags, throws or cushions. You can add as much or as little decoration as you choose.

YOU WILL NEED

round template

2 squares of red felt, about 8 x 8 inches

2 squares of blue felt, about 8 x 8 inches

fabric marker

pinking shears

dressmaker's pins

blue cord

needle and matching sewing thread

string

fabric item, such as a shoe bag or quilt

one *Find a round template: It could be a can lid, coin or anything similar. Place the template on the felt and draw around the template with a fabric marker. Cut around the circle with pinking shears.*

two *Pin two circles together, knot short lengths of cord and sew them onto the circles.*

three *Repeat with lengths of string. Sew the circles onto your shoe bag, quilt or other fabric items.*

DUSTPAN TIDY

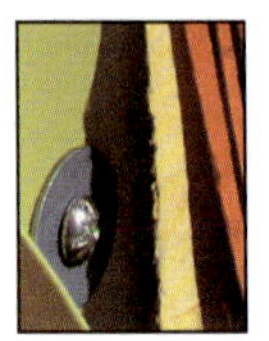

IF YOU HAVE TO excavate piles of paper, notebooks, lists and old letters every time you need a pen, then it is time to get the dustpans out. This project gives a new meaning to tidying up. Two metal dustpans can be spray-painted to match or in any color combination and attached with bolts. Use the dustpans for stationery, a small paper tray or, perhaps most suitably, for filing bills.

YOU WILL NEED

2 metal dustpans
4 metal washers
enamel car spray paint: lime green and metallic blue
newspaper
G-clamp
2 pieces corrugated cardboard
pencil
drill, with metal bit
2 nuts and bolts
pliers
screwdriver

one *Spray one dustpan and two washers lime green and the others metallic blue. Protect your work surface with newspaper and build up the color gradually with light puffs of paint. Let dry.*

two *Clamp the dustpans together, protecting the paintwork with cardboard. Hold the washers at the point where the dustpans meet and mark two equal positions with a pencil.*

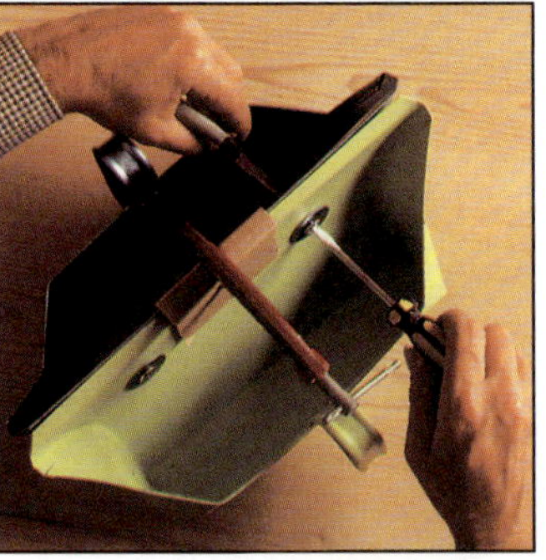

three *Drill through the marks on both dustpans. Place a washer on either side of a hole, hold the nut with pliers and tighten the bolt with a screwdriver. Repeat for the other hole.*

Punched-Metal Bucket

The idea of decorating metal objects with raised punched patterns has been around ever since sheet metal was invented about 300 years ago. Silver is probably best-known for this decorative treatment, but cheaper metals can also look very impressive. Bare metal buckets are ideal for this sort of pattern-making, and all you need is a pen to draw your guidelines and a hammer and blunt nail for the punching. You can practice your technique on any tin can to find the ideal sort of tap needed to make a good bump without piercing the metal.

YOU WILL NEED

bare metal bucket
felt-tipped pen (not water-based)
blunt nail (or center punch)
hammer
rag
lighter fuel (or similar solvent)

one *Draw your pattern on the inside of the bucket. These motifs come from South America, but any repeated curves or angles are suitable.*

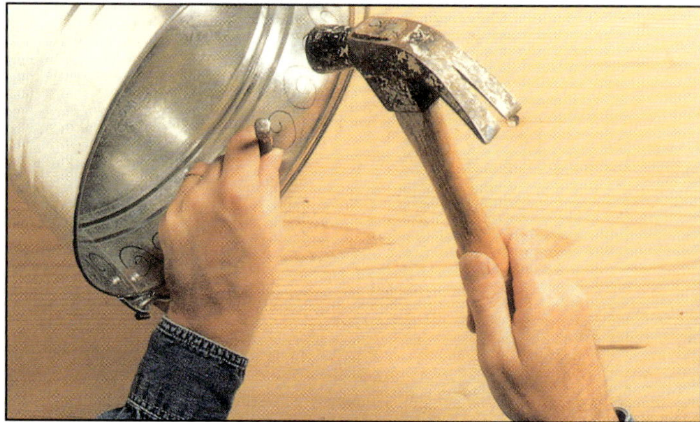

two *Rest the bucket on a piece of wood to protect your work surface. Tap the nail with a hammer, keeping the dents regularly spaced. About ½ inch is fine.*

three *Continue hammering the pattern all over the inside of the metal bucket.*

four *Use a rag and lighter fuel to clean off the pen pattern that is left between the punched marks.*

SNOWFLAKE STORAGE JARS

ALMOST EVERY KITCHEN COULD USE a face-lift every now and then. Rather than pay exorbitant prices for a completely new look, why not just cheer up your storage jars, simply and inexpensively, and give your kitchen a breath of fresh air? You can create a whole new atmosphere and a really individual look, by stamping patterns on your jars with acrylic enamel paint. The finish is quite hard-wearing and is tough enough to stand up to occasional gentle washing, but take note that it will not withstand the dishwasher.

YOU WILL NEED

pencil
tracing paper
spray adhesive
upholstery foam rubber
scalpel
dish cloth
glass storage jars
white acrylic enamel paint
plate
tile

one *Trace your chosen pattern shape, lightly spray it with adhesive and place it on the foam rubber. Cut around the outline with a scalpel. Cut horizontally into the foam rubber to meet the outline cuts and remove excess foam rubber.*

two *Clean and dry the glass jars. Spread a coating of paint onto a plate and make a test print on a tile to remove excess paint from the stamp.*

three *Holding the jar steady, press the stamp around the side of the jar.*

four *Rotate the stamp 90 degrees and make the second print directly below the first. Continue in this way, alternating the angle of the print.*

Blanket Chest

YOU CAN ALMOST GUARANTEE that every interesting pine chest has been discovered by now, stripped and sold for a profit, but there are still plain, solid work-chests around that can be used as a good base for this project. The blanket used for covering the chest is the utilitarian sort used by furniture moving companies as a protective wrapping. Any blanket would be suitable, but this sort has lots of "give" because of the way it is woven and so can be stretched for a smooth fit. The chest has a piece of upholstery foam on it so it doubles as a comfortable bedroom seat. The lid is held down by a leather strap—suitcase straps or old horse tack are ideal as they come in longer lengths than leather belts.

YOU WILL NEED

wooden chest
screwdriver
pliers
tape measure
blanket
dressmaker's scissors
staple gun
upholstery foam rubber, to fit lid
ruler
cutting board
craft knife
leather strap
upholstery tacks
small hammer
scrap cardboard

one *Unscrew and remove the hinges from the lid and remove any protruding nails or screws. Measure around the chest for the length of the blanket. Then measure the height of the chest. Double the height and add 5 inches.*

‹ two *Cut the blanket to size. Spread it out, and lay the chest on its side in the middle with an even amount of blanket on either side and 3 inches below the base. Cut from the front edge of the blanket, in a straight line, to the left and right front corners of the chest. Staple the cut section inside the chest.*

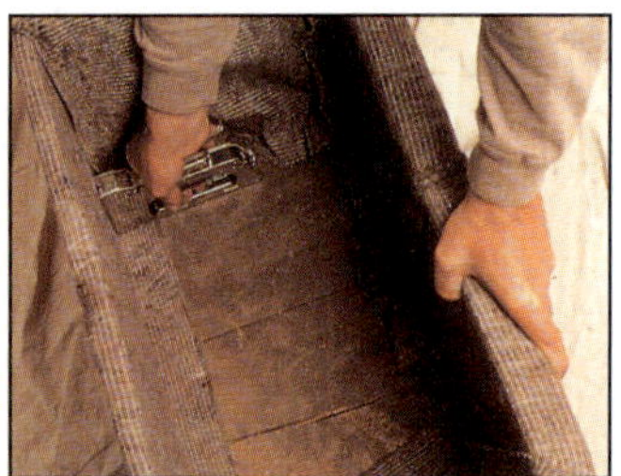

three *Smooth the blanket down the side and staple it under the base. Cover the rest of the chest in the same way. Fold the blanket around from both sides to meet at the back and staple it in place. Staple all the lining neatly inside.*

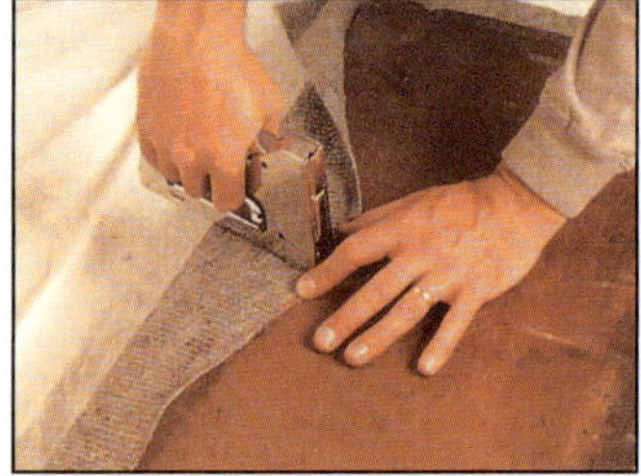

four *Cut a piece of blanket about 4 inches larger than the lid on all sides. Place the foam in the middle of the blanket with the wooden lid on top. Press down the foam, pull up the blanket on one side and staple it in place.*

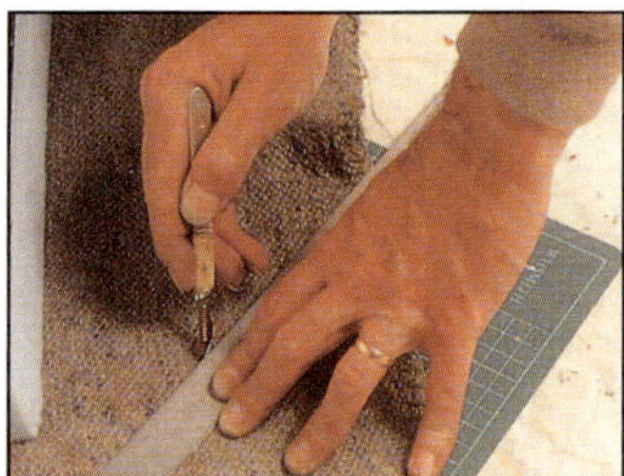

five *Cut a triangular section off each corner. Leave enough blanket to fold up and staple to the lid. Fold the cut edge up and staple it across the corner.*

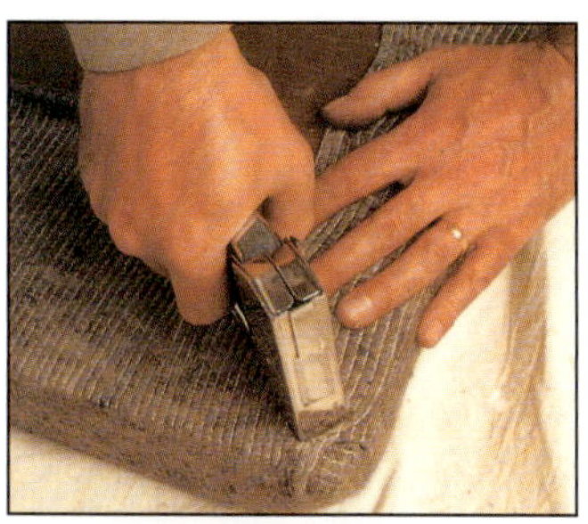

‹ **six** *Staple the side pieces over the first. Neaten by folding and trimming. Work on diagonal corners alternately.*

seven *Trim the chest and secure the fastening strap to the lower half with upholstery tacks. Use a cardboard strip as a guide to keep the spacing even.* ›

ORIGAMI BOXES

ORIGAMI IS THE JAPANESE ART of paper-folding where the most extraordinary three-dimensional objects are made from a single folded square of paper. This little box is a suitable project for a beginner, but it may take a couple of practice attempts before it suddenly "clicks." You can make the boxes any size you like, and use any paper that is not too flimsy. Wrapping paper is good as it creases well and is cheap and strong.

YOU WILL NEED

sheet of paper
scissors
double-sided tape (this breaks all the rules!)
selection of paper squares for practice (optional)

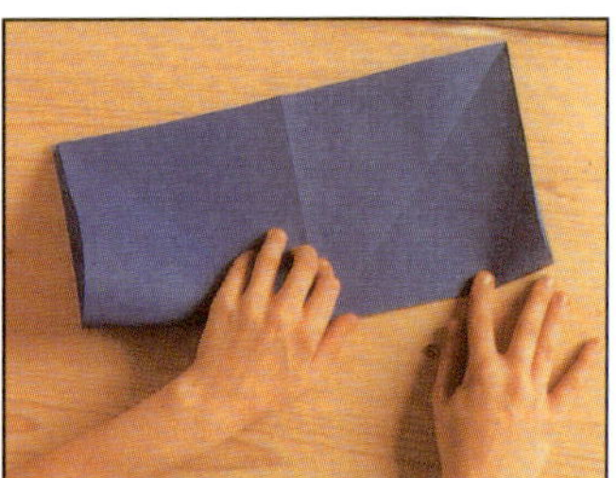

one *Fold and trim a sheet of paper to make a perfect square. Fold the square corner to corner. Open it to show the creases of four equal triangles. Turn it over and fold into four square quarters. Unfold it so you can see the creases of eight equal triangles. The center of the paper is Point A.*

two *Hold the model in the air and push all the sides together so that the corners meet in the middle. Flatten the model. Point A is now a corner of the flattened model. Keep it facing you.*

three *Fold the point opposite Point A over to meet it. Crease it along the mid-line. Now fold it back up to the mid-line and crease the fold. Unfold it again. Fold the same point up to the last crease, then fold it over again, up to the mid-line. Turn the model over and repeat this step.*

four *With Point A still facing you, take the top layer of the left-hand corner and fold it over onto the right-hand corner. You are now faced with a square. Fold the left-hand corner and the top layer of the right-hand corner into the center point, and crease. Bring the right-hand top layer over onto the left. Turn over and repeat.*

five *Point A now forms the base of a smaller triangle. Fold this up at the point where it meets the sides. Crease, fold it in the other direction and crease. Unfold. Insert your hand and splay your fingers while pushing up the bottom of the model, Point A. Fold down the two pointed sides level with the others and tuck the ends under. Secure with a small piece of tape.*

CIRCULAR PAINTED BOXES

THIS PROJECT EXPERIMENTS with three different paint effects. The first, rust, looks especially good when used on a material that doesn't naturally rust, such as wood. Verdigris is a natural substance that forms on the surface of weathered brass and is a beautiful turquoise-green color. The third finish used here is crackle-glaze, which looks a bit like lizard skin. This is the most time-consuming of the three paint effects because of the drying time needed between coats.

YOU WILL NEED

- 3 wooden boxes, with lids
- water-based paints: dark gray, 2 shades of rust, green-gray, stone, 2 shades of green and maize yellow (according to required finish)
- handful of fine sand
- plate
- paintbrushes
- 3 foam sponges
- clear matte varnish, crackle-glaze base varnish, crackle-glaze varnish
- alizarin crimson oil paint
- 2 rags
- turpentine

THE RUST FINISH

one *Mix sand into the dark gray base coat for texture. Apply two coats of paint to the box. Let dry. Dab on the darker rust color with a sponge. Cover most of the background.*

two *Dab on the lighter rust color. If you are in any doubt about how it should look, find some real rust and copy it. Finally dab in just a touch of green-gray. Do not overdo this as it should blend in rather than stand out as a sharp contrast.*

THE VERDIGRIS FINISH

Paint the box with the stone base coat color. Dab on the lighter green with a sponge. Cover most of the background with this. Dab on the other green using a sponge. Apply a coat of clear matte varnish to protect the surface.

THE CRACKLE-GLAZE FINISH

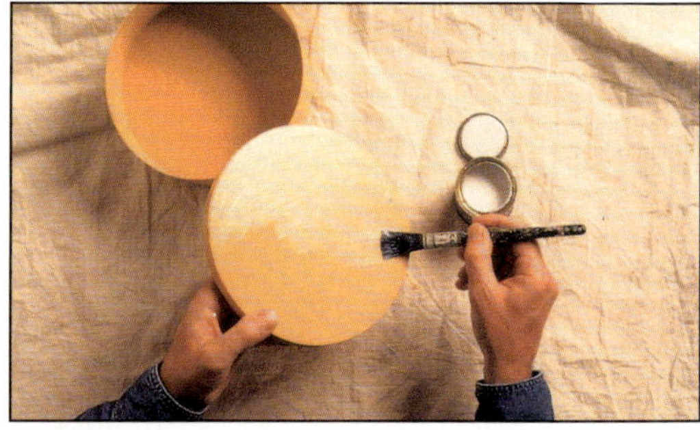

Paint a yellow base coat and a coat of crackle-glaze base varnish. When dry, apply a coat of crackle-glaze varnish. Let dry. Rub crimson oil paint into cracks with a rag. Dip a rag in turpentine; rub the surface so red paint remains in the cracks.

Button Box

Button boxes are an old-fashioned delight that should not be allowed to disappear altogether. There was a time when most homes had a cookie tin filled with an assortment of buttons for sewing and knitting projects. You can make your own button box to store these little treasures. The wooden box used here is an empty tea container with a sliding lid, covered with black felt and decorated with buttons.

YOU WILL NEED

wooden box with sliding or hinged lid
black latex paint
paintbrush
black felt
chalk
dressmaker's scissors
rubber-based fabric glue
craft knife
cutting board
buttons
glue gun with all-purpose glue sticks (or all-purpose glue)

one *Paint the box black, inside and out. Let dry. Put it on the felt and draw in chalk the shapes needed to cover it: a rectangle for the base and long sides up to the grooves for the lid; a strip to cover the two ends and the base a second time; and a strip for the lid, stopping short of the runners.*

two *Cut out the felt pieces. Then spread fabric glue onto the base and sides of the box and smooth the shorter strip of felt onto it. The felt will stretch a bit at this stage. Spread a thin strip of fabric glue along the top edge of the sides and fold the felt over it. Let it dry completely.*

three *Trim off any edges for a neat finish. Glue the longer strip of felt onto the base and up both of the ends in the same way. Trim off any excess. Cover the lid with felt, then begin arranging the buttons to make an attractive design.*

four *When you are happy with the design, use the glue gun to stick the buttons in place. The glue will set immediately, so work quickly and place the buttons accurately. Decorate the sides of the box with stripes of colored buttons.*

five *Glue a row of white and pearl buttons along the top edge of the sides to complete the design.*

Camembert Numbers

This project should be linked to a wine and cheese party or the befriending of a French restaurateur, as it involves nine Camembert boxes. It is always a relief to be able to recycle packaging, and these empty boxes are certainly given a new lease on life in the form of a stylish set of containers. Enlarge the numbers on a photocopier so they fit your boxes, and cut them out as stencils. If you find the task too daunting, trace the numbers onto the boxes and paint them in.

You will need

9 Camembert boxes
fine-grade sandpaper
clear matte acrylic varnish
number templates
craft knife
cutting board
spray adhesive
stenciling plastic or waxed stencil cardboard
enamel paint: 9 colors plus silver
paintbrushes: medium, stenciling, fine-pointed and square-tipped
compass and pencil (optional)
shellac button polish

1 2
3 4
5 6
7 8
9 0

one *Remove any paper labels from the boxes. Rub the wood with sandpaper to get rid of any rough edges. Apply a coat of clear matte acrylic varnish to all the boxes.*

two *Take the templates, or make your own, and enlarge them on a photocopier so the numbers are 3 inches high (or fit within a border of about ½ inch). Cut out each one.*

three *Stick the photocopies onto the stencil material with spray adhesive. Stick them underneath stenciling plastic, but on top of stenciling cardboard. Cut out, making the incisions away from the corners.*

four *Stencil a number on each lid in different colors. With a fine-pointed brush, paint a band about ½ inch wide around each lid. (If necessary, use a compass). With a square-tipped brush, paint a band of silver around the edges. When dry, rub them down lightly and apply shellac.*

STAR CUPBOARD

THIS ATTRACTIVE LITTLE cupboard fits in the moment you have finished it. While its style is individual, it does not scream out for attention, and it has that comfortable, lived in look. It was painted, stamped, then painted again and finally, it was given a coat of antiquing varnish and rubbed back with a cloth in places. It glows from all the attention and took just one afternoon to make. This style of decoration is so simple that you might consider transforming other furniture in the same way.

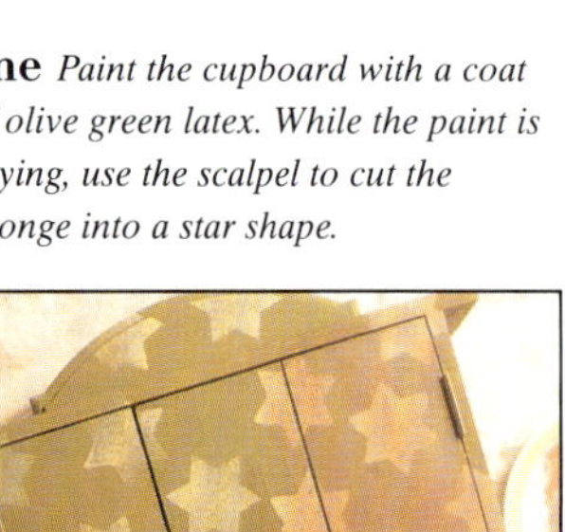

YOU WILL NEED

wooden cupboard
latex paint (olive green, off-white and vermilion)
scalpel
kitchen sponge
white glue
matte varnish (antique pine)
dish cloth

one *Paint the cupboard with a coat of olive green latex. While the paint is drying, use the scalpel to cut the sponge into a star shape.*

two *Pour some off-white latex onto a plate. Dip the sponge star into the paint and print stars all over the cupboard. Let dry.*

three *Make a mixture of two-thirds vermilion paint and one-third white glue and coat the cupboard liberally.*

four *Finish with a coat of tinted varnish, then use a cloth to rub some of the varnish off each star.*

LIZARD-SKIN BOXES

THESE SMART ANGULAR BOXES look crisp and exclusive, but they are, in fact, no more than paper-covered foam-core board. They make great containers for jewelry, barrettes or cufflinks, and they would add a touch of elegance to any desk or dressing table. When you make your own boxes, there are no manufacturing constraints, so you can make them any shape you like, however unconventional. Foam-core board is light and easy to cut and glue. Buy it at art and craft stores, and buy lizard-skin paper at specialty paper stores.

YOU WILL NEED

- foam-core board
- cutting board
- felt-tipped pen
- ruler
- craft knife
- glue gun with all-purpose glue sticks (or all-purpose glue)
- 3 different lizard-skin papers
- spray adhesive

one *Place the foam board on a cutting board and mark a four-sided angular shape for the base. Cut out the shape. Measure each side, then decide on the height of your box. Cut out four rectangular side sections to fit those measurements. Heat the glue gun and run a thin strip of glue along each base edge, then stick the sides on. The glue will set right away, so work quickly and accurately.*

two *Place the box on a sheet of foam board and draw around it. Add 1¼-1½ inches all around for the lid overlap. Cut this out. Do this again, taking off ½ inch all around, for the lower half of the lid. Glue the two lid sections together. Cut a strip of lizard-skin paper wide enough to line the inside and outside of the box and to fold underneath. Apply spray adhesive to the paper, then wrap it around the box.*

three *Cut down into the corners and fold the paper inside the box. Do the same underneath, smoothing the paper flat onto the box. Apply more glue where necessary.*

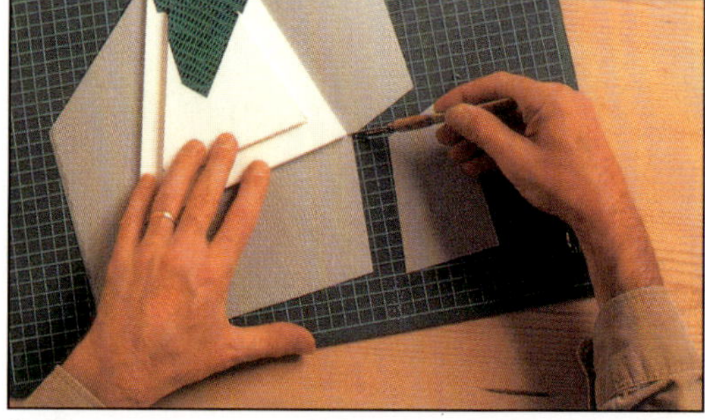

four *Cut out paper to cover lid. Glue in place and cut corners. Cut two identical shapes for a handle and glue together. Cover the handle with paper and glue to the top of the box.*

News on Shoes

Special shoes deserve a home of their own, and these sturdy wooden wine boxes can be made stylish enough to house anything from sturdy boots to Cinderella's glass slippers. The boxes were lined with different types of newsprint, which were layered and stuck down like papier-mâché. Select your newsprint to suit your shoes—put leather lace-ups in the pink financial pages, party shoes in comic strips and velvet pumps in the arts and literary pages.

YOU WILL NEED

wooden wine crates
sandpaper
white glue
paintbrushes
variety of newsprint
craft knife
clear matte varnish (or shellac)

one *Sand down one of the wine crates. Then mix white glue with water (50:50) and apply a coat to the inside.*

two *Apply another coat of the glue mixture, then smooth newsprint over the inside. Apply undiluted white glue along the top edges and smooth the paper over it. Let dry before applying more paper and glue at random.*

three *Let dry, then trim the paper along the outside top edges with a craft knife. Varnish the whole box with either clear matte varnish or, if you want an "aged" look, shellac. Let dry, then re-coat at least twice.*